D1737941

City, Class and Trade

City, Class and Trade

Social and Economic Change in the Third World

NIGEL HARRIS

I. B. Tauris & Co Ltd
Publishers
London · New York

Published in association with
The Development Planning Unit,
University College London

Published in 1991 by
I.B.Tauris & Co Ltd
110 Gloucester Avenue
London NW1 8JA

175 Fifth Avenue
New York
NY 10010

Published in association with
The Development Planning Unit,
University College London

In the United States of America
and Canada distributed by
St Martin's Press
175 Fifth Avenue
New York
NY 10010

British Library Cataloguing in Publication Data

Harris, Nigel *1935–*
City, class and trade, : social and economic change in the Third World.
1. Developing countries. Economic development. Social aspects
I. Title
330.91724

ISBN 1–85043–301–1

Typeset by Columns Design & Production Services Ltd, Reading
Printed in Great Britain by
WBC Print Ltd., Bridgend

Contents

Preface

The political transformation of Eastern Europe and the Soviet Union can be seen as only the latest stage in an even more remarkable change in world opinion: away from detailed economic management by the State to increased subordination of a growing array of activities to market criteria. It is often forgotten in the jubilation at the 'end of history' just how recent this is. In the 1950s, governments in Europe still expected to operate detailed controls, partly through major sectors of nationalized corporations and non-convertible currencies. By now, however, at least in rhetoric (and partly in practice), capitalism has come to correspond more closely than ever before in its history to the predominant economic theories of its operation.

Is the dramatic change in opinion merely a passing fashion? Certainly, there will be changes of opinion back to a more realistic emphasis on the importance of the State (and the embrace of the green issues by prominent conservative political leaders shows that there are newly discovered limits to what markets are supposed to be able to do). But the scale of the change suggests that it reflects a new reality. The partially closed national economy sustained the old political arguments and policies; those are now being rapidly superseded by the emergence of a single world economy, integrating the mass of economic activities without much concern for the country where the activity takes place.

It will take a long time for the implications of this momentous change to be fully understood. For example, prices in a partially or fully closed economy, other things being equal, will reflect local scarcities; and where labour is scarce, research will be directed to investments that save labour. But in a world economy, there is no scarcity of labour, so technology could be radically reoriented in the reverse direction (to save capital). Of course, immigration controls as well as other continuing restrictions still inhibit this outcome, but, in a competitive market context, sooner or later the relative scarcities must begin to reshape the priorities of the system.

Our capacity to understand the implications of the emergence of an integrated world economy is constantly obstructed by the inheritance of theory. The world has passed through the most intensely nationalist phase in its history – and in Eastern Europe and the Soviet Union, that phase has revived with great vigour – and, as a result, the characters in the world drama are invariably seen as national, countries. The world steel industry or wheat production or shirt-making disintegrates into national shares, even though this perception is increasingly at odds with a world production line that spans many countries. Thus, understanding the implications of the new world economy requires the analysis of both what is happening and how people identify it.

The essays in this book, all written in the 1980s, are broadly concerned with some of the practical and theoretical issues involved in this change in the world economy. Economic integration transforms the role of government. It shapes each country to perform a specialized role in the production of a world output (hence the preoccupation with exports) rather than producing at home a microcosm of the total world production for domestic consumption. Within each country, the decline in economic boundaries, the liberalization of trade, finance and capital movements, may perhaps shift the locus of international competition from governments to local areas, settlements and districts. As with countries, cities are then likely to become increasingly specialized, and will require, to be effective, greater degrees of administrative and financial autonomy in order to compete.

The first group of essays address this last topic in the light of the demographic transition in developing countries to predominantly urban societies. Perceptions of this process in the past have been dogged by many most destructive myths, some of which have inspired government policies in ways that have proved, at best, ineffective, at worst, disastrous. Simultaneous integration, the development of new divisions of labour, is likely to break down many of the distinctions of the past, between, for example, more and less developed countries, producing much greater heterogeneity. The appalling poverty of New York's Lower East Side now competes with some of the slums of Calcutta in terms of human misery; and the rich have always been universal.

In the 1950s, the nationalist perception in developing countries often made the quaint assumption that economic development was impossible through international trade and reliance on a domestic capitalist class. Trade would increase underdevelopment, it was thought, and domestic businessmen were little more than speculators.

In fact, the changes in the world economy, of which integration is one feature, have been so fundamental that it is difficult to know how anyone could have held such views. The last essays look at some of these issues in terms of the effects of international trade on selected developing countries and, in the middle section, on the emergence of assertive private business classes.

Economic integration – in terms of flows of trade, capital and labour – is examined relative to the emerging region of the Pacific Rim (in the last essay). The international movement of workers is also examined in order to explain why it takes place, why capital cannot be substituted for workers indefinitely.

Many of the essays are concerned with changing territorial specializations – between groups of countries, between localities within a country, and between the different districts within great cities. The system endlessly reproduces complicated patterns of complementary specialization, and for much of the time, we are out of date on what is happening. The patterns are produced in conditions of competition, so they are never indefinitely stable. This principle of continuous change is quite contrary to the operation of governments, administering stable patches of territory and a given share of the world's population. Frequently, the ethic of government collides with the continual changes in domestic economic activity that are generated by the world system, outside the national boundaries. The conditioned reflexes of the State, the product of past realities and theories, are often wrong. The melancholy fate of State planning, both economic and physical, bears witness to how the new world order has rendered important elements of public action redundant.

I am grateful to Tauris for allowing these essays to be exhumed from many a dusty grave. And even more grateful to the editors for the great work in turning them into a more presentable form.

Nigel Harris
London, June 1990.

Part I
CITIES

1

Economic Development and Urbanization: The Classical Tradition

INTRODUCTION

The famous account by Plato in *The Republic* to distinguish surface appearances from reality employed a striking metaphor. In a cave, a group of prisoners are chained from childhood by their necks and legs, so that they cannot move. They see on a wall in front of them only shadows cast by a fire burning behind them. The shadows are the only reality they know; they cannot know the real objects which cast the shadows. This seems analogous to the statistics on urbanization in developing countries, our shadows. Demography presents us with apparently hard data, but tells us little on why the data are as they are. This allows wildly different interpretations, and blind or perverse responses by governments.

DEMOGRAPHIC PROJECTIONS

The projections – with all their many faults – cry out for proper explanation. Much of Asia and Africa seems about to enter the fastest phase of that territorial–demographic transition that has long been accomplished in Europe and North America and is nearly complete in Latin America, the transition from being predominantly rural to predominantly urban. We have only to think of the unprecedented scale of the potential change over the next century if China, with over 1,000 million people, and India, with 800 million, pass through the steepest part of the curve.[1]

Consider some of the highlights of the United Nations projections.[2]

(i) The 500 million city dwellers of the developing countries in 1950 could have become 4,000 million by the year 2020, nearly half

Originally published as 'Economic development and urbanization' (the text of an inaugural lecture, given at University College London, 23 May 1988), *Habitat International* (Oxford), Vol. 12, No. 3, 1988, pp. 5–15.

of them living in cities with one million or more population. By the year 2020, there may be 750 million urban Africans (52 per cent of that continent's people); 2,200 million urban Asians (49 per cent); and 610 million urban Latin Americans (or 83 per cent).

(ii) Or take big city populations. In 1950, there were in developing countries 31 cities with a million or more inhabitants. By 1985, there were 146; and projected for 2025, 486. In 1950, there were just 5 cities of 4 million or more inhabitants in the developing world, but 28 in 1985, and a projected 114 for 2025. We shall hardly know their names.

(iii) Very large cities are becoming a feature restricted to developing countries. Of the 25 largest cities in the world in 1950, 11 were in developing countries. By the year 2000 this could be 19. Already it may well be that the very largest cities are now in developing countries – the Metropolitan Zone of Mexico City, the largest, with over 18 million people, or nearly three times the population of Greater London. Mexico City's population was not much more than a quarter of a million at the turn of the century, and about half a million in the late 1920s – consider the astonishing speed of change in one person's lifetime.

Of course, the *rates* of growth have fallen since the heyday of urbanization in the 1950s. Then, urban populations grew at just over 5 per cent *per annum*; now at just over 3 per cent. And there is evidence[3] that the population growth of the largest cities in a country is slowing down (regardless of the absolute size of the city), while that of smaller cities accelerates. Already, in Latin America, for example, the population growth of smaller cities is the same as or greater than in the large.

And the sources of growth have changed; it is no longer from migration. Sixty per cent of urban population growth in developing countries now comes from the natural increase of the existing citizens (disproportionately concentrated in the younger age groups). Between 8 and 15 per cent is attributable to changes of boundaries or definitions. And between a quarter and a third comes from net migration. Of course, these figures conceal wide differences. In Africa, rates of urban growth and inmigration are still high (although the numbers involved are much smaller than in Asia). Cities there are growing by 6 per cent *per annum*; and for the 35 major capitals that are doubling their population every 9 years, 8.5 per cent.

But let us return to the original question – what do these shadows on the wall mean? It is not enough to note the crude correlation between economic development and urbanization, or more narrowly, industrialization and the territorial concentration of the labour force. For the proposition is too general and ahistorical to tell us much about a particular country or time. However, in the 1950s, an historically specific thesis was created and proved remarkably influential. It was said that, in nineteenth century Europe, urban and industrial employment expanded, drawing workers off the land to rising city incomes while rural productivity could also grow. Today, however, the argument continued, it is rural poverty which drives migrants to the city where, given modern capital–labour ratios in industry, they cannot secure work.[4] In the one case, the cities were the engines of national growth; in the other, welfare centres for the rural poor. Later, others elaborated the case to explain the so-called 'informal sector'.

There are many things wrong with this case, but it cannot detain us here. In retrospect, it was a hasty misassessment to assume that matters had fundamentally changed so that excess labour supply accounted for urbanization. There was much evidence that urban labour demand remained the key factor.[5] However, the theoretical assumptions of the case were debatable. There was also an alternative route to understanding changes in the distribution of population, one that derived from classical political economy: the division of labour.

POLITICAL ECONOMY

Take, for example, the importance that Adam Smith (not to mention his forebears), writing well before there was much perception of economic development, attached to the division of labour, complementary specializations, as the basis for what we would call high productivity. In the main, he was concerned with this in units of production – the household, the farm, the workshop. But he also recognized specialization by different districts, mediated by exchange or trade. Furthermore, he formulated an important proposition of special significance today – the larger the market, the more differentiated can specialization become.[6] He also identified the peculiar strength of the town, for it allowed a much greater degree of division of tasks, of specialization, making it a place for the highest levels of labour productivity.[7] Smith linked what came to be known as comparative advantage, in this case linked to a particular district; exchange systems (including transport); productivity and the size of the market.

Ricardo had in the main different preoccupations, but he did develop the idea of comparative advantage in international trade (exchanging English cloth for Portuguese wine). The merits of this type of specialization were sufficiently great to offset the declining returns to agriculture.[8]

The division of labour was even more important for Marx than for Adam Smith. There was a technical division of labour, organized in the factory by the capitalists, and a social division of labour, organized by the market. One of the earliest forms of the social division of labour was the separation of urban and rural – as he puts it:[9]

> The foundation of all highly developed divisions of labour that is brought about by the change of commodities is the cleavage between town and country. We might say that the whole economic history of society is summarised in the development of this cleavage.

The arrival of modern manufacturing imposed on the social division of labour much more elaborate differentiations of skill – particularly in 'the territorial division of labour', as Marx calls it, 'in accordance with which particular branches of production become rooted in particular districts'.[10]

However, in contrast to both Smith and Ricardo, Marx's division of labour, while being decisive for growth of output and productivity, can also permit one territorial unit to exploit another, as he notes in his discussion of late feudal Europe in Volume 2 of *Capital*:[11]

> If the countryside exploits the town politically in the Middle Ages wherever feudalism has not been broken down by exceptional urban development – as in Italy; the town, on the other hand, exploits the land economically everywhere and without exception through its monopoly prices, its system of taxation, its guild organisation, its direct commercial fraudulence and its usury.

Thus monopoly power underlay an unequal exchange so that the towns appropriated a disproportionate share of the combined output.

POST-CLASSICAL ECONOMICS

Mainstream economics restricted questions of the territorial division of labour to the theory of international trade, bequeathing the concept as applied to society to Durkheim and sociology. There was a certain amount of work on territorial questions, a micro-analysis, and in the twentieth century, on flows of commodities (through

Leontief's input–output analysis), industrial location, changes in territorial activity and on regional questions, but the idea of territorial divisions of labour was at most implicit. Urban and economic geography raised interesting suggestions about the organization of territory and settlements, but usually without relating these to disaggregated economic specializations.

However, outside the mainstream of economic thought, territorial specialization recurred as an important economic and political issue, but in an increasingly simplified form. In the Great Industrialization Debate[12] in the Soviet Union, a particular division of labour between urban and rural was assumed by the leading theoreticians, Bukharin,[13] and his adversary, Preobrazhensky.[14] Mihael Manoïlesco, a Romanian economist, identified international trade relationships between more and less developed countries as necessarily exploitative for the weaker; this early version of what was to become known as the theory of unequal exchange was the argument for Eastern Europe to break away from the international division of labour, now identified as economic domination by the German Reich.[15] The Argentinian economist, Raúl Prebisch, with his sharp distinction between centres and peripheries, presented a not dissimilar case after the Second World War to explain the incapacity of Latin America to develop.[16] His case inspired a host of theorists and new concepts on unequal exchange.[17] From a different position altogether, in the first counter-attack of neo-classicial economics on import-substitution industrialization, Little *et al.* argued that protectionism caused overurbanization by tilting the terms of trade between urban and rural in favour of the city.[18] Michael Lipton presented a case that urban India exploited the peasantry.[19] Urban–rural was seen as an alternative to class analysis, and the argument was influential, much more so than the countercase, published in the same year by the then Chairman of India's Agricultural Prices Commission, Ashok Mitra, seeking to show that the rich peasantry were draining resources out of the cities.[20] For Harvard's E. A. J. Johnson, just as the metropolitan powers in the period of empire had exploited their colonies, so the city in developing countries exploited the countryside.[21]

PLANNING

It could hardly be expected that the people technically responsible for advising governments on what should be done with cities would escape this atmosphere of anti-urbanism. The best planners were preoccupied with the inadequate consumption of most of the citizens – the appalling conditions in housing, water supply, sewerage and other services. These were seen as emergency issues, whereas the opportunities for accelerated production arising from the concentration of the labour force were unseen. In consumption terms, each locality should be equal, not specialized. New towns were to be fully diversified, not oriented on one narrow range of activities. Within the city, the division of areas by function – the zoning of residential, commercial and industrial areas – was so highly aggregated it could not be related to the real economy.

If the conceptual approach was inadequate, the means of implementation could affect very little in conditions of rapid urbanization. Land-use controls could work only in upper-income areas. The brave Master Plans became, on the one hand, instruments of social segregation to protect the rich; on the other, public hypocrisy. For long, the planners complained that it was not the plans which were wrong, but only the implementation by administrators. Yet, only non-implementation saved the poor citizens from even worse disaster. Meanwhile, the poor, upon whom so much high-minded talk was lavished, remained stubbornly poor.

Much of policy was based upon the same demographic misspecification of the nature of the problems of the cities. Poor housing – or water supply or sewerage, or whatever – existed because there were too many people who wanted these things, not because incomes were too low or public authorities had failed to make adequate provision. Traffic congestion existed because there were too many people, not because too many private vehicles used or misused inadequate road space. The comfortable classes could thus protect their position.

The mistaken diagnosis led policy to a preoccupation with preventing people migrating to the cities when labour demand, often promoted by government stimulation of industrialization, impelled them to do so. In 1983, a United Nations survey of 126 developing countries showed the melancholy fact that three-quarters of the governments concerned were officially pursuing policies to slow or reverse migration. There was little evidence to support the idea that such policies had any useful effect (at tolerable cost), the costs even then were high, the benefits doubtful or negative. Neither popular welfare, nor equity, nor economic efficiency was advanced. It is ironic that, when the World Bank came to make its first report on China, it reproached the People's Republic for encouraging inequality and greater poverty by preventing people migrating from poor districts.[28]

The traditional measures of planning – land-use regulation at the city level, migration guidance or restriction at the national – cannot be made to work in conditions of fast urbanization in most developing countries. Increasingly, this stubborn fact has been forced upon governments as, despite all the statutes, regulations and planning offices, cities have continued to grow and grow in unanticipated ways. It has led in some cases to a greater preoccupation with how to make cities work better, how to guide territorial development to enhance productivity rather than seek – and fail – to impose an illusion of order.

People have also become much more aware that territorial distributions of economic activity summarize very complex forces. Those forces include much of the non-spatial macroeconomic policies of government as well as sectoral policies in external trade, industry, agriculture, tourism, transport, defence and so on. The urban is not a sector, capable of being handled separately: it is a summary of many sectors. It would not be sensible to seek to subject all sectors to a set of territorial priorities, even if we could agree on what those priorities ought to be. Yet without this, the old kind of spatial policies must fail.

There was much in common in the old methods of state planning in a command economy and physical planning. Both borrowed from the imagery of engineering as if an economy and a territory were machines, subject to simple technical measures, independent of markets, prices and external circumstances. That old world is dying, but the new is still far from clear. The high fashion for markets and a fictional version of private enterprise militates against both planning and the full use of public authorities to guide or stimulate development. But even if this were not so, the quality of local public agencies in many developing countries is quite inadequate to manage urban growth.

AGENCIES

Most developing countries – like some of the developed – have been subject to a long process of increased centralization in administration. The concentration of powers and finance in national governments has been advanced by the necessity to protect national independence and, if need be, fight to do so, as well as by efforts to industrialize. Centralization at one stage forced the generalization of innovation, raised local standards, conserved scarce skills, ensured measures of public accountability, etc. It also produced bureaucracies that frustrated local initiative and engendered administrative inertia. The dead hand afflicted not only local authorities, reduced to complete financial and administrative dependence on central governments, to demoralization and corruption, but also a wider circle of voluntary and community organizations, and the citizens themselves. The good soldier Schweik has now become a universal figure. However, there is increasing recognition that, after the first phase of economic development, national governments in all but the smallest states are unable to deal with the mass of complex detail throughout a country. The attempt to do so produces formidable inefficiencies and waste, an underutilization of the resources available, a reduction in popular welfare, and intense frustrations in the governed.

The liberalizing trend in the world has opened new possibilities here for the refashioning of local government to become agencies of local economic development, of managing urban development and of focusing the efforts of many other nongovernmental bodies. Both Right and Left of the political spectrum have become enamoured of the vogue for local self-reliance, even a measure of the withering away of the state. However, many states remain reluctant to wither. At the city level, they prefer to create powerful non-elected development authorities – a Calcutta Metropolitan Development Authority, a Metro Manila Commission and a London Docklands Development Corporation – which bypass local government. In many developing countries, what is developed in this way is then passed on for maintenance to a weak local authority; the new capacity begins to depreciate swiftly and immediately.

Nonetheless, moves towards strengthening and reforming local government are beginning: it is more often the decentralization of certain administrative functions rather than the creation of financial autonomy, but at least that might provide the basis for acquiring enhanced powers and increased revenues. A territorial division of labour requires effective local public agencies to initiate the tasks of development. The change of direction will require new definitions of local government, new skills and training. Here in Britain, with all the obstacles placed in the way, nonetheless local government is seeking to learn new lessons for a new world.

THE AGENDA

If the shadows, the United Nations demographic projections, are only half true, the tasks facing those concerned with these issues are daunting. The redistribution of a major part of the world's labour force over the coming century will require unprecedented increases in investment in infrastructure; in the training of people capable of linking issues of the built environment with the processes of rapid social and economic change. A new world of integrated manufacturing systems will require much more, not less, planning, much more anticipation of the innovations in transport and the giant throughput required of transport terminals to sustain a world division of labour, more attention to the unseen base of the manufacturing iceberg, the statistically unrecorded informal sector, and to the emergence of a single world financial system operating out of a string of world cities. In the field of education itself we can presume we shall see the emergence of a series of world universities, most often city-based.

The narrower agenda for those concerned with the built environment is no less ambitious – from the definition of new concepts to monitor the changing territorial distribution of labour to research and education in the management of settlement systems as important instruments in economic development, to the most appropriate design, technology and management of buildings, the changing balance between participation and public initiative, new patterns of employment, and the formidable threats to the urban environment.

With current resources, the tasks could not be undertaken. But cities will not grow without the growth of employment, statistically recorded or not, and thereby the incomes that potentially are capable of sustaining consumption. The problem becomes not an absolute shortage of resources in the face of blind influxes of faceless and starving millions – the old nightmare – but of developing the capacity to manage growing resources, and to do so without gross inequalities, the naked operation of class power and the hideous repressions so common today.

The new era is alive with rethinking, with revisionism. Many of the new ideas are deplorable, abandoning babes and bathwater together. But one must remind oneself of the Chinese character for great opportunity which means simultaneously great danger. In that dialectic has always lain the horror and magnificence of great cities, the threat and the promise. It is that spirit that leads me to believe that, despite all the appalling miseries of so many cities in developing countries, despite the issues of exploitation embedded in the division of labour, there are grounds for optimism. For 200 years, the world has laboured through the foothills of industrialization from those obscure beginnings in Lancashire; we are now ready for a world industrial revolution. The energies and ingenuities released in the first phases, giving rise to such astonishing material and technical accomplishments, are sure to be dwarfed by what is coming.

Thus, Plato's demographic shadows are not nightmares, but hints of a world where urbanization will be part of the completion of the process of universal emancipation – allowing all to be fed, well educated, to take the first steps on the long path of universal self-realization. Of course, it is all potential – until people seize it and make it actual. But still the shadows give us cause for hope that we can escape the imprisonment of the bad old past.

2

Urbanization and Economic Development: Territorial Specialization and Policy

INTRODUCTION

The 1988 report of the National Commission on Urbanization to the Government of India notes that, while India's urban dwellers have increased fourfold since 1947 (from some 50 to over 200 million), public attitudes to cities have remained ambivalent.[1]

> On the one hand, we see them as heroic engines of growth . . . On the other, these urban centres have also generated the most brutal and inhuman living conditions.

It suggests that the second observation has more substance for 'The urban centres . . . . should be generators of wealth; instead, they have degenerated into parasites looking elsewhere for support'.

The Commission is by no means alone in this second opinion. In possibly the majority of developing countries, cities are commonly seen as primarily problems, whether of welfare or potential political instability; they are also seen as rich and unproductive. At this stage, opinion comes close to early European mercantilism, seeing the urban sector as an unproductive parasitic force, draining resources out of the only truly productive activity, agriculture. However, while some such views lingered on in the nineteenth century, present-day analysts have tended to draw a sharp contrast between nineteenth-century urbanization in the now developed countries and modern urbanization in developing countries; then cities were supposedly productive, now they are not.

This paper argues that, while the content and function of cities have indeed changed, their overall role remains much as it was in the nineteenth century. Nor is the poverty so apparent in the cities of

Originally published as 'Urbanization and Economic Development' as DPU Working Paper No. 19, Development, Planning Unit, University College London, January 1990.

developing countries today a new phenomenon. The social conditions of the urban poor today are, by the main measures available, a remarkable improvement on those experienced in, say, British cities in the early nineteenth century. Furthermore, urban productivity is now high, and the contribution of cities to national development is almost certainly greater than in the last century. It follows that, if this argument is valid, developing country governments and aid donors need to take the cities very much more seriously.

ECONOMIC ACTIVITY AND URBANIZATION

The association of urbanization and changes in economic activity is not at all a simple one, both because of the complexity of factors underlying the physical concentration of populations and because of the formidable statistical problems at stake. Each country – and countries are of enormously different sizes – has a unique historical inheritance of settlements (for example, in some farmers have traditionally lived in towns; in others, manufacturing is traditionally rural-based), and a no less unique physical endowment. Furthermore, we have no satisfactory single statistical measure of the structural change a national economy goes through as it develops; changes in gross national product per capita or gross domestic product do not allow us to distinguish between the structural change implied by economic development, and economic growth (where no structural change is necessarily implied). Urbanization is beset with even greater problems, since it refers to the concentration of population (not the labour force) within quite arbitrarily established administrative boundaries, themselves subject to radical changes from time to time: there is no common international standard for the definition of 'urban' in national censuses – at the extremes, urban can refer to settlements with 2,500 or more inhabitants or 50,000 or more.[2] Moreover, there is no agreement on what should be properly grouped together as the urban economic unit – New York City or the New York Metropolitan Region, central Tokyo or the Tokyo Region (with 24 million inhabitants).[3]

Given these difficulties, it would be surprising if a very close relationship could be established. Nonetheless, a number of successful attempts have been made to express the association in comparisons between countries.[4] Figures 2.1 to 2.3 illustrate the association with the most recent data available. Figure 2.1 compares GNP per capita and the proportion of national population which is urban for 120 countries in 1987. The straight line represents the trend in the relationship for the series. As can be seen, there is a

Figure 2.1: GNP per capita by urban population 1987

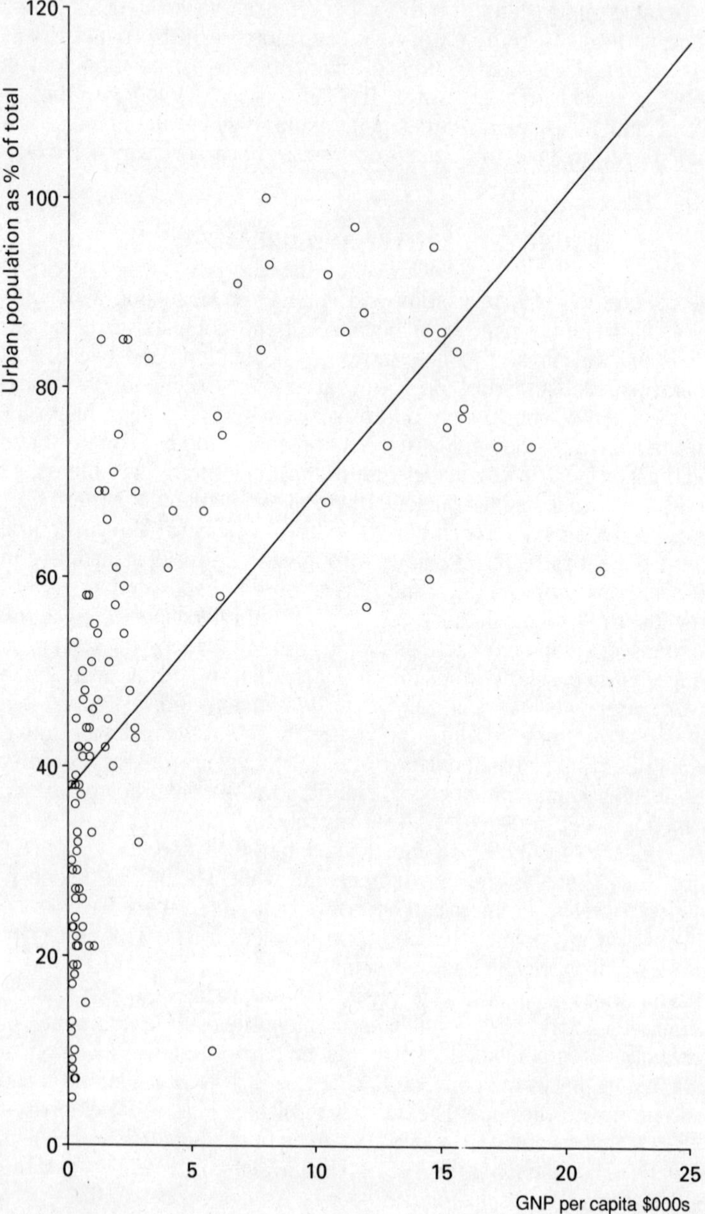

Figure 2.2a: Comparison of rates of increase in GDP and urban population 1965–80 and 1980–87. Low income countries

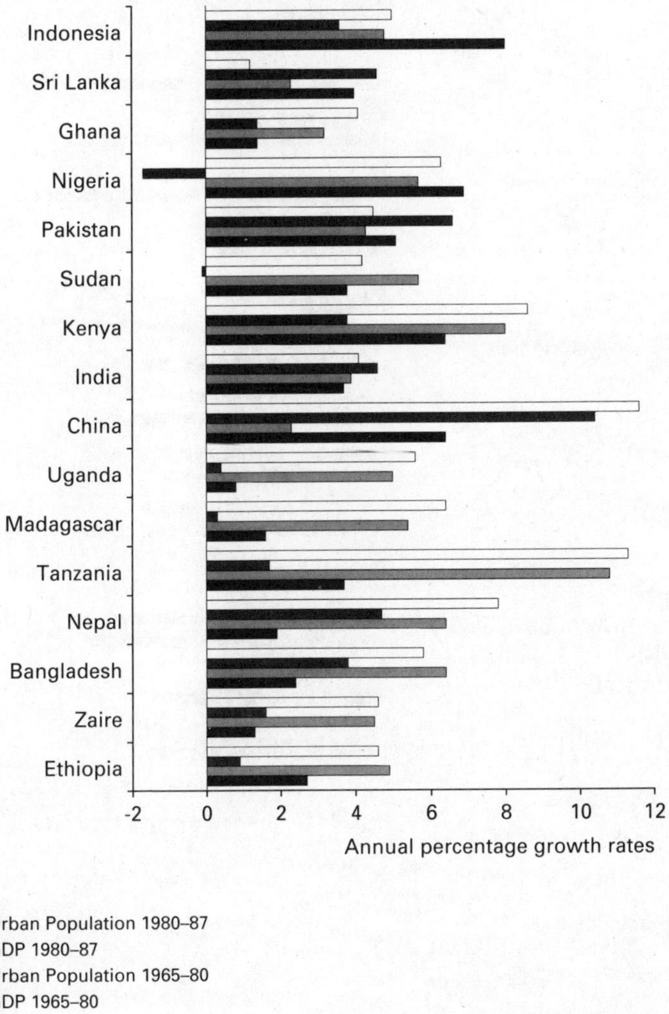

Indonesia
Sri Lanka
Ghana
Nigeria
Pakistan
Sudan
Kenya
India
China
Uganda
Madagascar
Tanzania
Nepal
Bangladesh
Zaire
Ethiopia
-2
0
2
4
6
8
10
12
Annual percentage growth rates
Urban Population 1980–87
GDP 1980–87
Urban Population 1965–80
GDP 1965–80

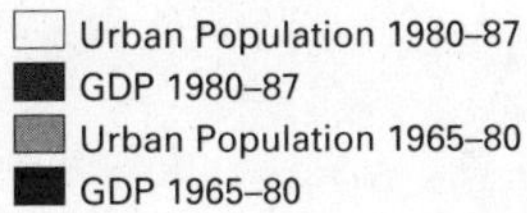

Rates of increase of GDP and of urban population, 1965–87, ascending order from the lowest per capita GNP level, countries with 10 million or more population (where data available)

Source: *World Development Report 1989,* World Bank, Washington DC, 1989,

Figure 2.2b: Comparison of rates of increase in GDP and urban population 1965–80 and 1980–87. Lower middle income countries

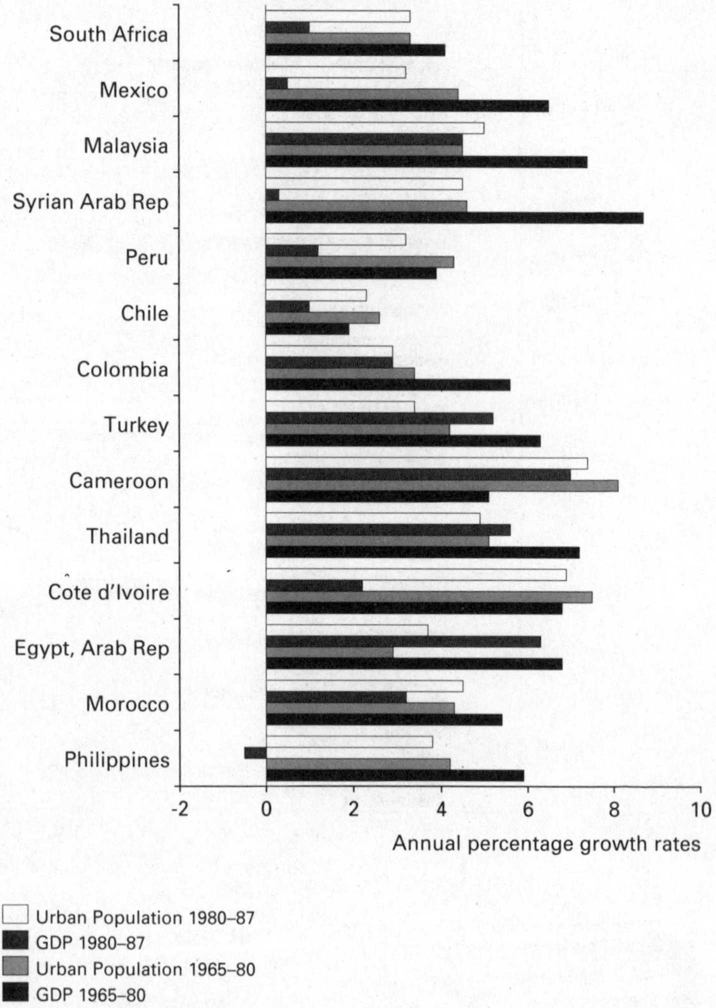

South Africa
Mexico
Malaysia
Syrian Arab Rep
Peru
Chile
Colombia
Turkey
Cameroon
Thailand
Côte d'Ivoire
Egypt, Arab Rep
Morocco
Philippines
-2
0
2
4
6
8
10
Annual percentage growth rates
Urban Population 1980–87
GDP 1980–87
Urban Population 1965–80
GDP 1965–80

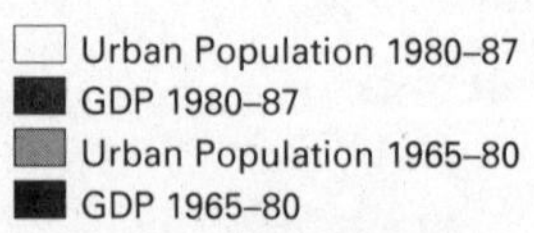

Rates of increase of GDP and of urban population, 1965–87, ascending order from the lowest per capita GNP level, countries with 10 million or more population (where data available)

Source: *World Development Report 1989,* World Bank, Washington DC, 1989,

Figure 2.2c: Comparison of rates of increase in GDP and urban population 1965–80 and 1980–87. Upper middle income countries

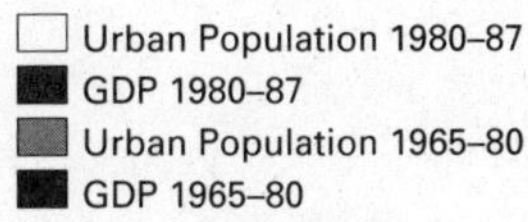

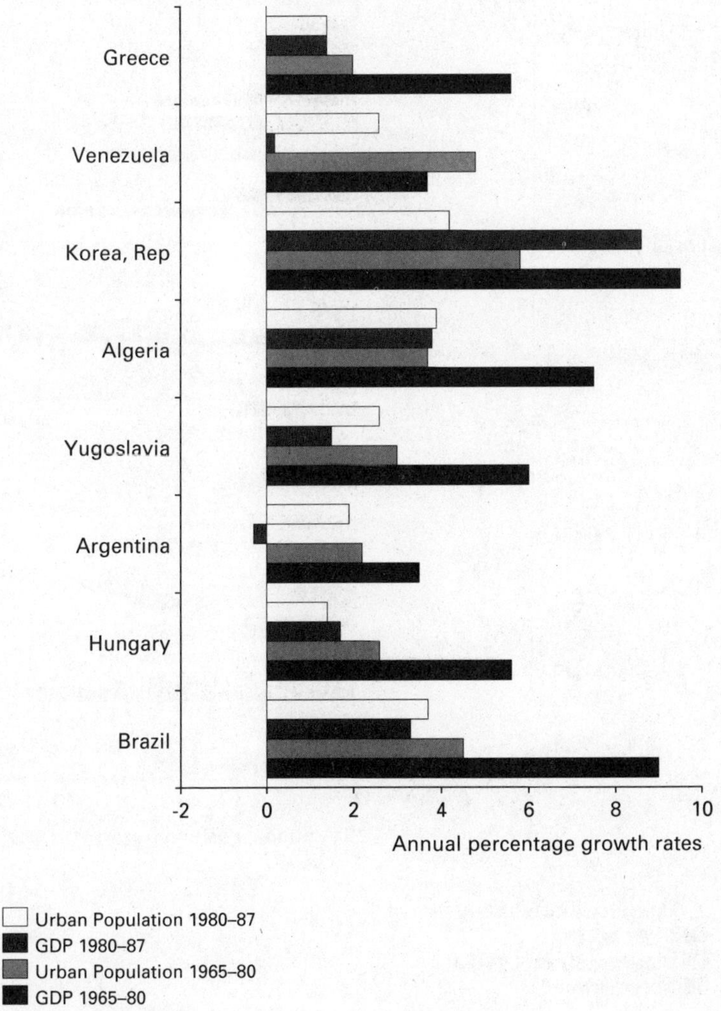

Rates of increase of GDP and of urban population, 1965–87, ascending order from the lowest per capita GNP level, countries with 10 million or more population (where data available)

Source: *World Development Report 1989,* World Bank, Washington DC, 1989,

Figure 2.2d: Comparison of rates of increase in GDP and urban population 1965–80 and 1980–87. High income countries

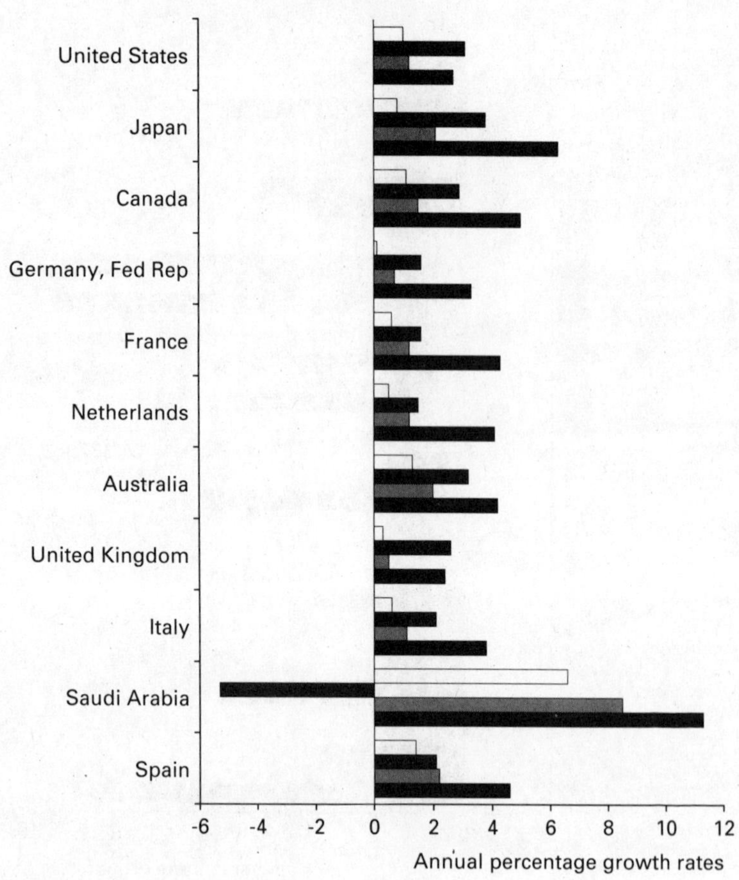

Rates of increase of GDP and of urban population, 1965–87, ascending order from the lowest per capita GNP level, countries with 10 million or more population (where data available)

Source: *World Development Report 1989,* World Bank, Washington DC, 1989,

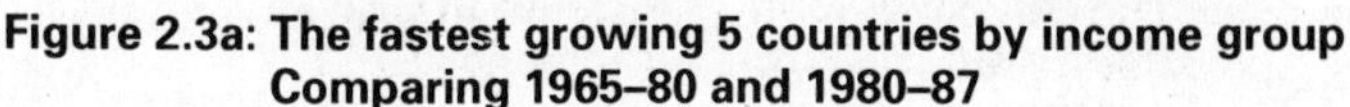

Figure 2.3a: The fastest growing 5 countries by income group Comparing 1965–80 and 1980–87

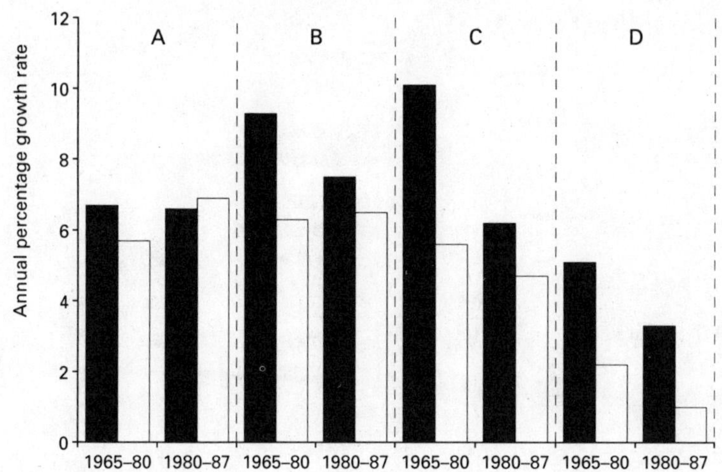

■ % increase GDP
□ % increase urban population

The fastest growing 5 countries (rate of increase of GDP), 1965–80 and 1980–87[a], compared to rate of increase in urban population.

A – Low-income countries
1965–80: Average rate of growth of 5 countries (China, Kenya, Lesotho, Nigeria, Indonesia). 1980–87: Average rate of growth of 5 countries (China, Chad, Lao PDR, Burkino Faso, Pakistan).

B – Lower-middle income countries
1965–80: Average rate of growth of 5 countries (Dominican Republic, Ecuador, Botswana, Syrian Arab Republic, Malaysia). 1980–87: Average rate of growth of 5 countries (Yemen Arab Republic, Egyptian Arab Republic, Thailand, Cameroon, Botswana).

C – Upper-middle income countries
1965–80: Average rate of growth of 5 countries (Brazil, Algeria, South Korea, Gabon, Oman). 1980–87: Average rate of growth of 5 countries (Brazil, Panama, Algeria, South Korea, Oman).

D – High-income countries[b]
1965–80: Average rate of growth of 5 countries (Spain, Ireland, Canada, Japan, Norway). 1980–87: Average rate of growth of 5 countries (Australia, Canada, Japan, Norway, United States).

a. Excluding members of COMECON group.
b. Covering only OECD members

Source: *World Development Report 1989.*

Figure 2.3b: The slowest growing 5 countries by income group Comparing 1965–80 and 1980–87

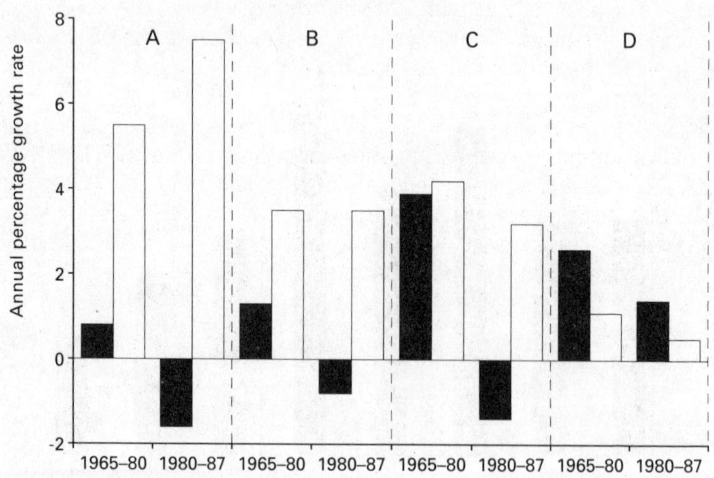

% increase GDP
% increase urban population

The slowest growing 5 countries (rate of increase of GDP), 1965–80 and 1980–87[a], compared to rate of increase in urban population.

A – Low-income countries
1965–80: Average rate of growth of 5 countries (Chad, Zaire, Niger, Uganda, Ghana).
1980–87: Average rate of growth of 5 countries (Mozambique, Niger, Togo, Nigeria, Liberia).

B – Lower-middle income countries
1965–80: Average rate of growth of 5 countries (Senegal, Nicaragua, Jamaica, Chile, Lebanon). 1980–87: Average rate of growth of 5 countries (Bolivia, Philippines, Nicaragua, El Salvador, Guatamala).

C – Upper-middle income countries
1965–80: Average rate of growth of 5 countries (Uruguay, Panama, Argentina, Venezuela, Libya). 1980–87: Average rate of growth of 5 countries (Uruguay, Argentina, Gabon, Venezuela, Trinidad and Tobago).

D – High-income countries[b]
1965–80: Average rate of growth of 6* countries (New Zealand, United Kingdom, United States, Switzerland, Denmark, Sweden). 1980–87: Average rate of growth of 7* countries (Ireland, Netherlands, Belgium, Austria, Sweden, France, Federal Republic of Germany). (* because of identical growth)

a. Excluding members of COMECON group.
b. Covering only OECD members

Source: *Ibid*

reasonably close association (the correlation is 0.6557), but with quite a wide scatter of 'exceptional' cases. It is also apparent that the association varies considerably at low and high incomes; low-income countries appear as relatively 'overurbanized' (above the line), and the few higher-income countries are 'underurbanized' (that is, below the line). In the middle ranges, the fit is closer, but with a tendency towards the 'overurbanized'.

Figure 2.2 provides a bar chart for 49 countries with populations of 10 million or more, comparing rates of annual *growth* of GDP and urban population for two periods, 1965–1980 and 1980–87. The same general conclusion follows; there is a roughly ordered scatter with some wide divergences (which may of course be due to extraordinary definitions or poor data rather than representing real deviations). Finally, Figure 2.3 presents the same relationship for the five countries in each income group (low, lower middle, upper middle, and high) with the highest and lowest rates of growth of GDP in the same two periods.

It is apparent from the bar charts that, with high rates of economic growth, urbanization increases. However, at high *levels* of per capita income – which are also points where usually a high proportion of the population is already urban – the association is weak; urbanization is slow, and relatively unresponsive to changes in economic growth (very roughly, the increase in urban population is always well below the rate of economic growth, and most commonly about half the rate). At the other extreme, with low levels of per capita income (where a low proportion of the population is urban), the reverse situation seems to occur; relatively small increases in economic growth may produce disproportionate increases in urbanization. The fit between the two variables is closer in the middle ranges, but then fades as income rises. However, in the low-income case, where the rate of economic growth between the two periods declines, urbanization not only does not increase, the relationship may become perverse. In Figure 2.3, for the slowest growing group of low-income countries, a low rate of growth of GDP (averaging 0.8 per cent annually) in the first period went with a growth of urban population of 5.5 per cent per year; in the second period, a negative economic growth rate (−1.6 per cent) went with an extraordinary urban growth rate of 7.5 per cent. Thus, the relationship is non-symmetrical in the low-income group (a point confirmed for some individual countries with high rates of urban growth and low or negative rates of economic growth, like Tanzania with an urban growth rate of 11.3 per cent, or Mozambique, with 10.7 per cent, but economic growth rates of 1.7 and −2.6 per cent, all in the 1980s). Of course, aggregation of the groups of five may have produced some of the anomalies, and, even if this is not so, we have little idea of the lags in, or changing ratios of, changes in the output of goods and services and associated urban employment effects.

In both low- and high-income groups, inmigration is an important source of growth in the urban population, but in the low-income countries, relatively high inmigration goes with high rates of natural increase, whereas in the high-income, the rate of natural increase is low, and the proportion of migrants high. In the middle-income countries, natural increase predominates, particularly where the urban population is dominated by young inmigrants from the past phase of urban growth. The middle-income countries, however, have also had much higher rates of economic growth, and this has generated significantly higher rates of urbanization than the high-income. The lower-middle share features with the low-income; countries with high economic growth have maintained rates of increase in output well ahead of urban growth, but economically slow growing countries have experienced a reverse phenomenon (even, in the 1980s, matching a −0.8 per cent product decline with a 3.5 per cent urban growth). In the upper-middle group, the trends approximate to high-income patterns, but with much higher rates of economic growth (though again, in the 1980s, for the slow growers, a −1.4 per cent annual decline in output with a 3.2 per cent urban increase). For this group, the rural population is now small enough to decline absolutely with urbanization, indicating that urban labour markets (and migration between cities) dominate the national picture.

Thus, in sum, the association of economic activity and urbanization varies with the 'stage of development'. Of course, the generalization applies only to the years examined and is not meant to imply some ahistorical relationship. Urbanization can decline sharply, and even the size of the urban population can shrink in certain circumstances (during war or extended periods of economic contraction). Furthermore, historically, the composition of GDP has varied enormously, and so, necessarily, the relationship of output to location. However, the rough generalizations hold for the type of national outputs characteristic today, despite a few striking exceptions (for example, China, governed by relatively strict migration controls up to 1980 but not afterwards). They do not rule out very different patterns – from the dispersed spatial patterns of Taiwan or Kerala, to the highly concentrated ones of South Korea and West Bengal.

TERRITORIAL SPECIALIZATION AND ECONOMIC DEVELOPMENT

The mechanism linking economic development and urbanization is the labour market. With economic development, employment is redistributed beween sectors, and since different locations are or become the sites for different sectors of production, so the labour force is also territorially redistributed. The physical concentration of workers appears to be an important initial phase in the process of raising the general level of social productivity; once concentrated, the workers and their families then become an additional element in sustaining growth in demand. Of course, this generalization is based upon a high level of abstraction, and, as noted before, historically the content of the process has been very different, and each country is in some sense unique (with, therefore, a unique relationship to external markets). There are no grounds at this stage for assuming that one pattern of territorial organization is better than another.

Thus, settlements can be seen as a physical bunching of the labour force (with supportive capital equipment and infrastructure) in response to the disproportionalities in the growth of output which are implicit in the process of economic development. Cities produce an output of goods and services where, in conditions of relative economic backwardness, productivity is disproportionately enhanced by physical concentration. Of course, not all urbanization is related directly to expanded output in the ordinary sense. Many other modern economic activities require some physical concentration of factors – finance and commerce, wholesale trade, some high value retail trade, warehousing and markets, transport terminals, government, higher education and higher-level health and cultural facilities. The reverse is also true: the transformation of some types of output requires physical dispersal – for example, high productivity but extensive agriculture, some forms of manufacturing (for example, sugar refining, timber processing, etc.). Furthermore, dependence upon the physical concentration of the factors of production varies widely relative to changes in technology, the adequacy of infrastructure, communications and a labour force with relevant skills outside the cities (or willing to move at acceptable cost). But it seems generally true that the more backward economically a country is, the more vital it is for national output that there should be at least one major concentration of workers with infrastructure of a reasonably high standard.

In the study of international trade, a well-known set of theories holds that, under conditions of relatively free trade, countries come to specialize – and trade – in particular goods and services, making different contributions to a world output. The theory of comparative advantage has even greater validity within countries where the barriers to trade are usually much less important and the market is freer. Such a separation of locality specializations would occur without economic development, but development considerably enhances the process (by unifying the territorial area economically, overcoming internal socio-political and physical barriers to domestic trade, reducing transport costs and local self-sufficiency, expanding output as well as introducing many more new forms of output). In the stereotypical case, out of subsistence peasant agriculture emerge wheat-growing districts, cotton tracts, sugar fields; the old market towns or traditional mining centres become heavy or light engineering cities, garment-making districts, administrative centres, etc. In a competitive system, these specializations are not necessarily stable indefinitely, but at any moment of time, they allow us to perceive the territorial interactions which go to make up the national output – and so the connections between a changing composition of output and spatial organization.

Urban productivity during economic development depends upon the fact that the activities which begin or already take place in cities gain disproportionately from scale economies.[5] These may be internal to the industry or the result of the urban agglomeration itself (or some combination of the two). They are of many different types: the low cost of the communication of innovations, market information, etc. between firms; labour market economies in searching for and matching diverse and scarce skills to demand, creating combinations of skills, reducing the need to hold workers in offseasons; economies of specialization through long runs of making only specialized inputs to the output of other firms; economies in the provision of common services. Furthermore, the urban command of transport networks offers the cheapest access to the largest market sizes and thus the potential for the greatest economies of scale in production.

The concentration of population makes for great economies. But it also makes for greater costs, represented, for example, in higher wages, higher land costs, greater congestion, etc. To meet these higher costs, city firms have to utilize the factors of production more efficiently. The lower costs of non-urban locations – given equal provision of infrastructure – allow less efficiency. In the developed countries, some of the large old industrial cities showed in the 1960s and 1970s a declining capacity to meet the higher costs, a problem exaggerated in the contraction of 1979–81 and leading to the rapid decline of urban manufacturing.[6]

Thus, the degree to which scale economies are possible in the newly created and changing output of goods and services of a developing country broadly determines the growth of the urban sector, the distribution of the urban population between settlements of different sizes and the patterns of specialization by locality. Of course, other factors affect the issue – for example, the availability of natural resources, the availability and pricing of infrastructure, transport costs (for the inputs to, and extra-city traded output of, the city), income and consumption patterns, government policy, trade relationships,[7] etc.

As the output of goods and services changes from the traditional (natural fibre textiles, warehousing, processing and transport of agricultural and mining goods, food processing, leather and wood manufacture, printing and publishing, retail and personal services) to the non-traditional (heavy machinery, transport equipment, chemicals, synthetic fibre processing, electrical and non-electrical equipment, pulp and paper, etc.), so the roles and relative sizes of cities change. It may be – as Mills and Becker have noted for India[8] – that manufacturing proper is of declining significance within urban boundaries, but rapid industrialization, even when the factories are located outside the cities, depends heavily upon urban services – from finance, markets and transport terminals to research and scientific support.

Settlement systems in countries with a long history of cities are usually very stable. The inherited system accommodates the new forces, or at least endeavours to do so. The cost of creating new cities is very high, and even when such cities are created, they are often quite unable to emulate the services of older cities for a long period of time. Thus, new settlements are not created at anything like the speed with which older ones are growing into larger and larger size classes, so producing a constantly more 'unbalanced' distribution of settlement by size.

If the growth of cities in industrializing economies is a function of the changes in national output, then the disaggregated pattern of national output – which sectors and sub-sectors grow relatively more or less swiftly (with their respective employment multipliers) – determines which cities grow fastest. The composition of the output of each city is thus as unique as that of a country, and the cities as a whole form a system of interdependent production locations (not at all the same as what geographers call 'urban hierarchy').

Henderson[9] has made some important progress in identifying the patterns of territorial specialization in a number of countries (the United States, Brazil, and China). In the case of the United States, he estimates that between 50 and 60 per cent of the city labour force is engaged in the production of goods and services which are not traded outside the city (the proportion varies relative to, among other factors, how far transport costs lend a 'natural' protection against imports from outside). The remaining 40 per cent is engaged in the 'export base', the specializations traded by the city. Of the 243 urban areas of the United States with a population of 50,000 or more in 1970, about half specialized in particular sub-sectors of manufacturing, while the rest were engaged in the provision of non-industrial services – from those pertaining to agriculture, to government, banking and commerce, medical and educational services, etc.

Henderson seeks to demonstrate that different population sizes of cities indicate different 'peak sizes' for the complex of specializations in the city's externally traded output of goods and services. In particular, he argues that in the United States, for example, the peak size for one of the most rapidly growing sectors, 'business and professional services', is very high, suggesting that as the American economy shifts towards a greater share of this sector in its national output, an increasing proportion of the population is likely to live in, or close to, the largest cities. The same factor may be, to differing degrees, at work in most large cities of the world, tending to increase the average size of the large city in developing countries.

He also argues that the largest cities specialize in the production of those goods and services where the greatest scale economies are available. The radical reduction in transport costs since the Second World War has perhaps increased the number of industries where such economies are exploitable, breaking down the former protection of activities located in smaller settlements (as for example, in the last century, the railways broke down the protection of village handloom weaving in India and created a much larger market for Bombay mill output). There are, of course, other forces enhancing the economic superiority of the largest cities in developing countries – for example, the important inheritance of colonially created port cities, the economic necessity to concentrate the first major efforts in infrastructure, the availability of skilled labour in a situation of great skill scarcities, the dependence upon imported manufacturing inputs and services, all of which encourage in the first stages a relative lack of territorial specialization between different cities (that is, many more specializations are located in one place, whereas in a developed country they would tend to be distributed in a number of cities). Furthermore, as is well known, there are perverse effects of macroeconomic policy and pricing in encouraging 'excessive' growth of the largest cities.

These may be some of the elements explaining the relatively high proportion of the urban population in developing countries living in the largest city (see Tables 2.6–2.7 below) (as compared to the more developed countries). It seems that the largest cities in all income groups are the more appropriate environment for the location of the characteristic forms of current economic activity, but whereas this tends to be a multiplicity of cities in developed countries, it may be only one very large city in a low-income country; and this last result may be a direct function of the relative scarcity of resources.

However, in many countries, the largest cities (regardless of their absolute size) seem to be experiencing slowing rates of growth. In the more developed countries, urbanization continues (in the OECD group, the 'urban' proportion increased from 72 to 77 per cent between 1965 and 1987), as does the concentration of the urban population in cities of half a million or more people. However, of the 14 largest developed countries, five experienced a decline of population in cities of half a million or more (and one stayed the same). Furthermore, despite some recent revival of growth, the very largest cities, particularly those heavily dependent in the past upon manufacturing, have lost population. The disproportionate decline in manufacturing employment in developed countries has had exaggerated effects in the urban sector. However, just as it now seems that 'deindustrialization' in fact concealed enhanced specialization in manufacturing,[10] the byproduct of an increasingly integrated world economy which, if the theory is correct, must produce greater specialization, so 'deurbanization' concealed not so much a decline of cities but rather enhanced territorial specialization within the sector of 'quarternary producer and administrative services'. Nor is the phenomenon restricted to the developed countries. Mills and Becker note that the contribution of large cities to differentials in manufacturing productivity in India was declining compared to medium-sized cities, and that this may have been a key factor in the relative stagnation of the largest cities in terms of population growth and the increasing role of smaller settlements.[11]

Once the criterion of output is introduced in the study of cities, it is implicit that each city is unique, so there can be no 'optimum' population size for cities in general. Indeed, other things being equal, each city can be assumed to be optimal for its particular output of goods and services. Or, to turn the proposition round, there are no grounds for assuming that the peculiar output of a particular city could be produced by increasing or reducing the population living within it. Cities cannot be other than temporarily 'too big' or 'too small', and there are a multiplicity of optima relating to different outputs. The largest cities may be, for certain historical periods, more efficient in the use of resources than small ones, but that is more efficient in producing a different output. In the same way, smaller cities are more efficient at producing what they produce. It is implicit that the production functions involved are unstable, subject to sudden and swift changes, so that optima similarly cannot be assumed to be stable. Furthermore, although technologies are often relatively rigid in the combination of factors required to produce a particular output, the total social process of production can vary very widely – so that different city population sizes may, in different contexts, be based upon the same volume of output of goods and services at the same prices. In policy terms, we have no defensible grounds for asserting that one size of city or one combination of settlements is economically superior to another.

It is usually easier to identify the specializations of smaller cities. Larger cities are characterized not only by greater complexity but by a greater speed of change, making analysis difficult. However, in territorial terms, the same principles apply within metropolitan areas as apply to national settlement systems. The city's output is determined by the interaction of specialized but closely interdependent urban districts. The most evident of these is the central business district, usually with a physical identity (high-rise buildings) which is the product of its specialization in banking, finance, investment and commerce, linked to wholesale markets and thus warehousing, transport terminals (trucking, rail, seaports). In many large cities, the business district is not necessarily distinct from the area of retail stores, hotels, clubs and theatres. Usually in developing countries it is also closely interwoven with a mass of petty manufacture, trading and finance, the 'informal' sector. The threads lead outwards from the central complex to other areas of specialized manufacture, servicing and repair, and specialized retail trade. In pre-industrial cities, patterns of territorial specialization have long been familiar – the quarters of silversmiths, harness makers, sempstresses, etc. In the modern city, the same process produces similar differentiation of modern products by streets. The rapid growth and dynamic change of many urban areas in developing countries make for greater instability in the formation of territorial specialization. Nonetheless, the principle remains the same, indicating that the urban districts are not simply homogeneous housing areas that ought to be provided with a standard package of consumer services, but interdependent and specialized contributors to a city's output.

The possibility of territorial specialization enhancing productivity depends upon the openness of the trading system, a market economy. However, there are many well-known reservations here. Public authorities intervene at many different levels and often without being particularly concerned with territorial issues. In a fully State-directed economy, it becomes a matter for research to identify how far in practice spatial differentiation nonetheless emerges within the framework of public control. In such a context, the generalizations advanced here may have to be radically amended.

Agriculture

The sectors of high productivity in a developing economy play an important role in forcing the pace of change in the rest of the society. The more dynamic agricultural sectors have, other things being equal, multiple effects on the rest of agriculture and on the cities. The more expansive sectors of urban activity are similarly important for agriculture, particularly in the rural areas surrounding the growing cities. Here the improving farmer can develop the capital, credit and technical basis to experiment with innovative high value intensive farming. The city labour market offers part-time work in the agricultural offseason for cultivators; some urban labour-intensive activities are decentralized to rural locations. Increased rural incomes make possible further diversification. Thus, despite the frequent assertion that 'trickle-down' economic effects no longer occur, there is substantial evidence that this is not so.

Furthermore, there are economic effects in agriculture which are more general, not simply related to areas physically contiguous to a city. Concentrated urban markets with a relatively high growth of income provide expanding demand for agricultural outputs, and this forces the pace of agricultural specialization and helps to impel raised productivity. City-related manufacturing usually provides part of rural consumption as well as engineering, chemical and other inputs to agriculture. High levels of urban productivity today – compared to the developed countries in the nineteenth century – mean that enhanced national investment from urban savings can be available for direct improvement in rural areas (particularly in infrastructure).

In sum, the need for urbanization in developing countries as a means to modernize agriculture is today probably greater than ever before. No possible transformation of agriculture could conceivably employ the expected rural labour force, so that employment in the cities (including those resulting from the growth of existing small towns) and off-farm (non-agricultural but still rural) must be the main means to ensure some work for all. Urban development is not an alternative to rural development: each is necessary to the other.

Productivity

To summarize, the heart of the process of economic development is the establishment of mechanisms for a continuing rise in the productivity of the factors of production. This involves a radical change in the structure of an economy and the quality and composition of the labour force. The sharp differences in productivity between sectors and sub-sectors of the national output are key factors in producing or enhancing territorial differentiation (and territorial differentiation in turn enhances the growth of productivity). The sectorally different potential for scale economies generates and sustains different sizes of settlement.

Careful studies suggest that national rates of natural population increase bear little relationship to the rates of growth of urban populations. Nor is urban growth related to capital transfers to cities nor rural land scarcity.[12] Rural poverty does not in general drive people off the land (although, of course, there may be particular cases where this is true). Thus, changes in the rates of overall population growth or improvement in rural conditions (which may be desirable on other grounds) are unlikely to have significant effects on the growth of urban populations. Even lowering the urban rate of natural increase may make little difference to the growth of the urban population, for, if labour demand continues to be buoyant, increased inmigration will make up any losses. The most important factor in reducing the growth of the urban population would thus be a sharp relative decline in urban productivity (other things being equal, of course).

Despite the perception of disordered and impoverished cities, urban productivity has become, by historical standards, very high today. So much so that the nature of economic development appears to have been changed; the growth of the contribution of modern manufacturing and services to GDP can continue at high levels without substantial changes in the employment of the labour force in modern activities. By the output criterion, a number of Newly Industrializing Countries are now more 'industrialized' than the industrialized countries, even though a sizable share of their labour force remains engaged in low productivity agriculture.

A related feature of this phenomenon is the growing and disproportionate contribution of the cities to national output in a number of developing countries. World Bank figures suggest that nearly 60 per cent of the gross national products of developing countries is now generated in urban areas (by one third of the labour force), and 80 per cent of the increment in national outputs.[13] In low-income India, the National Commission on Urbanization reports that the cities and towns contributed 29 per cent of GDP in 1950–51 and 37 per cent in 1971–2.[14] The equivalent figure for 1980–81 has been put at 47 per cent, with a projection for 1994–5 of 58 per cent. The same source estimates the differential in value added between rural and urban workers in India at 1:2.7 in 1970–1, 1:2.87 in 1980-81, with a projection to 1:3.34 for 1994–5.[15]

In middle-income countries, the economic role of cities and towns appears to be even greater. For example, in Turkey, it is said that

Table 2.1 *High-growth developing countries in the 1980s (4% or more)*

	1. Rate of change in GDP, 1980–7 (manufacturing)		2. Rate of change of exports 1980–7	3./4. Manufactured exports (machinery) and transport eq.) 1965		1987	
Low-income							
Chad	5.1	(8.5)	—	4	(0)	—	(—)
Nepal	4.7	(—)	5.1	22	(0)	70	(2)
Lao PDR	5.3	(—)	—	—	(—)	—	(—)
Burkina Faso	5.6	(—)	4.9	5	(1)	2	(1)
PR China	10.4	(12.6)	11.7	46	(3)	70	(4)
India	4.6	(8.3)	3.6	49	(1)	69	(10)
Pakistan	6.6	(8.9)	8.4	36	(1)	67	(3)
Sri Lanka	4.6	(6.2)	6.5	1	(0)	40	(2)
Lower-middle income							
Yemen AR	5.6	(14.2)	−4.0	0	(0)	78	(63)
Egypt	6.3	(6.1)	8.4	20	(0)	19	(0)
Thailand	5.6	(6.0)	10.2	4	(0)	53	(12)
Congo PR	5.5	(9.7)	3.9	63	(2)	16	(1)
Cameroon	7.0	(8.5)	9.7	5	(3)	10	(5)
Botswana	13.0	(4.5)	—	—	(—)	—	(—)
Turkey	5.2	(8.2)	17.1	2	(0)	67	(7)
Mauritius	5.5	(10.9)	11.1	0	(0)	40	(2)
Jordan	4.3	(3.1)	5.9	18	(11)	55	(14)
Malaysia	4.5	(6.3)	9.7	6	(2)	40	(27)
Upper-middle income[a]							
S. Korea	8.6	(10.6)	14.3	59	(3)	92	(33)
Oman	12.7	(37.9)	—	—	(—)	7	(5)

[a] Two city-States, formerly classified as upper-middle income countries and with average rates of growth of 4 per cent or more – Singapore and Hong Kong – are now included by the World Bank in the high-income group.

Columns: 1. Annual rate of increase of GDP, 1980–87. 2. Annual rate of increase in exports, 1980–87. 3. and 4. Manufacturing exports, 1965 and 1987, with the proportion of exports provided by machinery and transport equipment in brackets.

Source: World Development Report 1989, Tables 2, 14 and 16.

the urban contribution to GDP is of the order of 75 per cent (having risen from 19 per cent in the 1950s and 50 per cent in the 1970s). Of course, the methodology for these calculations is difficult, for they rest upon assumptions about rural and urban pricing and macro-economic policy (including, for example, import protection and interest rate subsidization) which can easily distort the final outcome. However, without placing much weight upon the precise quantitative differences, the broad orders of magnitude are suggestive of the changed role of modern urban economic activities in national development, and are thus part of the agenda for public action.

TRENDS IN THE WORLD ECONOMY AND TERRITORIAL SPECIALIZATION

Given the unprecedented economic growth in the quarter of a century following the Second World War and the simultaneous process of decolonization for the majority of developing countries, the great surge of growth in urban populations is hardly surprising. With high economic growth has come an unprecedented expansion in infrastructure and industrialization, changing the world shares of these items. In the second case, up to 1980, when world gross manufacturing output (excluding the Comecon group) increased by something of the order of three and a half times, the share of developing countries grew from 12.7 to 17.9 per cent.

Furthermore, despite the severe problems confronting many developing countries and affecting the growth in world trade in the 1980s, a number have continued to experience rapid growth. Table 2.1 lists the twenty developing countries with rates of growth of GDP in the 1980s of 4 per cent or more. They include eight low-income countries, with three of the most heavily populated countries in the world (China, India and Pakistan). In brackets is shown the rate of growth of manufacturing output for fifteen of the twenty, eleven of them with annual average growth rates of a remarkable 8 per cent or more. In exports, nine of the eighteen for which there are data also had rates of growth of 8 per cent or more. Furthermore, most countries had made substantial increases in the proportion of manufactured goods in their exports; by 1980, for the nineteen for which there are data, in eight manufactured goods contributed 50 per cent or more of the total (including four of the low-income group for which data are available), and for six, machinery and transport equipment, a rough surrogate for skill intensity, constituted 10 per cent or more of the total.

Table 2.2 looks more closely at the 25 developing countries with

Table 2.2 *Growth of manufacturing, selected countries 1980–87*

	1. Rate of growth of manufacturing	*2. % Manufacturing in GDP – (a) Machinery & transport equip. (b) Textiles & clothing*			*3. Gross domestic investment*
Low-income			*(a)*	*(b)*	
Chad	8.5	15	(0)	(40)	—
Burundi	6.6	9	(—)	(—)	5.4
China	12.6	34	(26)	(13)	19.0
India	8.3	20	(26)	(16)	3.7
Benin	4.6	4	(0)	(16)	−12.7
Kenya	4.3	11	(14)	(12)	−2.3
Pakistan	8.9	17	(8)	(21)	7.4
Lesotho	12.9	15	(0)	(20)	—
Sri Lanka	6.2	16	(—)	(—)	−5.1
Indonesia	7.8	14	(10)	(11)	4.1
Lower-middle income					
Senegal	4.3	17	(6)	(15)	1.1
Yemen AR	14.2	12	(—)	(—)	−10.0
Egypt	6.1	14	(13)	(27)	2.7
Côte d'Ivoire	8.2	16	(—)	(—)	−14.2
Thailand	6.0	24	(14)	(17)	3.9
Congo, P. Rep.	9.7	8	(3)	(13)	−3.8
Cameroon	8.5	13	(7)	(13)	3.3
Botswana	4.5	6	(0)	(12)	−1.5
Tunisia	6.1	15	(7)	(19)	−3.8
Turkey	8.2	26	(14)	(15)	4.8
Mauritius	10.9	24	(3)	(39)	10.8
Malaysia	6.3	—	(23)	(5)	−1.0
Upper-middle income					
Algeria	8.5	12	(11)	(20)	0.6
S. Korea	10.6	30	(24)	(17)	10.0
Oman	37.9	6	(—)	(—)	18.4

Table 2.2 continued

	1. *Rate of growth of manufacturing*	2. *% Manufacturing in GDP – (a) Machinery & transport equip. (b) Textiles & clothing*			3. *Gross domestic investment*
High-income					
OECD Group	3.2	30	(—)	(—)	3.1
United States	3.9	20	(35)	(5)	5.0

Columns: 1. Annual rate of growth of value added in manufacturing, all countries with a rate of 4 per cent or more, 1980–87. 2. Manufacturing as a proportion of GDP in 1987; % of manufacturing value added from (a) machinery and transport equipment sector; and (b) textiles and clothing sector. 3. Gross domestic investment, rate of change, 1980–87.

Source: Ibid., Tables 2, 3, 6 and 8.

annual rates of growth of manufacturing output of 4 per cent or more in the 1980s. Fifteen of them experienced growth of 8 per cent or more. By 1987, the share of manufacturing in GDP for nine of them was equal to or above that in the United States, and for ten, machinery and transport equipment made up 10 per cent or more of the value of manufacturing output. Only in investment were there signs of economic slowdown (nine of the twenty for which there are data had negative rates).

Finally, Table 2.3 presents data on the 25 developing countries with rates of growth of exports in the 1980s of 5 per cent or more. Fourteen experienced annual increases of 8 per cent or more; for nineteen, manufacturing contributed 40 per cent or more of total exports, and for eleven, machinery and transport equipment made up 10 per cent or more of total exports.[16]

Thus, in sum, at this crude level of aggregation, we can see that the growth of manufacturing and of exports for a significant number of developing countries persisted through the 1980s. For developing countries as a whole, manufactured exports increased on average by 12.4 per cent between 1967 and 1973, by 11.3 per cent between 1974 and 1979, and by 11.2 per cent between 1980 and 1984. Furthermore, the increase in the skill content of manufactured exports has persisted; for the leading Newly Industrializing Countries,

Table 2.3 *Growth and composition of developing country exports in the 1980s*

	1. *Rates of growth exports, 1980–87*	2. *Manufactured exports, % of total exports*	3. *Machinery & transport equipment*	4. *(Textiles & clothing)*
Low income				
Bangladesh	6.2	50	17	(—)
Nepal	5.1	72	2	(37)
Mali	6.6	29	1	(—)
Burundi	8.3	15	0	(—)
China	11.7	70	4	(—)
Pakistan	8.4	67	3	(41)
Sri Lanka	6.5	40	2	(25)
Mauritania	11.2	2	0	(—)
Lower-middle income				
Senegal	6.7	15	4	(—)
Egypt	8.4	19	0	(12)
Thailand	10.2	53	12	(18)
Cameroon	9.7	9	5	(1)
Paraguay	13.8	12	0	(0)
Ecuador	5.5	4	1	(—)
Turkey	17.1	67	7	(33)
Colombia	7.5	21	1	(4)
Mauritius	11.1	40	2	(—)
Costa Rica	5.9	40	7	(—)
Malaysia	9.7	40	27	(3)
Mexico	6.6	47	28	(2)
Upper-middle income				
Brazil	5.6	45	17	(3)
S. Korea	14.3	92	33	(25)
Portugal	12.2	80	16	(32)
Greece	6.6	54	3	(32)
Taiwan	13.5	93	30	(17)

Table 2.3 continued

	1. Rates of growth exports, 1980–87	*2. Manufactured exports, % of total exports*	*3. Machinery & transport equipment*	*4. (Textiles & clothing)*
High-income				
Israel	7.3	85	18	(7)
Singapore	6.1	72	43	(6)
Hong Kong	11.4	92	22	(34)

Columns: 1. Average annual growth rate of merchandise exports(%), all countries with an annual rate of 5% or more, 1980–87. 2. Manufacturing as a percentage of total exports, 1987. 3. Machinery and transport equipment exports as a share of total exports 1987. 4. (Textiles and clothing exports as a share of 'other manufactures' exports, 1987).

Source: Ibid., Tables 14 and 16.

the OECD estimates the increase in the skill content of manufactured exports as follows:[17]

		'high'	'medium'	'low'
Manufactured exports				
	1964	2.2	15.9	81.6
	1984	25.0	21.6	53.2

Of particular significance in this context is the fact that the two largest countries in the world in population terms are among the group of low-income countries experiencing relatively high rates of growth of industrial output and manufactured exports. The relevant figures are:

	China		*India*	
Rate of increase, p.a.:	1965–80	1980–87	1965–80	1980–87
(a) GDP	6.4	10.4	3.7	4.6
(b) Manufacturing output	9.5	12.6	4.4	8.3
(c) Manufactured exports	5.5	11.7	3.7	3.6

While China's breathtaking pace of growth may now be temporarily checked, India's much less dramatic increases may be slowly accelerating; in 1988 Indian real GDP grew by 9 per cent (18.8 per cent for agriculture, and 9.3 per cent for industry), with an expectation of between 6 and 7 per cent for 1989 (for the two sectors, 6–7 and 9.5 per cent). The implications of such rapid growth for both countries in terms of urbanization need hardly be emphasized.

The content of the growth of developing countries, however, is in constant change. As the leading exporters seek to upgrade the skill intensity of exports, other less advanced developing countries replace them in important sectors or become the location for production by firms from the original exporting country. In textiles and clothing, probably the sector governed by the fiercest competition, Taiwanese and Korean capital is now spreading to new locations in South East Asia, while half the garment output of Hong Kong firms is now said to be produced by some 2 million workers in south China. The case of Mauritius is by now well-known; Hong Kong capital has been important in raising manufacturing production (of garments) to an annual growth rate of 11 per cent in the 1980s, with manufactured exports rising from an annual increase of 3.1 per cent between 1965 and 1980 to 11.1 per cent in the 1980s. Furthermore, the growth of world trade in manufactures can continue to stimulate the growth of employment in new areas in countries which, in other terms, suffer from some of the worst macroeconomic difficulties; thus, while Mexico's GDP increased by barely 0.5 per cent annually in the 1980s, employment in the in-bond plants along the US border expanded from some 127,000 to 470,000 today.[18]

The major part of the continued growth of this trade is with the developed countries, and, particularly in the 1980s, with the United States. Indeed, dependence upon OECD markets has increased radically for most exporters. The relationship is highly asymmetrical; thus, India, named under the so-called 'Super 301' clause of the US 1988 Trade Act, sends nearly a fifth of its exports to the United States (and receives 11 per cent of its imports), whereas for the United States, imports from India constitute no more than 0.6 per cent of total imports, and exports to India, 1 per cent of total exports. Many developing countries are similarly vulnerable to any increase in protectionism in the OECD group, and this becomes a factor in understanding the forces at work shaping urban development.

While it is expected that the growth of world trade will slow after 1988 (a record for the 1980s, when the volume increased by 8.5 per cent), there are still high growth prospects for particular exports. In the 1980s, for example, office equipment trade increased by 15 per cent per year; garments by 10.5 per cent; motor vehicles by 9 per cent; household appliances by 8.5 per cent and machinery and transport equipment by 6 per cent.[19] In 1987, garment exports, of particular significance for many low-income developing countries, expanded by an extraordinary 30 per cent.

How does all this relate to cities? First, it would appear that many of the underlying forces which precipitate and sustain urbanization in developing countries retain their vigour. This is not simply a matter of continued high rates of growth of manufacturing, which, in the case of the formal sector, may be increasingly located outside the areas of the largest cities (but connected to them in ribbon development along major highways) or in smaller cities within the metropolitan region. The urban effects of the growth of formal sector manufacturing may also be felt in the expansion of associated activities – informal manufacturing, commerce and finance, business and professional services, and the growth of internal communication networks. Furthermore, the long-term trend for world trade to expand significantly faster than production implies a disproportionate growth in the means of transport, the central networks of which are most often urban based, and which sustain a wider pattern of physically concentrated services – warehousing, handling yards, vehicle workshops, etc. While this last point is of lesser significance for seaport facilities, since docks now tend to handle crude raw materials and have few multiplier effects for city activities, it is particularly important for one of the swiftest growing sectors of commodity movement, air freight. The tonne–kilometre growth of air freight rose from 3,350 million in 1960 to 31,470 in 1979. In developing countries, airport activity influences both the location of manufacturing (for low weight–high value goods, particularly garments) and parts of horticulture (flowers, fruit and vegetables). In the developed countries, the reduction in wholesale and retail stocks as well as 'just-in-time' stock systems in manufacturing also increase the flow of air freight. The more general growth of air transport is also related to the continued rapid increase in international tourism, and it is to be expected that this will also continue to influence urban development in developing countries.

Many of these forces assume that macroeconomic policy, especially on pricing, is favourable to the processes involved, and that governments do not pursue actions which, in particular, price labour at levels which nullify one of the comparative advantages of many developing countries. At present, the trend appears to favour realistic pricing and, in particular, floating or regularly adjusted exchange rates, as part of a general package of liberalization. This currently also includes widespread efforts to privatize activities formerly in the public sector. While arguments concerning both liberalization and privatization are primarily concerned with relative efficiency – most frequently identified with lower costs – the overall impact, if fully pursued, is likely to make market determination of activities more universal than ever before in the history of industrial society. The implication would be not only an increasingly trade-led pattern of specialization by country, but also, within countries, increasingly specialized cities. The process would limit the capacity of governments to shape the domestic environment independently of international prices as well as increasing the need for local flexibility. This is possibly part of the background not only to privatization but also to the decline in traditional physical planning and to measures of administrative decentralization and the taking on by voluntary or non-governmental bodies of quasi-public functions.

In sum, then, the forces impelling population concentration in developing countries would seem likely to continue to be strong, particularly in low-income countries. However, urbanization may now be marked by increasing differentiation of settlements by specialized function and increased dependence upon foreign markets. There seem to be several self-reinforcing processes at work here: liberalization of the external economic boundaries of countries (including floating exchange rates), increased export orientation, and increased movement of goods, privatization and administrative decentralization. The development of quasi-entrepreneurial local authorities, on the lines of, say, the US model, may then be seen as an important reaction to these changes. Urban management thus faces a quite new agenda – relating to the specific peculiarities of a particular city, rather than dealing with an example of an homogeneous class of cities, defined by population size. Of course, governments are still groping towards a definition of the proper division of labour between national and local agencies in order to secure measures of intersubsidization between rich and poor areas in pursuit of common minimum standards, but whatever the final resolution of this question, it would appear that local government will be required to make radical changes.

Sub-Saharan Africa

The increased heterogeneity of the Third World is nowhere more apparent than in the contrast between the group of countries experiencing relatively high growth, discussed in the last section, and many of those in Sub-Saharan Africa. Table 2.4 lists the 19 countries of Sub-Saharan Africa which experienced rates of change of per capita Gross National Product between 1965 and 1987 which were negative or below 0.5 per cent (or, in three cases, where the change in GDP in the 1980s was negative). Sub-Saharan Africa as a whole is, of course, heterogeneous and includes eleven countries with higher annual rates of growth in the 1980s (with the best performances for Botswana, 13 per cent; Cameroon, 7 per cent; and Mauritius, 5.5 per cent). It is also true that there are countries in other regions with negative rates of growth in the 1980s (for example, Haiti, Bolivia, Nicaragua, El Salvador, Guatemala, etc.).

Columns 2 and 3 of Table 2.4 give some idea of agricultural performance. Only three of the 19 had, by 1987, a negative average rate of change (although this included the catastrophic Mozambique at −11.1 per cent) since there had been an upturn in output in 1985; indeed, the growth rate between 1985 and 1988 was three times the average for the period 1970–85.[20] However, only six countries were able to improve per capita food production on 1980 (but then Sub-Saharan Africa was not unique in this – 22 of the 42 low-income country group were by 1987 below the 1980 level). Of the 15 countries where there were data, all except five experienced some growth in manufacturing. In exports, almost all experienced severe decline; only Sudan, Mauritania and Senegal attained substantial growth. For Sub-Saharan Africa as a whole, the volume of exports increased by 16 per cent in the 1980s, but revenue declined by 10 per cent (and debt-servicing obligations more than doubled). However, after 1984, the trend of 1970–84 was reversed with an increase in Sub-Saharan Africa's share of world exports. Finally, in gross investment, the picture is at its bleakest, particularly in Mozambique (−23.1 per cent per year). The effects could be felt long into the future.

The different diagnoses of the origins of the economic crisis are well known but are not relevant to the theme of interest here – the effect of this slump upon urban development. In this connection the key issues are public responses to the crisis in terms of the overall decline in the public sector, the slump in urban incomes from increased unemployment and cuts in real wages and salaries, and the contraction in manufacturing. The decline in development spending – halved, for example, in the first half of the 1980s in Malawi, Ghana and Tanzania – and in public infrastructure maintenance, let alone new construction, has been disastrous. It has been made even worse by the appropriation of an increasing part of reduced export earnings to service debts, so making it impossible to import key components or replacements for public infrastructure and equipment. The effects in agriculture – on irrigation dams, rural roads, railways, power generation, etc. – could severely affect the capacity to expand exports. A recent report on Zambia's transport network[21] illustrates the deleterious effects of the current difficulties upon a longer

Table 2.4 *Sub-Saharan Africa: countries with poor growth rates (0.5% or less, GNP per capita 1965–87)*

	1. GNP per capita, increase '65–87 %	*2. Incr. agric. output '80–7* %	*3. Per capita food prod. 1985–7 (79–81: 100)*	*4. Incr. in mfg. '80–7* %	*5. Incr. in export '80–7* %	*6. Gross domestic investment '80–7* %
Ethiopia	0.1	2.1	89	3.8	−0.6	2.0
Chad	−2.0	2.6	104	8.5	—	—
Zaire	−2.4	3.2	99	0.6	−3.4	1.3
Mozambique	(−2.6)[a]	−11.1	84	—	—	−23.1
Tanzania	−0.4	3.8	9	−3.5	−7.4	−5.6
Madagascar	−1.8	2.2	97	—	−3.1	−4.5
Zambia	−2.1	3.2	97	0.8	−3.3	−9.3
Niger	−2.2	2.8	87	—	−4.8	−15.0
Uganda	−2.7	−0.5	123	−0.9	2.7	—
Somalia	0.3	2.8	102	−0.5	−7.7	2.7
Togo	(−0.5)[a]	0.8	89	—	−3.0	−6.4
Sierra L.	0.2	1.6	98	0.6	−2.1	−7.1
Benin	0.2	2.5	114	4.6	−0.1	−12.7
C. African R.	−0.3	2.4	94	0.3	1.0	14.6
Sudan	−0.5	0.8	100	1.6	4.2	−4.0
Nigeria	(−1.7)[a]	0.6	105	−2.1	−5.1	−14.8
Mauritania	−0.4	1.5	90	—	11.2	−5.5
Liberia	−1.6	1.2	96	−5.0	−2.6	−16.7
Senegal	−0.6	4.2	105	4.3	6.7	1.1

[a] Increase in GDP, 1980–87, for two countries where GNP per capita not available, and for Nigeria, in order to record the effect of falling oil prices in the 1980s.

Columns: 1. Average annual growth rate (%) GNP per capita, 1965–87. 2. Average annual growth rate (%) in agriculture, 1980–87. 3. Average index of food production per capita (1979–81: 100), 1985–7. 4. Average annual growth rate (%) in manufacturing, 1980–7. 5. Average annual growth rate (%), exports, 1980–87. 6. Gross domestic investment (% change), 1980–87.

Source: Ibid., Tables 1, 2, 4, 8 and 14.

tradition of poor maintenance – the railway rolling stock and track halved, the stock of trucks disastrously reduced (private hauliers refuse to collect produce from the villages because the deterioration of rural roads now imposes too much damage on their vehicles), village storage facilities so depleted that there are heavy losses in a normal harvest, etc.

The World Bank and International Monetary Fund placed primary emphasis upon cutting public expenditure, eliminating price biases in favour of non-tradable goods and against the traditional exports of agricultural goods (exaggerated where governments maintained a public monopoly of the domestic trade in exported commodities), reassessing overvalued exchange rates, etc. Structural Adjustment Loans were therefore designed to achieve staged reforms in these elements and to shift the balance in favour of tradable goods and, in particular, agriculture and exports. It was initially thought that the reform package would be fairly swift in its effects and the loan programme would be quickly completed. The resulting change in the balance between urban and rural incomes, it was thought, would reduce or reverse rural–urban migration. However, in practice, the length of time required to implement reforms has been extended almost indefinitely because of the difficulties in execution; as the World Bank has noted, 'where economic structures have been in place for some time, the pain of adjustment can be enormous'.[22]

Table 2.5 lists the 36 larger countries of Sub-Saharan Africa, indicating those which have received a World Bank Structural Adjustment Loan. However, only six countries received a loan before 1985, so that it might be considered premature to expect effects for the majority of countries after such a short period of time. Nonetheless, there is so far no correlation between accepting a loan and reduced urban population growth; indeed, 18 of the countries listed experienced increased urban growth rates in the 1980s in comparison to the preceding period 1965–80, including four of the six in receipt of loans before 1985. In a number of cases, urban wages have declined – indeed, they have been declining in many countries in real terms since 1970 – but without this apparently reducing the growth of urban population (indeed, in both Tanzania and Ghana, where a substantial decline in real urban pay is recorded, there is an increase in urban population growth rates).

If the current trends persist, United Nations projections, also included in Table 2.5, suggest that by 2025 there will be very large urban populations in a number of countries (for example, Nigeria, Zaire, Tanzania, Kenya, etc.). Furthermore, as the last column of the table indicates, 70 to over 80 per cent of the growth in urban populations is expected after 1987.

Table 2.5 *Sub-Saharan Africa: rates of growth and size of urban population at different dates and the proportion of growth still to occur*

	Urban Population					% of growth 1950 –2025 occurring after 1987
	annual increase		*size (mns.)*			
(i) Low-income	*1965–80*	*1980–87*	*1950*	*1987*	*2025*	
Ethiopia	4.9	4.6	n.a	n.a	n.a	n.a
Chad[a]	7.8	7.8	0.1	2.0	8.0	81
Zaire[a]	4.5	4.6[c]	2.0	12.0	58.0	83
Malawi[a]	7.5	8.6[c]	0.1	1.0	8.7	90
Mozambique[a]	9.4	10.7[c]	0.1	3.0	20.0	84
Tanzania[a]	8.7	8.3	0.3	6.2	47.0	87
Burkina Faso	4.1	5.3[c]	0.1	0.6	6.0	91
Madagascar[a]	5.3	6.4[c]	0.4	3.0	15.0	85
Mali[a]	4.3	3.4	0.3	2.0	10.0	87
Burundi	6.0	9.2[c]	0.1	0.5	3.0	85
Zambia[a,b]	7.2	6.6	0.2	4.0	19.0	81
Niger[a]	7.0	7.5[c]	0.1	1.2	9.0	88
Uganda[a]	5.0	5.0	0.2	1.7	17.0	91
Somalia[a]	5.5	5.5	0.2	2.0	8.0	80
Togo[a,b]	6.6	6.9[c]	0.1	0.8	5.0	86
Rwanda	7.5	8.1[c]	0.04	0.5	5.0	92
Sierra Leone[a]	4.3	5.0[c]	0.2	1.0	4.0	78
Benin	9.0	7.9	0.1	2.0	9.0	82
C. African Rep.[a]	4.3	4.7[c]	0.2	1.0	5.0	77
Kenya[a]	8.0	8.6[c]	0.3	4.8	42.7	89
Sudan	5.7	4.2	0.6	5.0	25.0	83
Lesotho[a]	7.8	7.2	0.01	0.3	2.0	84
Nigeria[a]	5.7	6.3[c]	3.5	25.0	179.0	88
Ghana[a,b]	3.2	4.1[c]	0.6	5.0	27.0	84
Mauritania[a]	9.2	7.9	0.02	0.8	4.0	81
Liberia	6.2	5.9	0.1	1.0	5.0	83
Guinea[a]	5.3	5.7[c]	0.2	2.0	8.0	83
(ii) Middle-income						
Senegal[a,b]	2.9	3.8[c]	0.1	3.0	11.0	78
Zimbabwe	6.0	6.3[c]	0.3	3.0	17.0	87
Côte d'Ivoire[a,b]	7.5	6.9	0.4	5.0	21.0	80
Congo[a]	3.4	4.6[c]	0.3	0.8	3.0	83
Cameroon[a]	8.1	7.4	0.4	5.0	21.0	78
Botswana	12.4	8.1	—	0.3	2.2	89
Mauritius[a,b]	2.5	0.8	0.1	0.5	1.0	63
South Africa	3.3	3.3	n.a	n.a	n.a	n.a
Gabon[a]	6.7	6.7	0.1	0.5	2.0	75

[a] in receipt of one or more World Bank Structural Adjustment loans.

[b] in receipt of such a loan before 1985.

[c] rate of urban growth increase between the two periods.

Source: First four columns, from Table 32, *World Development Report 1989*, ranked by per capita income, ascending. Other columns from *The Prospects of World Urbanization*, United Nations, New York, 1987.

Thus, it appears that for low-income countries, a significant fall in urban incomes may not necessarily produce a decline in rural–urban migration in the short term. Of course, outmigration from rural areas is affected by many factors other than simply the income differential; for example, the size and distribution of land holdings and household incomes. Furthermore, changes in the differential between average earnings may not indicate the gap obtaining between comparable occupations. Enhanced rural incomes for the minority of farmers with a marketable surplus (provided the means exist to get the crops to market) could, with inappropriate pricing of farm machinery, lead to a reduction in rural employment; and the enhanced consumption of farmers could stimulate the urban production of goods and services. Certainly, Turkey – an inappropriate model in other respects for comparison with most of Sub-Saharan Africa – offers a well-documented example where a high rate of urban growth coincided with a severe decline in urban wages and salaries (between 1979 and 1984).

It is too early to draw firm conclusions concerning the implications for urban populations of structural adjustment reforms in Sub-Saharan Africa. However, because of the notorious complexity of factors at stake and the known high propensity of low-income countries to rapid urbanization even with poor rates of economic growth, a certain scepticism would seem appropriate in considering the prognosis of stability or decline in the rate of growth of urban population. Governments would be most unwise to frame their policy stance on such an assumption.

THE URBAN OUTLOOK

In 1800, the urban–rural division of labour is estimated to have produced a world urban population of about 25 million people (or some 3 per cent of the total). By the 1980s, this had become 1.8 billion (thousand million) or about 40 per cent of the much larger total.[23] In 1900, only in Britain was a majority of the population living in urban areas; now all the developed countries are in this situation, as well as 12 of the 18 upper-middle income countries, 15 of the 35 lower-middle, but only one (Zambia) of the 42 low-income countries.

Classifying countries by income level, however, is misleading. By regions, other important differences emerge: 70 per cent of Latin Americans are urban, between 25 and 27 per cent of low-income Africa and Asia, and 37 per cent of East Asia. Furthermore, within regions, the range of variation is considerable: 85 per cent urban in Argentina and 46 per cent in Paraguay (or 33 per cent in Guatemala);

53 per cent in Zambia and 12 per cent in Ethiopia; 69 per cent in South Korea and 13 per cent in Bangladesh. The picture is misleading for another reason, for differences in countries' absolute size of population are concealed in proportions. Thus, two countries – China and India – have a combined relatively low urban proportion (33 per cent), but, in absolute terms, they have between 616 and 620 million urban dwellers (or 12 per cent of the total world population), equal to 53 per cent more than all the inhabitants of Latin America, and 40 per cent more than the inhabitants of Sub-Saharan Africa.

The magnitudes involved today are unprecedented, but the trends are not historically unusual. Even quite moderate rates of economic expansion thus seem likely to sustain those trends over the next thirty years. If this is so, then virtually all developing countries where at present a minority of the population is urban will make the transition to predominantly urban societies. At that stage, urban labour markets will dominate the whole society and rural populations will decline absolutely. The process is exaggerated today since the rates of economic growth in developing countries are considerably higher than those experienced by the developed countries in the nineteenth century, and the effects of this on urbanization seem to be greater. Furthermore, there appears to be a long-term trend of redistributing the world's labour-intensive manufacturing capacity to the less developed countries.

Projections rest upon changeable assumptions, inevitably incorporate errors of data (or estimates where data are lacking) and, in the case of the urban, non-comparable definitions. Furthermore, they provide spuriously exact population results for very complex processes which are imperfectly understood. The longer the period of projection, the greater the chance that minor errors at the outset become large deviations by the end of the period. Thus, inevitably, projections of the urban population could never be borne out except by pure coincidence. Nonetheless, the broad magnitudes involved give us some sense of the possibilities.

In the past forty years, the urban populations of developing countries have grown at rates of between 3 and 5 per cent annually – from a total of 300 million people to 1.3 billion by 1980. In the 1970s, the numbers increased by nearly 300 million. Currently, cities and towns in developing countries accommodate on average some 45 million new inhabitants each year (compared to 7 million in the developed countries). The United Nations medium-variant projections estimate that the urban total should reach 4 billion by the year 2020.

After 2010, it is projected that the rural populations in developing countries will decline absolutely. By 2020, over half of all Africans will live in cities and towns; just under half of all Asians; and over eight in every ten Latin Americans. In countries with large populations, this could produce – as we saw in Table 2.5 for Sub-Saharan Africa – absolutely very large urban populations:

Projected urban population (millions)

	1950	1987	2025
India	62	215	658
Bangladesh	2	14	79
Pakistan	7	32	119
Indonesia	10	46	152

Big cities

As mentioned earlier, existing large cities are tending to grow less rapidly than other classes of settlement, but an increasing proportion of urban inhabitants live in the largest cities, since the faster growing smaller cities are joining the class of large cities. By the year 2000, it is projected that just under half of all urban inhabitants in developing countries will live in cities of one million or more people. Accordingly, the number of larger cities will increase on an unprecedented scale. In 1950, there were 31 cities of one million or more people in developing countries (only five of them had a population of 4 million or more). By 1985, there were 146 in the one million class, and 28 with 4 million or more. The projections for 2025 are 486 and 114. Already, the world's largest cities are becoming a feature of developing countries rather than, as in the past, the developed.

In the smaller low-income countries, this process often produces the growth of one city only, a phenomenon geographers have come to call 'primacy'. Table 2.6 indicates the increases and decreases in primacy for low-income developing countries over the past two decades. The declines may reflect no more than reclassifications. As can be seen, large countries tend to score rather low in primacy, indicating that the issue is partly related to size of country. However, there are also some striking increases (as in Zaire, Tanzania, Uganda, Guinea, and wartorn Mozambique). The middle-income countries have, interestingly, much higher scores than the high-income, suggesting that the sheer speed of urbanization may produce greater concentration today rather than the dispersal of urban growth points that occurred with slower urbanization in the developed countries of the nineteenth century.

Table 2.7 shows the concentration of urban population in cities with half a million or more people for countries which had at least one

Table 2.6 *The proportion of urban population living in the largest city, low income developing countries, 1960 and 1980 (%)*

Increases	1960	1980	*Decreases*	1960	1980	*Constant*	1960	1980
Ethiopia	30	37	Nepal	41	27	China	6	6
Zaire	14	28	Lao PDR	69	48	Burma	23	23
Bangladesh	20	30	Madagascar	44	36			
Mozambique	75	83	Mali	32	24			
Tanzania	34	50	India	7	6			
Uganda	38	52	C.Afr.Rep.	40	36			
Sierra L.	34	47	Sri Lanka	28	16			
Kenya	40	57	Yemen PDR	61	49			
Sudan	30	31	Afghanistan	33	17			
Pakistan	20	21						
Haiti	42	56						
Nigeria	13	17						
Ghana	25	35						
Indonesia	20	23						
Guinea	37	80						
Low income	11	13						
Lower-middle	31	34						
Upper-middle	27	27						
High-income	19	19						

Source: World Developoment Report 1989, Table 31.

Table 2.7 *The proportion of the urban population in low-income developing countries living in cities of half a million or more people in 1960: 1960 and 1980 (%)*

	1960	*1980*		*1960*	*1980*
Zaire	14	38	Nigeria	22	58
Bangladesh	20	51	Indonesia	34	50
China	42	45	Low-income	30	43
India	20	39	Middle-income	34	47
Pakistan	33	51	High-income	47	55

Source: Ibid.

such city in 1960. Here the forces of concentration are much more clearly illustrated, with, for example, a more than doubling for Bangladesh and Nigeria. It is striking that the low-income countries, on this measure, were in 1980 approaching a comparable level for the high-income countries of 1960. In regional terms, Sub-Saharan Africa moved from 7 per cent of its urban population in cities of half a million or more people to an astonishing 41 per cent in 1980.

However, simultaneously, the largest cities are spreading their populations to the metropolitan periphery and beyond, and almost all experience some decline of inner city populations (although most recently this process seems to have been reversed in the developed countries).[24] Smaller cities up to 100 kilometres from the old large cities seem now to be experiencing some of the highest population growth rates. The process must partly be related to the tendency for formal sector manufacturing to seek new low-cost locations outside metropolitan areas, a process made possible by the extension of highways, communications and power supply to larger regions.[25] Larger manufacturing plants, with standardized output, now tend to locate well away from built-up areas, leaving metropolitan districts to forms of manufacturing reliant on close proximity to rapidly changing market demand (most typically, high fashion garments), on linkages to other firms, and on innovation ('incubator' plants). In developing countries, much of this activity is in the informal sector. Furthermore, the disproportionate growth of services seems to be affecting large cities in developing countries as well as those in developed. It now appears to be the case that, contrary to earlier estimates, new technology in information-related industries is likely to increase concentration of activity rather than decentralize it by enhancing central control functions and making them more heavily dependent on locationally specific information sources.

The more macroeconomic policy reforms permit increased competition between different settlements, the more likely it is that, in low-income countries, informal sector production will become competitive with sectors of modern manufacturing both domestically and in international trade. This may not necessarily mean operation in urban locations, for important sectors of informal sector manufacturing are based in villages (for example, bidi or match making in India). But the less traditional forms of petty manufacture are usually more dependent upon manufacturing linkages and services available only in the cities. Thus the sharpening of specialization of output by city as the result of trade liberalization could enhance the concentration of non-traditional informal sector activities in cities. Such a growth would take place at the same time as the development of modern knowledge and information-processing industries in the metropolitan regions of developing countries, creating much sharper differentiation within the cities (the model here might be named after Los Angeles which combines a vigorous growth in both high-technology industries and backward black economy manufacturing, employing many illegal immigrants).

As noted earlier, settlement systems tend to appear as exceptionally stable, although historically the functions and relative sizes of the constituent cities radically change. For example, it has been suggested that India possessed in 1586 some 3,200 towns and 120 cities,[26] a total not far from the existing 3,245 urban settlements and 216 'urban agglomerations'. The stability is, of course, partly an illusion, but it indicates that the system does not recreate itself continually to accommodate new functions and forces, but rather, economic change is fed through an existing geography of settlements. The costs are high of starting afresh (as opposed to reutilizing and incrementally expanding the inherited capital endowment of existing settlements), but recycling the old settlements imposes rigidities on the process of change which frustrate both governments and inhabitants.

Migration

While the numbers of urban dwellers in developing countries continue to grow absolutely, the rates of growth have been falling consistently since their peak in the 1950s – from an annual rate of 5.2 per cent in the last half of the 1950s to 3.4 per cent in the last half of the 1970s. However, the decline reflects in the main the experience of middle-income countries, and the overall results for low-income countries have been transformed by the enormous surge of growth since 1980 in China (where the former tight migration controls were apparently relaxed). For the low-income group, average annual growth rates have risen from 3.5 per cent between 1965 and 1980 to 8.8 per cent in the 1980s (with China's rate of growth in the 1980s at 11 per cent annually). As we have seen, from a low base point, rates of growth in Sub-Saharan Africa are also high.

Up to the early 1980s, the components of urban population growth in developing countries as a whole were dominated by the rate of natural increase of the urban population itself, providing some 60 per cent of growth. Another 8 to 15 per cent was due to the redrawing of urban boundaries or the reclassification of settlements, and between 25 and 32 per cent to net migration. However, the general aggregate figures are not very helpful since they cover such a range of diversity. Even within countries, the heterogeneity is marked. For example, the aggregate picture in low-income India is: natural increase provides 41 per cent of urban population growth, migration 40 per cent, and reclassification, 19 per cent. However, the more urbanized States are closer to a middle-income model in that nearly 70 per cent of migration is urban-to-urban, indicating that urban labour markets are more important for migration than rural–urban relationships. In the poorer States, rural-to-urban migration still provides nearly half the migration flows.

If we ignore the problems raised by reclassification and the definition of 'urban' and assume that urban and rural fertility and mortality rates are the same, we can estimate the relative contribution of migration to urban growth in the low-income countries. The results are presented in Table 2.8. The problem of including China in the aggregate figures for the low-income group and for East Asia is immediately apparent, particularly given the low rate of Chinese natural increase – nearly 90 per cent of urban population growth now derives from migration (compared to 4 per cent between 1965 and 1980). However, there are other inferences. In general, the proportions of migration are surprisingly stable between the two periods for most countries, but span a very wide range. For Sub-Saharan Africa, only five of the 27 countries increased the migrant proportion between the two periods, but this was sufficient to produce an increase for the region as a whole. However, for 14 countries (and Sub-Saharan Africa as a whole), the migrant share was 50 per cent or more in both periods (and for 11, between 20 and 50 per cent). For the nine Asian countries where data were available, five increased the migration share between the two periods (which produced an increase for both regions of East and South Asia), and in four cases, this was 50 per cent or more in both periods. Of course, it should again be stressed that omitting the effects of reclassification exaggerates the migration residual by possibly between 8 and 15 per cent, and that this is not systematic – it affects different countries differently.

The conditions of migration are very varied, so it is wrong to seek strong generalizations, particularly because there are few studies of the migrants who fail to stay in urban areas: we have data only on those who succeed. However, demographically one would expect migrants to do better than city-born natives after the initial learning process. Since they are an unbalanced population – concentrated in the active age groups, better educated, healthier and better motivated than average. The evidence is that 75 per cent of migrants who stay in the cities improve their standard of living. Nor, it seems, does the distinction between migrants and non-migrants help to explain urban poverty, housing conditions or employment, certainly not in comparison with age, sex and educational level.

Table 2.8 *The contribution of migration to urban growth.*[a] *1965–80 and 1980–87, for low income countries in Africa and Asia (%)*

Sub-Sarahan Africa	1965–80	1980–87	*Asia*	1965–80	1980–87
Ethiopia	45	48	Bangladesh	56	52
Chad	74	71	Nepal	63	65
Zaire	38	33	Lao PDR	64	61
Malawi	61	56	China	4	89
Mozambique	73	75	India	41	49
Tanzania	69	69	Pakistan	28	31
Burkina Faso	49	51	Sri Lanka	22	−25
Madagascar	54	48	Indonesia	50	58
Mali	51	29	Burma	28	4
Burundi	68	70	Vietnam	—	33
Zambia	58	46			
Niger	61	60			
Uganda	42	38			
Somalia	51	47			
Togo	55	51			
Rwanda	56	59			
Sierra Leone	54	52			
Benin	70	60			
C. African Rep.	56	47			
Kenya	55	52			
Sudan	51	26			
Lesotho	71	63			
Nigeria	56	46			
Ghana	31	17			
Mauritania	75	66			
Liberia	52	44			
Guinea	64	58			
Low-income	34	75			
Middle-income	39	35			
Combined	38	68			
High-income	36	22			
Sub-Saharan Africa	51	54			
East Asia	26	86			
South Asia	40	44			
Latin America, Carib.	36	31			

[a] *Assumptions:* (i) reclassification of settlements and redrawing of urban boundaries does not affect the outcome; (ii) urban and rural fertility and mortality rates are the same.

Source: World Development Report 1989, calculated from Tables 26 and 31.

POLICY ISSUES

The problems

The rapid growth of urban populations in conditions of great poverty can swiftly exhaust the capacities to meet their growing needs. Urban life and, in particular, the maintenance of rising levels of urban productivity, rely heavily on an interconnected set of efficiently provided services – power, transport, communications, water supply and sewerage, housing, health and education. They do not easily keep pace with demand when cities grow rapidly, particularly given an inheritance of weak financial and administrative management in many cities.

Yet, as suggested earlier, national economic development depends heavily, and increasingly, on the continued growth of urban productivity. To ensure this, the cities must be made to work efficiently and to do so within the severe resource constraints that characterize low-income countries. However, enhancing the specialization of cities and rural districts raises some of the policy issues which are most difficult for governments to resolve. The consumption needs of a poor population are frequently in painful collision with what seems to make common sense in terms of the pursuit of production and productivity, and it is no consolation to the hungry to be advised that the reward for present abstinence is to be fed some time in the remote future. There are other major obstacles to sensible national spatial planning, for where the factory is to be located is not merely a contribution to national output, it is also a source of work and incomes for one group of people rather than another, and a source of political prestige for one official or deputy rather than another. Inevitably, real planning must be a continuous compromise rather than a unilateral rationality.

Furthermore, the spatial effects of macroeconomic policy are imperfectly understood. A whole range of publicly determined or influenced prices – exchange rates, tariffs, taxes, interest rates – influence the balance between urban and rural sectors, and between different settlements, but the magnitudes and final ramifications are unknown. Import-substitution strategies of industrialization have been criticized for stimulating excessive urbanization,[27] for institutionalizing 'urban bias'[28] but again, short of abandoning such policies altogether, it is unclear how far they can or should be varied for spatial ends. The grounds for determining these policy choices are held to be concerned with much more important issues than simply territorial distributions; population redistribution then becomes no more than one incidental result. Other priorities – on infrastructure provision, on credit targeting and local authority finance – may likewise be decided on criteria which have little relationship to territorial distributions. Thus, inevitably, explicitly spatial policy (in terms of regions, industrial location, and city planning) can play no more than a marginal role in determining the final territorial outcome.

Underlying many of the more obvious problems of cities is the endemic and seemingly obstinate character of poverty. It is not a separate issue from that of productivity, since a rising urban contribution to national development is profoundly affected by the implications of very low incomes – poor diets, poor health, poor housing, an inability to secure shelter or necessary services or contribute to adequate local authority provision, etc. The standards of health of the young in urban slums are sometimes among the worst in a country, and thus predetermine in part the abilities of the future adults.

In absolute terms, the problem is set to get worse. As populations become increasingly urban, so the general problem of poverty will become predominantly an urban one. World Bank projections from 1980 suggest that there will be a decrease in rural households in the worst poverty up to the year 2000 (from 83 million in 1975 to 57 million), while urban poor households will more than double (from 34 to 74 million). Thus, on this projection, the majority of poor households will be urban based by the end of the century. Of course, in urban areas generally there tends to be a reduced proportion of poor, so that the transition may also include a decline in the share.[29]

Much work has been undertaken in identifying the nature and causes of poverty,[30] and its relationship to urban labour markets. The central problems are often associated less with unemployment or underemployment (meaning that workers have more time to work if work is available) than with working for excessive hours at very low rates of pay. This in turn often reflects low skills, training, and capital per worker, as well as an excessive supply of workers competing for work.

It is thus hardly surprising to find that the poor have a particular demographic character. For example, in India – with officially between 51 and 57 million urban dwellers below the poverty line (or one in four of the urban population)[31] – a 1987 survey[32] shows that over two-thirds of poor households consist of women and children; the households tend to be large (5.9 persons), and disproportionately drawn from scheduled tribes and castes and minorities. Programmes of poverty alleviation are frequently misdirected because they are aimed at increasing work that the poor cannot do or instituting programmes that are skew of the specific characteristics of the poor.

Other urban problems are painfully well known in the fields of power provision, the availability of land and services, etc. In transport, the capacity to move and move increasing distances speedily and at low relative cost is fundamental to the activity of the metropolitan area. As cities grow, movement tends to increase disproportionately (by some 10 to 15 per cent per year). The problems of expanding expensive physical facilities in this connection is compounded by those in managing the existing infrastructure – road space and transport equipment, rail operations and rail stock, terminals, etc. Subsidies to avoid the political problems of effective management can then spread what was initially a transport issue into the general field of public finance.[33]

The problems of financial management and mobilizing adequate resources are daunting in countries with rapidly expanding cities. The sums involved in poor societies appear far beyond existing capacities. For example, assuming a per capita expenditure of no more than Rs.1,000, it has been estimated that Indian cities will require expenditure up to the year 2000 of the order of Rs.300 billion (or US$25 billion).[34] Such calculations may be a useful input to long-term estimates of public expenditure, but they can be politically damaging and encourage people to believe that there must be some alternative to adequate urban provision. It might be analogous to estimating the food consumption needs of the expected increment in urban population without simultaneously estimating the increase in income generated by the new urban dwellers. For there can be no sustained urbanization without a continuing increase in urban labour demand, in jobs which, despite low levels of productivity by international standards, represent in aggregate an improvement in productivity for the country as a whole. Thus the income to support adequate infrastructure at appropriate standards is, in principle, generated simultaneously with urban growth itself. The real problem is not the absolute costs of the growth of the urban population, but rather establishing the political will and institutional mechanisms to raise part of the income increment for the provision of services.

The point has more general significance. For without effective institutions and competent staff, good ideas and sensible policies cannot be implemented. It is here that probably the greatest problems arise. It is becoming generally agreed that national governments are poorly equipped to deal with local problems, let alone promote local entrepreneurial initiatives and innovations appropriate to increasingly specialized settlements in a swiftly changing competitive environment. The local arms of national line agencies are thus frequently unable to do more than, at best, maintain routine functions, let alone cope with accelerated urban growth. Local authorities, on the other hand, have frequently been deprived of financial and managerial powers, while being entrusted with additional responsibilities but impeded at every stage by tighter restrictions. The results are often corruption and inertia. Yet it is here that the most important reforms appear to be required if cities are to respond to their heightened role in national economic development.

Policy

Governments in developing countries – like some of those in nineteenth-century Europe – have frequently identified cities as first and foremost problems, challenges to national political power or concentrations of disorder and deprivation, rather than opportunities for economic development. Quite often the better-off urban classes have identified inmigrants as threats to 'their' city, slums as threatening crime and violence, the poor as spreading epidemics, even street vendors and overcrowded streets as nullifying the benefits of private vehicles, etc. Furthermore, the greater publicity afforded conflict in urban areas and the need for political leaders to take special measures to secure the cities encourages a belief that the urban inhabitants are greedier than the rural, exploiting a quasi-monopoly position to levy rents from the countryside. An anti-urban culture is at least as impressive as 'urban bias' among the urban upper classes.

Separately, a more sophisticated critique of urbanization has also emerged. For example, the heavy debts of some middle-income countries have been identified as resulting from the extraordinary investment programmes required for urban infrastructure.[35] W. Arthur Lewis cites in this connection the fact that average per capita local government spending in Bogota is seven times that of the four municipalities of 50 to 90,000 population in the central region of Colombia, implying the use of the political leverage which derives from concentrated populations to achieve a privileged position.[36] In fact, as a critical reply notes, very little of municipal spending is directed at servicing the resident population; it is rather a contribution to national economic growth (in ports, highways and transport terminals, warehousing, national markets, hospitals, universities, etc.). Its validity can only be assessed relative to the returns to the society as a whole, not simply average levels of cost by settlement. The same argument is familiar in Europe where, for example, it is sometimes asserted that France subsidizes Paris where the evidence suggests the reverse.[37]

A broader vindication of the critique of cities in contemporary developing countries has, however, gained much wider currency.[38]

Here it is argued (or implied) that the standard relationship between economic development and urbanization was established in nineteenth-century Europe. Then, supposedly, as urban (and industrial) employment (with rising average productivity) and incomes expanded, workers were drawn from the countryside to urban opportunities and thus made possible simultaneous increases in rural productivity. On this account, the cities were then truly 'engines of national economic development'. By contrast, in the modern period, it is said, unprecedented levels of rural poverty, arising from dense populations and high rates of population increase, drive the poor from the countryside to urban sanctuaries. The capital intensity of modern manufacturing makes it impossible to employ the stream of rural inmigrants who then end up as unemployed. The cities become welfare centres for the rural poor, who, with the urban masses, use their political leverage to secure even further benefits, now at the expense of the countryside.

Later the case was further elaborated. Poor unemployed migrants were driven to initiate informal sector activities where the marginal productivity of labour was close to zero (as indeed, it was said to be in agriculture). As already mentioned, the critique of import-substitution industrialization strategies added a further dimension. For the subsidization of interest rates and provision of other incentives for investment in manufacturing along with protection against manufactured imports were said to have lowered the returns to agriculture and so the levels of rural wages. The enhanced capital intensity of urban manufacturing reduced the potential rate of creation of urban jobs, but raised incomes for those employed. The resulting urban–rural wage gap encouraged excessive rural–urban migration to urban unemployment, and a neglect of the comparative advantage of cheap rural labour.

It was a powerful case that, in parts, had strong appeal for governments and seemed to correspond in some measure to the instinctive perceptions of the better-off urban classes: neither the 'City Beautiful' nor the urban engine had survived inmigration. The case still persists in some contexts as we saw in the quotation at the beginning of this paper from the Indian National Commission on Urbanization.

However, as more empirical evidence has accumulated, the argument has come to seem ingenious but, in certain key essentials, false. For example, the data on urban unemployment are in general rarely adequate to detect a secular trend to increase, nor do they show significantly higher rates for inmigrants (but rather the reverse). Urban wages have experienced considerable fluctuations, and in Sub-Saharan Africa, as we noted earlier, appear in many countries to have been declining since 1970.[39] There is no unequivocal evidence that the real level of urban wages has been or could be politically fixed. It is not the rural poor who migrate to cities, and, in many situations, urban-to-urban migration is more important. Rural incomes are not uniformly below urban levels; in aggregate they are, but in comparisons of like occupations and allowing for a higher urban cost of living, the picture is often more ambiguous. Formal sector incomes and conditions are not systematically above informal ones, nor do the self-employed necessarily earn less than the employed. Indeed, in practice, the formal and informal are not very easy to distinguish.[40] Peter Gregory has put together these elements, along with many others, in a powerful critique of the overall argument as it affected macroeconomic policy in Mexico up to 1982.[41]

In fact, it appears that, while the content of urban economic activity has changed radically, it still remains true that a growing and changing composition of output selects a particular type of migrant: urban labour demand sustains migration, not those expelled from impoverished agriculture. If macroeconomic policy and pricing accurately reflect real scarcities, we have no grounds for assuming, in general, that the volume of migration or the size of cities is economically wrong. And if policy and pricing do not reflect scarcities, the remedy lies in the reform of policy rather than in redistributing population.

Those entrusted with direct responsibility for planning cities and settlement systems came from a different intellectual tradition, but reached surprisingly similar conclusions. Physical planners saw as one of their central tasks the territorial distribution of population. It was argued that maldistribution was a primary source of deleterious 'imbalances', both in absolute terms, the population size of large cities, and in terms of population densities. Together, these two imbalances were a primary source of the social problems of cities – the shortage of adequate services, congested streets, poor housing, squatting and slums, etc. In general, big cities were bad, suffering from 'overpopulation' or 'population saturation', particularly in the form of a primate city (as geographers refer to it). In sum, poverty and other manifest urban problems were, in an important sense, locational questions, and could be remedied, or at least ameliorated, through relocation.

The remedies flowed from the diagnosis. The control of land uses, the establishment of aggregated functional zoning and population density targets within the city, went with attempts to decentralize economic activity and population to smaller settlements, sometimes in backward regions, and to encourage rural development in order to discourage migration.

Governments frequently found the case persuasive and committed resources and staff to implementation. Thus, for example, a 1981 United Nations survey of 126 governments in developing countries found that 123 'continued to be far from satisfied with their migration trends and patterns of population distribution, and many considered population distribution issues to be among their most important problems'.[42] Three-quarters of the governments concerned claimed to be pursuing policies to slow or reverse migration, as part of a strategy of decentralization.

Possibly one of the most strict in this respect was the Government of the People's Republic of China, exercising in the 1960s tight control over migration to the cities, periodic removal of urban inhabitants for relocation in rural areas, and directed redistribution of labour. Others pursued part of the programme. For example, both Tanzania and Indonesia sought at various times to control migration to the largest cities. The Government of the Philippines in the early 1960s tried to charge inmigrants to Manila a substantial fee for entry to public schools (free education was available only to existing urban residents). The measure proved difficult to enforce, weakened by corruption, and without significant effects upon the rate of inmigration. Many other countries have, from time to time, tried to expel sections of the urban population, whether the unemployed or squatters (thus Congo, Niger, Tanzania, Zaire, South Korea, India, etc.). Rural development schemes have often been vindicated in terms of their effects upon rural outmigration, but are rarely evaluated and even more rarely shown to have affected migration. Indeed, there is some evidence that village improvements (particularly in rural education and communications tend to increase outmigration, since both the average and marginal propensity to migrate increases with education (sensibly enough since the gains from migration rise with educational level).[43]

Many countries have introduced programmes to encourage the growth of small and intermediate cities as alternatives to the growth of large cities (Brazil, India, Peru, Thailand, China, etc.). These may have had useful effects in improving the provision of services to hitherto neglected households, but there is no evidence that they have significantly affected the growth of large cities. The same propositions apply to new towns which, in general, seem to have been 'successful' where activity is redistributing itself spontaneously within metropolitan regions.

Recent studies of industrial location policies affecting Seoul, São Paulo and Bogota-Cali[44] also encourage scepticism about the claimed benefits of decentralization measures. The policies appear to work only when spontaneous redistribution is taking place, in which case the policies are superfluous. Furthermore, as an alternative to tackling the problems of metropolitan areas directly, such programmes have nothing to contribute.

In general, spatial policies have a surprisingly poor record in achieving their stated purposes (although equally surprising is the rarity of evaluation with any rigour or attention to opportunity costs). They can carry a high social and financial cost. The reasons for the poor performance are not obscure. Population size and distribution would not seem to be the source of either poverty in general or of the specific problems of a city. These do not seem to be pre-eminently locational questions (although there may in some cases be relevant locational issues). Nor are there any clear criteria for what an improved, let alone optimal, population distribution would be. There are no self-evident reasons why urban primacy should be held to be deleterious, nor the growth of small and intermediate cities beneficial, to society at large. Some analysts have argued that the per capita costs of public services are lower in the second than the first, and in some respects (pre-eminently housing) this is correct. The few studies which purport to demonstrate that cost differences should be the basis for policy have sometimes become quite influential.[45] However, before embarking upon such a course, a government would require to be reassured that rates of return to the society would not suffer as a consequence of relocation to a greater degree than any economies in expenditure. In general, it appears that in the past the benefits have risen significantly faster than the costs as city populations increase; and in some cases, cities have even experienced declining costs per capita in the provision of social overhead capital because productivity has risen faster with the increasing scale of provision.

Identifying the spatial economy, not by disaggregated function or role within the whole, but by settlements of a given population size, gives a spurious homogeneity to classes of settlement (say, cities of 100,000 population). The output which is the basis for settlements, rather than settlement population size, ought to be the criterion of policy. Furthermore, even if redistributing population could be made effective at acceptable cost, it could only contribute to popular welfare or economic growth by accident. Some of the same observations apply to regional policy and the assumption, so important for 'growth poles', that physical contiguity has self-evident benefits.[46] In a market system, governments have less chance of predicting future locations, which cities or towns will grow, than they have of predicting the future output of the economy.

However, many governments have remained surprisingly loyal to an approach which suggests that they have within their power the capacity to determine territorial distributions of population and activity, and that this can be achieved at tolerable cost and will have self-evident economic and social benefits. There are still many people who believe that the distribution of public investment in a developing country can determine the territorial outcome,[47] even though the evidence does not support such a proposition, and many of those who have examined the question most closely express scepticism.[48]

The approach is doubly regrettable, for a preoccupation with unrealizable population redistribution obscures the performance of those tasks which can and need to be undertaken. The speed of urbanization requires a national policy response in terms of ensuring that cities contribute to national development as effectively as possible, the timely provision of services and settlement management, programming public investment, evaluating and seeking to counteract the unintended and undesired spatial effects of national economic policy, ensuring the movement towards effective administrative and financial management, and removing the barriers to movement. Within the city, the need for a coherent approach to improvement and effective management is everywhere apparent.

Facilitation

The poor results of past action as well as the daunting scale of the problems of existing cities (in conditions, for many governments, of increased financial austerity) have encouraged attempts to rethink the appropriate role of government. This has led to efforts by some governments to withdraw from the direct provision of certain urban services and housing, and to concentrate on facilitating actions by private firms, non-governmental or self-help organizations. This has tended to shift attention away from one-off projects to medium-term programmes and sector level policy reforms (including decontrol), from new additions to capacity to the rehabilitation and maintenance of existing capacity. There has been a comparable move away from the regulation of land uses and ambitious attempts to determine the territorial distribution of population to seeking to ensure that the cities become increasingly efficient (whatever their population size), from an emphasis on order to one on economic growth.

In the most ambitious version of this change, some countries are seeking medium-term economic policy packages for a national settlement system, the heart of which is a projection and programme of investment needs for urban infrastructure with institutional mechanisms for the co-ordination of the public agencies involved. The UNDP-funded Indonesian National Urban Development Strategy is possibly the most ambitious example here, but other attempts have been made in Egypt, Pakistan, Malaysia and Peru.

Management

The emphasis on government as facilitator makes urgent the need for effective local government. Yet in many countries, this is one of the most notorious areas of government incompetence. Often, local authorities are burdened with large financial deficits (in extreme cases, equal to 5 per cent of the GDP) but are unable to expand their revenue sources because of the pre-emptive claims of central government. In some cases, the local administration cannot even collect the revenue to which it is entitled. Often they have been given new responsibilities without changes in finance or staff. So bad has the problem become in some countries that central government officers despair of the possibility of reform and seek methods to bypass local government (through, for example, statutory development authorities).

Other innovations may include, as we noted earlier, measures to privatize some local government functions, provided the policy framework is conducive to this. Even then, in poorer countries, there may be difficulties because capital markets are limited, public agencies often have unattractive rates of return and specific services do not attract eager buyers who can sustain services at an acceptable standard and price. Nor is it altogether clear that privatization will result in the provision of services to poorer localities at present not supplied at all. There are also administrative problems in ensuring that monopoly positions are not exploited. It is therefore still necessary to make local authorities and public utilities work more efficiently.

In the case of local government reform, greater financial and legal autonomy appears a precondition for effective financial management.[49] Some governments are now beginning to move in this direction. Furthermore, other innovations are being introduced to support this process – the provision of stable automatic transfers from the centre on objective criteria, the possible establishment of municipal banks, an easing of the restrictions on municipal borrowing from private capital markets, etc. With a strengthened financial basis, reforms of management systems, improved pay to recruit and hold competent staff, continuous training, etc. become feasible methods of enhancing the capacity of local government to manage the process of rapid urbanization.

URBANIZATION AND AID

International aid to developing countries is a small element in total savings and investment (for example, in comparison with a total developing country investment in infrastructure and housing of the order of $100–150 billion annually), and it is therefore important that it is used to exploit the 'comparative advantage' of the donor and to achieve the maximum effect. In the past, aid was often seen as primarily a capital transfer, a means to add to the capacity of a developing country, to relieve a critical bottleneck. The approach fostered some well-known problems – the highway built to standards and specifications that assumed, wrongly, a local capacity (in terms of finance, skills and institutions) to maintain it. Rapid depreciation of aid projects is sadly common in many developing countries.

This experience, as well as the rethinking of government roles on the part of aid recipients, shifted attention to the importance of technical support, the facilitation of activities rather than the direct provision of capacity. This led in some cases to a shift from financing projects to sustaining medium-term programmes of self-reinforcing measures. In the urban field, this was part of the background to the World Bank's Urban Development Programmes which were directed at a locality and combined measures in the fields of housing, health care, education, employment stimulation, small business development, transport and land.

However, the programme, like the project, can still operate in isolation without much spread effect. The exemplary case too often proved no example at all. Thus, the World Bank's sites and service schemes not only proved poor in terms of cost recovery (they could not house the poorest people at costs they could afford), they were not replicated. The Bank now argues that the locality programme cannot be effective if the policy framework is wrong and if the implementing institutions are poor. Attention has shifted towards policy (finally resulting in general support for the balance of payments while structural adjustment is pursued), and downwards to the reform of institutions and their financial management, and the relationships to bodies outside the public sector. In the Bank's case, this has led to a reassessment of the original diagnosis: low incomes are not the result of a lack of employment but of the very low productivity of labour in the work that the poor do. Aid, it is concluded, must therefore make a shift of emphasis from the attempt to tackle urban poverty directly to efforts to improve urban productivity (as the only sustainable means to improve the condition of the poor).

This change of emphasis fits much more closely the comparative advantage of aid donors. For this is not in the absolute size of funds mobilized, but in the fact that they are foreign exchange and therefore provide exceptional access for developing countries to international experience. Thus, aid ought to become technical assistance-led rather than capital-led. And technical assistance is becoming less the transmission of well-codified techniques (local capacities for training in many developing countries are increasingly able to fill this need), and rather more the transfer of technical innovation, research results, policy reconsiderations and concerns less easily defined – organization and management.

In the case of the urban sector, the weakness of public sector agencies has been described. If they could be strengthened (and their functions redefined), the effects would be much greater than those achieved by an aid donor substituting itself for an inadequate set of agencies (as, some might argue, the World Bank did in Calcutta through the Calcutta Metropolitan Development Authority).[50] An institutional approach encourages the combining of elements in complementary packages over the medium term – consultancy, research, training, the twinning of agencies, as well as supporting capital aid. One of the Bank's innovatory loans in this field combined training and consultancy to local authorities with selected capital aid used as the incentive to undertake the programme.

There are problems involved in this approach. For the aid donor, it is much more politically exposed to be so closely involved with an agency. A capital project disposes of large sums in a form relatively easy for a donor to administer, and produces an output which can be politically and diplomatically impressive. Policy advice, training, enhancing the capacities of institutions are less easy to manage, monitor and evaluate, and involve much greater administrative inputs for the disposal of quite small sums of aid. Thus, if the change of emphasis is to be made effective, it will require not only changes in the organization of the aid donor's administration but greater reliance on bodies outside the donor agency.

There has been considerable aid in the past which has had important effects in urban areas, although not classified as such. Aid to ports, manufacturing industry, suburban railway systems, bus systems, highways, water supply and housing, tourism and so on, may be predominantly urban in effect. But the urban has tended to be narrowly defined as old-style town and country or physical planning which, as has been argued earlier, is not the appropriate focus. On the other hand, the spatial economy, urban and rural, is a vital element in national economic development and is not primarily a matter of *physical* ordering. There is a case for aid donors more consciously co-ordinating the elements of their activity which relate to the urban in order to see how far they can be mutually reinforcing or reveal gaps, the filling of which could have disproportionate development effects. They also allow the possibility of learning. There are vital lessons to be learned from the experience of other donors, particularly affecting the new stress upon the role of agencies. Thus, for example, the fifteen years in which Calcutta has been the centrepiece of the World Bank's urban lending provides an unrivalled set of lessons on the efficacy of the methods employed, the strengths and weaknesses, which in turn provides the basis for new policy directions.

This paper has endeavoured to show that urbanization in developing countries is going to be of increasing significance as the low-income countries enter the demographic transition to predominantly urban societies. The role of government is of particular importance in utilizing the necessary increases in income which are one of the results of the process in order to create the means to ease this transition, and aid has a particular role in helping in the management of that process. An urban strategy – whether as a national economic policy framework for settlements or development plans for particular cities – is one of the means of assisting governments to anticipate events which now appear inevitable, of concentrating the efforts of relevant public agencies in enhancing the productivity of cities and of seeking to minimize the damage to popular welfare which can result from rapid urbanization. The role of external assistance in implementing such a strategy can be of particular importance.

3

Some Trends in the Evolution of Big Cities: Case Studies of the USA and India

The city has represented wealth, civilization and power for over three thousand years. In the nineteenth century, power came in part to mean industry, and 'industry' and 'urban' became almost synonymous; the physical equipment of cities seemed almost to be no more than part of the capital base of industrial production, and similarly subject to the obsolescence of particular forms of industry. It was understandable that urbanization could be seen as empirically one of the most accessible surrogate measures of industrialization, and thus of the growth of wealth, of employment and incomes, of 'modernization'.

In the developing countries, however, once cities began to grow swiftly in the 1950s, there was much more pessimism. Indeed, the identity between industry (alias progress) and urbanization came under severe challenge;[1] city growth was the result, it was said, of the poor being driven off the land to the relative security of the cities, not the growth of the urban demand for industrial labour: the Third World was 'overurbanized', and its cities 'unnatural'. Some came close to the spirit of horror of the Victorian bourgeoisie in the presence of what it had created. However, whereas Marx (and subsequently, Lenin) saw the growth of cities as the source of progress and ultimate emancipation, their followers in the post-war period – pre-eminently, Mao Tse-tung and Fidel Castro – saw the cities as no less threatening than the ruling order.[2] The world was apparently agreed.

Furthermore, the belief that an alternative way of life was possible – as embodied in town and country planning – achieved greater success after the Second World War than ever before. Instruments, it seemed, were available to public authorities to order the distribution of population and activities in conformity with that

Originally published under the same title in *Habitat International (Oxford), Vol. 8, No. 1, 1984, pp. 7–28.*

belief. The confidence that the market could be shaped in predetermined ways connected with the sense of horror, and increasing numbers of governments introduced the statutory and institutional requirements to make effective the vision of a world well-ordered and green.

However, the actual behaviour of populations only in part coincided with the perceptions of the planners. The evaluation of the effectiveness of policy was nowhere well enough developed to produce unequivocal conclusions, and was never free of those perverse results which dog the applied social sciences. Does a low city unemployment rate indicate high employment, or a city so poor that the unemployed cannot afford to stay in the urban area? Does a declining city population indicate the effectiveness of planning or a slump, an increase in welfare or a decrease?

Interpretation is afflicted by just those surrogates, the nineteenth century deities that, in the twentieth century, became false gods. Settlement patterns are, we presume, the spatial responses to a particular structure of economic activity, a spatial labour market and a spatially distributed system of production. These underlying forces are in continuous change so that we would expect the same of the settlement 'superstructure'. The words remain the same – villages, towns, cities. But the infinite elasticity of concepts should not lead us to assume that what the concepts mean remains the same. Like so many social institutions – the family, farming, industry – their significance can be radically transformed without budging the use of the term;[3] the appearance of constancy is illusion. As the economy changes, so does the significance of 'city'; the contingent factors which forced one division of labour can change.

THE UNITED STATES

These observations become relevant in seeking to understand the new wealth of data produced by the 1979–82 census rounds. The emerging patterns of population distribution need to be matched against the past and future aspirations of policy and planning if public action is to come closer to effectiveness and relevance. In particular, two cases are examined here, not because either is in any way 'representative', but because each is a major component of the opposite ends of the per capita income spectrum. In both cases, we assume that the distribution of population is a response to the changing demands of national production. In that oversimplified form, the generalization is clearly false; or rather, grows increasingly weak, the higher the per capita income. Higher incomes make possible greater mobility and therefore a greater spatial dissociation between residence and work; they also make possible a much larger dependent population which may be, as used to be said of modern industry, 'footloose'; the relatively affluent pensioner is not tied to the location of the pension office. Nonetheless, we would expect some conformity between work and residence for a major part of the population, even if the reservations have to be extended.

The first striking feature of the 1980 United States Census[4] – now well known – is that for the first time in the recorded history of the country, a majority of Americans live in the south and west, not in the north-east and north-centre. Furthermore, the urban sector as a whole is expanding less fast (10 per cent growth of population for the decade) than the rural counties (15 per cent); that is, nationally, the USA is 'deurbanizing'.

There are, however, some diverse patterns. Table 3.1 distributes the cities which had, in 1980, populations of 100,000 or more in order to identify the different rates of growth. 'Deurbanization' is the central parameter of the table, and is defined as covering those cities growing at less than the rate of natural increase of the American population as a whole. A number of features stand out in examining the fortunes of the 290 cities (or Standard Metropolitan Statistical Areas) concerned:

(a) Contraction

Fully 137 (or 47 per cent) of the cities are, in population, either contracting absolutely (there are 25 of these, ten of them with populations of one million or more) or relatively. Indeed, of the 38 large cities in the USA (one million or more population), 21 are 'deurbanizing'; if we could make due allowance for boundary changes, particularly in the southern States, it is possible that even more large cities would join the 21. Furthermore, 53 of the 120 smaller cities (100–199,000 population) are also 'deurbanizing'. All the contracting cities are located in the north-east and north-centre, so that the regional redistribution is also an urban–rural change.

(b) Slow growth

A further 102 cities (or 35 per cent) are increasing in population only slowly (that is, by between 11.4 and 31.4 per cent for the decade). Of these, all but ten are below one million in population size, and 72 of them below 400,000.

Table 3.1 *USA: Distribution of Standard Metropolitan Statistical Areas, with populations of 100,000 or more in 1980, by population size and population growth, 1970–1980 (numbers)*

1980	*Rates of population growth (1970–80) (numbers of settlements)*						
	'Deurbanization'		*'Slow'*		*'Moderate'*	*'Rapid'*	
Size of population	*Negative* 1.	*0–11.4%*[a] 2.	*11.5–21.4%* 3.	*21.5–31.4%* 4.	*31.5–41.4%* 5.	*41.5% or more* 6.	*Totals*
(a) 7 million or more	1	2	0	0	0	0	3
(b) 3–6.9 million	2	2	0	0	0	0	4
(c) 2–2.9 million	3	3	0	2	0	1	9
(d) 1–1.9 million	4	4	3	5	3	3	22
(e) 0.7–0.99 million	1	9	4	1	1	1	17
(f) 0.5–0.69 million	4	9	4	3	1	3	24
(g) 0.4–0.49 million	1	5	5	3	3	1	18
(h) 0.3–0.39 million	3	12	9	2	3	0	29
(i) 0.2–0.29 million	0	19	11	4	3	7	44
(j) 0.15–0.19 million	3	18	14	2	3	5	45
(k) 0.1–0.14 million	3	29	19	11	6	7	75
Totals	25	112	69	33	23	28	290

[a] 11.4% is the national rate of natural increase, 1970–80.

Source: calculated from Table 4, Rank of Standard Consolidated Statistical Areas and Standard Metropolitan Statistical Areas in the United States, 1980 and 1970, in: *1980 Census of Population*, Supplementary Reports PC 80–S1–5, *Standard Metropolitan Statistical Areas and Standard Consolidated Statistical Areas 1980*, Bureau of the Census, US Government, Washington DC, 1980, pp. 50–53.

(c) High Growth

Twenty-eight cities are expanding at rates for the decade of above 41.4 per cent (or four times the national rate of natural increase); four of these each have a population of one million or more – Houston (Texas), the largest, with two others in Florida and one in Arizona. Of the full 28, eleven are in Florida, four in Texas, three each in California and Washington State, and the rest in other Western States (Arizona, Nevada, Utah, Idaho, Colorado). Again, if we could allow for boundary changes, some of these high-growth cities might also become closer to the low-growth type.

In sum, in this somewhat cursory examination, it seems that Americans have for the past ten years been increasingly dispersing their residences away from the old main centre of population – from the north to the south and the west (a much older process than simply the last decade); secondly, away from cities to rural counties; thirdly, from more 'advanced' to more backward areas. Furthermore, the population is continuing to disperse away from existing city areas to the periphery and beyond. This process is at its most extreme in the north-east and north-centre; St Louis lost 28 per cent of its 1970 population; Buffalo 23 per cent; Detroit and Pittsburg, 21 per cent each; and New York City 10 per cent (compared to New York State's 4 per cent). It is a part of a process noted throughout much of this century.[5]

Thus, the dominant picture is one of 'deurbanization', and of a shift in growth from the larger cities to the smaller and to the rural areas. Marx's division of labour is apparently being replaced by something quite new, contrary to the expectations of followers of Marx, for example, some of whom held that this division of labour could only be overcome by a fundamental transformation of society (a view faithfully reproduced in Mao's discussions of the 'Three Great Differences').[6]

SPECULATIONS

What factors might underlie this type of spatial redistribution? One of the obvious observations is that while the level of per capita income in the north remains above average, the rate of growth in the past decade has been poor. By contrast, in eight of the ten southern States, per capita income has increased faster than the national average, increasing fastest in the poorest States. It seems that in the past phase of transformation of the American industrial economy, the south played the role attributed to the Newly Industrializing

Countries, attracting selected elements of more mobile industries, those dependent upon geographically specific raw material sources (farm output, oil and petrochemicals in Texas, for example), or those where labour costs were a relatively high proportion of total costs (such industries were thus able to utilize the relatively low wage levels, poor trade union organization and sympathetic State governments of the south). The process of redistribution also reflects – particularly in Florida – an increasing proportion of the population which is aged and with access to relatively high pension levels, allowing them to move to more favourable climates and thus provide a demand for a larger servicing economy, particularly manned by relatively low-income and immigrant labour.

The process could not take place, however, unless other changes had occurred. The upgrading of the infrastructural provision in the south (highways, air and sea ports, power, water, etc.), perhaps because it was more recent, more modern than the depreciated stock of the north, was a precondition, as also was an improvement in southern educational standards, bringing them closer to the national average; or rather, the provision of both elements in selected localities of the south. This would be particularly important for urban locations, contrasting the old and depreciated infrastructure of the north with that in the south, and the tax levels in the north required to renovate the equipment there in comparison with the costs of development *de novo*. Past cuts in maintenance budgets, as for example in New York, would exaggerate this contrast – particularly in the New York case, where there are severe political difficulties in extending the city's borders to capture the tax revenue of the wealthy suburbs.

These factors may go part of the way in explaining the regional redistribution as well as 'deurbanizing' trends. In sum, they represent a dissociation of 'urban' and 'industrial'. The process presupposes a measure of homogenization of the conditions of production on the land surface so that plant location could, in theory, be less constrained by the past factors governing distribution. However, there is another important feature. Higher productivity and higher incomes have made possible a higher degree of daily mobility by the workforce. Residences and workplaces have become more dissociated.

Redistribution presupposes, however, larger processes, including the changing structure of the American economy – between industry and services, and within industry, the creation of a new generation of manufacturing processes with different locational characteristics (and the decline of older ones). 'Deindustrialization' is a well-known phenomenon. As manufacturing output has continued to rise, the proportion of the labour force required to produce it has declined; indeed, the absolute numbers of manufacturing workers have also tended to fall in almost all the developed countries.[7]

The statistics are a little misleading. They seem to imply that those employed in manufacturing manufacture, and those outside have little to do with it. In fact, an increasing proportion of manufacturing employment is 'non-productive' (that is, white-collar employees: clerical, technical and supervisory), and a large and possibly growing proportion of those in 'services' are directly related to making manufacturing possible or disposing of its output, whether in research, trading, storing, financing or moving. Thus, a change in the ratio of direct to indirect manufacturing employment may reflect no more than that the growing productivity of the manufacturing worker proper depends upon a larger and larger number of non-manufacturing workers. The firepower of the modern soldier depends on a growing army of suppliers.

Manufacturing is only one part of national output. What has grown disproportionately in employment terms is services and, while an important part of that is related directly to manufacturing, a growing part is not. 'Services' is an ill-charted concept, particularly when we are concerned with the relatively unexplored area of the changing locational characteristics of different types of economic activity. In the British case, between the first half of the 1960s and 1976, there was a loss of 1.3 million jobs in manufacturing and a gain of 1.5 million in 'professional and scientific'; (since there was a net growth in the labour force, unemployment also rose). In the USA, a majority of the non-agricultural labour force has been employed in services for a long time – 63 per cent in 1961, 68 per cent in 1971, 72 per cent in 1981.[8] In Japan, the service sector increased its share of total employment from 35 per cent in 1965 to just under 55 per cent in 1980 (the sector's share of national income rose from 35 to 54 per cent). Stagnation and slump since 1974 have afflicted manufacturing much more severely than services, so the trend has been exaggerated; thus, between October 1982 and one year later, of the estimated gain in non-agricultural employment in Japan, two-thirds was in services. Lest it be thought that the process is restricted to the developed countries, it might be noted that many of the Newly Industrializing Countries exhibit comparable processes; for example, the share of the South Korean labour force engaged in services rose between 1960 and 1980 from 25 to 37 per cent.[9]

Service employment draws more heavily on low-paid female labour; often it involves 'traditional' female jobs – clerks, typists, nurses, health care workers, teachers, child care and social workers, cleaning and household workers. In Britain, 41 per cent of employed women work in community, social and personal services, and 21 per cent in wholesale and retail trade, hotels and restaurants. Much of the work is part-time; 40 per cent of British women workers were part-time in the mid-1970s (in 17 per cent of all jobs). Much of this work is likely to be city-based, but insofar as major employment units, whether industrial or servicing, choose non-urban locations, such employment does not obstruct the movement.

A much greater disaggregation of services data – indeed, a satisfactory conceptual framework with which to disaggregate – would be needed to assess accurately the locational implications of the overall growth in the service economy. However, it seems that, whereas in the recent past large units of servicing activity required a relative physical bunching of their labour force (thus favouring urban locations), this may now be declining. The average size of units in terms of employment may be declining, and the mobility of the labour force rising. Furthermore, new technology may increase these tendencies. The development of innovations in telecommunications and data processing systems, tapping worldwide information sources at almost any location, threatens even those complexes of service activity *par excellence*, central business districts, which hitherto have been dependent on physical concentration for 'knowledge in a hurry'.[10]

The interconnecting threads may be obscure, but it is not unreasonable to assume a relationship between 'deurbanization' and 'deindustrialization', and thus to speculate on the underlying forces for the results of the US Census. The changing composition of industrial output has a more obvious significance in terms of location. The old heavy industries – and the textile trades – which were prodigious consumers of physically concentrated labour forces a century ago, have been declining for much of this century, a process only exaggerated in the current phase of stagnation in the industrialized countries. The decline of the European and American steel industries is well known, producing commensurate spatial effects in Alsace–Lorraine, the Benelux countries, and Indiana–Ohio. Shipbuilding and coal-mining are similar cases. One of the more striking examples is that of the old heart of German capitalism, the Ruhr; between 1966 and 1976, nearly half a million jobs were lost in the region; outmigration took another 330,000, and even then, the regional unemployment rate was double the national average.

Thus, the changing composition of output also means a changing location of production. The transition from the industrial core of the British economy of the late nineteenth century (textiles, iron and steel, coal, shipbuilding) to that of the period after the Second World War (vehicles, light engineering, petro-chemicals) was also a shift from the north-east, north-west, and Scotland to the West Midlands and south-east. The process similarly afflicts urban–rural distributions. Like New York, Greater London lost a third of its manufacturing employment in the two decades after 1950. In the 1970s, this emerged as also an 'inner city' problem, sifting the inner population to leave behind relatively poor groups in derelict or declining districts. Montreal, Paris, Frankfurt, Osaka, Stockholm, all seem to have lost 15 per cent or more of their inner city populations in the 1970s (and Lyons lost over a fifth).

Within the process is another. Increasing levels of labour productivity with a relatively slow growth of output imply declining labour inputs per unit of output. There seems also to have been a decline in workers per unit of production, a trend that would further reduce the need for the physical concentration of the labour force.

In sum, the redistribution of the American population may reflect many of these common processes. We are very far from being able to weight the relative contribution of each: the spread of infrastructure and education, the mobility of the labour force, the changing 'economic mix' (industry, services, etc.) and 'industrial mix' of the American economy, the changing employment size and labour inputs in the units of production, etc. The results, however, appear to be a continuing decline in the need to concentrate the labour force in specific spatial areas. Production, power, finance can be centralized without the physical concentration of the population – or at least, not on the same scale of concentration. The old division of labour appears to be coming to an end.

INDIA

The USA is not an economic island. It is, to an increasing degree, integrated in a global economy,[11] so that the processes of domestic redistribution of the labour force are intimately related to the American role in a world division of labour. The factors affecting the domestic redistribution may thus in part affect all countries, each in a different way, depending upon its specialized role. How far can we see common and differing elements in countries very remote in most respects from the situation in the USA? The Indian case is instructive in this respect.

The Indian Census results of 1981[12] are provisional (the figures exclude Assam, Jammu and Kashmir, as well as a number of cities), but they still provide us with a crude entrypoint to the changes taking place. In 1981, some 160 million Indians (or 24 per cent of the total population) lived in 3,245 settlements defined as 'urban', of which 2,230 had a population of under 20,000 each. Some 60 per cent of the urban population – or 94 million people – lived in 216 'Urban Agglomerations' of 'Class I' size (that is, each with a population of 100,000 or more). Of these, only twelve had a population of one million or more.

Thus, in the first instance, there is a striking contrast between India and the USA. In the latter, there were 290 cities with 100,000 or more population, covering 166 million people (with an average size of city of 572,383); of these 290, 38 had a population of one million or more, with 55 per cent of total population of the 290. India, with three times the total population of the USA, had 216 comparable cities, with 94 million inhabitants (and an average size of such cities of 435,185). Its twelve cities with one million or more population included 27 per cent of Class I city population.

Table 3.2 presents a distribution of the cities of India which, in 1981, had populations of 100,000 or more, classified according to their respective rates of population growth between 1971 and 1981. As one would expect, the table is, in comparison with Table 3.1, sharply shifted to the right, a shift which would be much more pronounced if the vertical columns were comparable in both tables instead of being governed by very different local rates of natural increase – 11.4 per cent for the USA as compared to 24 per cent for India. However, the overall picture of urban growth in India is not a uniform phenomenon, and certainly not an 'urban explosion'. In contrast to the American figures, there are no negative growth rates in the Indian list. But there is, by the standard defined here, 'deurbanization'; that is, city population growth rates below the national rate of natural increase.

(a) Deurbanization

Two States are of particular interest here, Uttar Pradesh and Tamilnadu. Uttar Pradesh is India's largest State, with some 20 million 'urban' population (increasing by 61 per cent in the decade). Half these city dwellers live in Class I cities (whose population increased in the decade by 46 per cent). The State supplies the large city, one million or more population (1(a) in the table), in the Deurbanization category. This is Lucknow, the State capital. It also supplies Agra in 1(d), and there are two other Uttar Pradesh cities in smaller size groups.

If we take column 2 of the table, the slower of the 'Slow' group, Kanpur in Uttar Pradesh is one of the two large cities in 2(a) (West Bengal's Calcutta is the other). The city in 2(d) is also from this State, Varanasi, and in the smaller size categories, there are a

Table 3.2 *India: Distribution of Class I cities (with a population in 1981 of 100,000 or more) by population size and population growth, 1971–81 (numbers)*

1981 Size of population	*Rates of population growth (1971–81) (number of settlements)*								
	'Deurbanization'	*'Slow'*		*'Moderate'*	*'Rapid'*	*'Very fast'*			
	0–24%	*25–34%*	*35–44%*	*45–54%*	*55–64%*	*65–74%*	*75% or more*	*Data not available*	*Total*
	1.	*2.*	*3.*	*4.*	*5.*	*6.*	*7.*		
(a) 1 million or more	1	2	4	2	2	0	1	0	12
(b) 0.9–0.99 million	0	2	0	0	0	0	2	0	4
(c) 0.8–0.89 million	0	0	0	1	0	0	0	0	1
(d) 0.7–0.79 million	1	1	1	0	1	0	0	0	4
(e) 0.6–0.69 million	0	2	0	2	2	0	1	1	8
(f) 0.5–0.59 million	1	0	3	1	2	0	1	3	11
(g) 0.4–0.49 million	0	2	1	1	2	0	2	0	8
(h) 0.3–0.39 million	1	3	7	2	2	1	3	2	21
(i) 0.2–0.29 million	0	7	13	6	3	0	4	0	33
(j) 0.15–0.19 million	5	6	3	6	5	0	0	4	29
(k) 0.10–0.14 million	12	24	13	15	8	2	6	5	85
Total	21	49	45	36	27	3	20	15	216[a]

[a] The total is effectively 201 (216–15). 24% was the national rate of natural increase, 1971–81; the urban population increased by 45%, and the population of Class I cities by 57%.

Source: Calculated from Provisional Population, Table 4, Population, Growth Rate, Sex Ratio and Literacy Rate of Cities and Urban Agglomerations with Population of 100,000 and above, in Census of India, *Provisional Population Totals, Rural–Urban Distribution,* Series–1, India, Paper 2 of 1981, R. Padmanabhan, Delhi, 1982, pp. 65–71.

further ten cities from this State. Closer examination would allow us to locate these settlements on the map, perhaps contrasting the relatively higher rate of economic growth of the west (close to Delhi and a beneficiary of the Green Revolution) with the poor areas of eastern Uttar Pradesh.

Tamilnadu in the south had an urban population of 16 million in 1981 (it had increased by 28 per cent in the preceding decade), with 9.9 million (or 62 per cent) living in Class I cities (that had increased by 38 per cent since 1971). The State is of particular interest since it grew rapidly in economic and urban population terms in the decade preceding 1971. In the Deurbanization column (1) of the table, (f) is the Tamilnadu city of Salem, and (h) is Tirunelveli. Of the 17 cities in the size groups below this, fully seven are from Tamilnadu (no other State had more than two). In the first of the Slow columns (2), the two cities in (b) are both from Tamilnadu – Coimbatore and Madurai, as also is one of those in (e). In (j), two of the six cities are from this State, but only one in (k) (compared to four each from Uttar Pradesh and Gujerat). Finally, Madras, India's fourth largest city, only just gets into column 3 at 35 per cent.

(b) High growth

It is in columns 5 to 7 of the tables that India is most sharply distinguished from the USA. Only 15 of the American cities had rates of growth above 54 per cent for the decade in comparison with 50 in India. The 15 included two cities of one million or more population, but in the smallest category (line (d) in Table 3.1) – Phoenix (Arizona) at 55 per cent, and Fort Lauderdale, Hollywood (Florida) at 63.5 per cent. Of the 50 Indian cities, only one – Bangalore (Karnataka) – was in this size class, with a population growth for the decade of 76 per cent. The class immediately below this in Table 3.2, (b), contained two more – Patna, the State capital of Bihar (87 per cent growth), and Surat in Gujerat (85 per cent). Most of the remaining smaller cities were single industry (usually, heavy industry) or raw material extracting settlements or State capitals – Bhopul (Madhya Pradesh, 75 per cent); Ranchi (Bihar, 96 per cent); Chandigarh (81 per cent); Rourkela (Orissa, 86 per cent); Bokharo (Bihar, 144 per cent); Bhubaneshwar, Orissa, 108 per cent), etc.

The geographical spread of high growth settlements is striking. Many of them are from the existing dominant centres of relatively dense population; they are, as it were, on the 'periphery' and in the relatively more backward areas (Rajasthan, Orissa, Bihar, etc.). However, as we have seen, the spread did not reach as far as Uttar Pradesh – with three (one in line (i), two in line (k)) – or Tamilnadu with one (in line (i)) respectively.

However, if we separate the 50 by States, the highest number of high growth cities are contained in three geographically contiguous States of central India – Andhra (with eight), Maharashtra (with six) and Karnataka (with five). Maharashtra, with the largest share of India's urban population (17.5 per cent) and three of the 12 largest cities – Greater Bombay, Pune and Nagpur – is of particular interest because its share of the increase in India's Class I urban population is below average (15.9 per cent). However, this small relative decline seems to conceal a wider dispersal of its big city population to smaller cities, or rather, growth is taking place more vigorously away from the larger existing settlements. A number of the State's smaller high growth settlements are, like Pune, closely related to Bombay's manufacturing economy: for example, Ulhasnagar, Nasik, Thane, Aurangabad. Perhaps this 'spillover', as the hydraulic imagery has it, is affecting areas beyond Maharashtra's borders in neighbouring States, which include, in addition to the two mentioned, Gujerat.

The phenomenon of the relative contraction of Greater Bombay is shared by all three of the oldest and largest industrial States of India. Thus:

	1981 Percentage share of the all-India Class I population	Percentage share in the increase of Class I population, 1971–81
1. West Bengal (including Calcutta) 2. Maharashtra (including Bombay) 3. Tamilnadu (including Madras)	39.8	28.5

If we include with the three the third largest city in India, Delhi, then the share of Class I population in 1981 rises to 45.9 per cent, and the share of increase to 34.6 per cent.

Grouping adjacent States is a quite arbitrary phenomenon in the absence of separately identified data, but it brings out how far the decline of the old large cities is masked by regions of associated growth. Thus:

1. *West Central India*

	1981 share of Indian Class I population			Share in the 1971–81 Class I population increase		
(a) Andhra Pradesh	7.1			7.7		
(b) Karnataka	6.7	20.3		7.8	22.7	
(c) Gujerat	6.5		37.8	7.2		38.6
(d) Maharashtra	17.5			15.9		

We can compare this with three other smaller State groupings:

2. *South India*

(a) Kerala	2.7	13.2	3.1	6.0
(b) Tamilnadu	10.5		2.9	

The relative decline in Tamilnadu is well illustrated in this form, and in no way masked by the higher growth of Kerala.

3. *Eastern India*

(a) Bihar	5.0		6.3	
(b) Orissa	1.4	18.2	1.7	17.7
(c) West Bengal	11.8		9.7	

4. *Northern India*

(a) Uttar Pradesh	10.9		9.4	
(b) Haryana	1.7	21.0	4.0	22.0
(c) Punjab	2.3		2.5	
(d) Delhi	6.1		6.1	

Source: Table 3, *ibid.*, p. 59.

Thus, while there has not been any dramatic reordering or redistribution of the urban population regionally – certainly nothing to compare with the final achievement of a southern majority in the USA – there are important trends. High urban growth has benefited the outlying States, while the older industrial States are in relative decline. Furthermore, there may be emerging a much larger macro industrial–urban region in the centre of India, covering three or four States.

Contrary to popular impressions, India's largest cities are not growing particularly rapidly,[13] with the sole exception of Bangalore. Of the twelve cities with one million or more population nine are growing at rates below that for the Class I population as a whole (57

Table 3.3 *Shares of the Class I population held by the largest cities (1 million or more population in 1971) in 1971 and 1981, and shares of the increase in Class I population, 1971–81*

	Share of the Class I population, 1971 (%)	*Share of the Class I population, 1981 (%)*	*Share of the increase in Class I population (%)*	*Index of variation: (c) × 100 / (a)*
	(a)	*(b)*	*(c)*	*(d)*
Calcutta (UA)	11.6	9.8	6.3	54.3
Greater Bombay	10.0	8.8	6.7	67.0
Delhi (UA)	6.1	6.1	6.1	100.0
Madras (UA)	5.3	4.6	3.3	62.3
Bangalore (UA)	2.8	3.1	3.7	132.1
Hyderabad (UA)	3.0	2.7	2.2	73.3
Ahmedabad (UA)	2.9	2.7	2.3	79.3
Kanpur (UA)	2.1	1.8	1.2	57.1
Pune (UA)	1.9	1.8	1.6	84.2

Figures have been rounded
UA: Urban Agglomeration.

Source: Ibid., calculated from Statement 20, p. 44, and Table 3, p. 59.

per cent); Delhi is growing at exactly that rate, Jaipur slightly above it (58 per cent), and only Bangalore at an exceptionally rapid rate. Eight of the twelve were growing more slowly than the rate of increase of the urban population as a whole (46 per cent). Thus, a *declining* proportion of India's urban population lived in the largest cities in 1971.

With 45.7 per cent of the Class I population in 1971, the nine largest cities took only a third of the increase in Class I population between 1971 and 1981. Of the three newcomers to the large city group in 1981 – Nagpur, Lucknow and Jaipur – only Jaipur was growing above the rate for the Class I population, and then only slightly above, and Lucknow was growing at a rate below that of natural increase for the country as a whole. Thus, the picture of relative stagnation in the population sizes of big cities in India – Bangalore excluded – would not be changed in substance by the inclusion of the newcomers.

In Table 3.3 the index of variation (column (d)) shows that Calcutta and Kanpur were the slowest growing of the big cities, with Bombay and Madras in the next group. Hyderabad, Ahmedabad and Pune come next, with Delhi exactly on the growth rate for the Class I population as a whole.

Much can change in the coming decade, but the trend appears to be strongly towards the relative decline of the larger cities as their numbers increase.[14] The smaller cities entering the class of large ones have not qualitatively changed the performance of the group as a whole. India's large cities seem to be slowing at a much earlier stage than was seen in the USA; if the trend persists, it would suggest an urban spatial configuration in India quite unlike the historical experience of Western Europe and North America (and quite contrary to many contemporary expectations). It is paradoxical, however, that both American and Indian big cities are slowing together.

The census results so far for India do not permit us to identify in detail the dispersal processes of particular cities, particularly in order to assess how far the population of inner-city districts is falling relatively or absolutely, a phenomenon familiar in the cities of Western Europe and the USA. Nonetheless, crude figures exist to show that the large cities are experiencing some redistribution between the old municipal areas and the larger urban agglomeration. For the twelve largest cities, the picture is as shown in Table 3.4 (pp. 86–7).

In the decade preceding 1971, all cities except Delhi and Lucknow (excluding Greater Bombay for which there are no comparable data available) registered ratios of over 100 in column 3, indicating redistribution away from the municipal area. Paradoxically, while Delhi and Lucknow joined the majority group in the decade 1971–81, three cities seem to have reversed the trend of the previous decade – Kanpur, Pune and Nagpur. It is possible that a redrawing of municipal boundaries would help to explain this effect. None of the city areas are declining as swiftly as Calcutta, with an MC rate of growth of population well below the rate of natural increase. Of course the 'MC' population is a quite misleading measure for comparable studies since it scarcely coincides with the old city area everywhere and, as in the case of Calcutta, does not include all the old city area proper. Nonetheless, closer examination of the primary enumeration districts when the data become available will allow us to confirm how far this trend is borne out, how far inner-city districts are beginning to lose population not only relatively but also absolutely (as was the case of Fort North in A Ward of Greater Bombay between 1961 and 1971),[15] and how far these trends are likely to become exaggerated by the time of the next census.

In sum, then, on the results at present available, it seems that while India – with a per capita income far below that of the USA and a population three times larger in a smaller land area – is very different from North America, there may be some common processes at work. India's Class I urban population appears to be in some senses 'dispersing', or rather, the urban population is growing more swiftly outside the existing centres. The largest cities are tending to stagnate in terms of population growth (whereas the American cities are contracting) with redistribution from the old city areas to the Metropolitan Region (and possibly beyond). This process is very far from being recorded, as it is in the USA, as a growth of rural population, albeit in non-agricultural occupations, but of more rapid growth in smaller cities, particularly 'on the periphery' and within the west-central region. Certainly there is no generalized 'urban explosion' taking place, nor are the masses of rural poor endlessly streaming towards the existing big cities. Furthermore, India may already be undergoing the same processes that have affected urban America – of course, powerfully mediated by local circumstances and substantially 'to the right' in terms of Table 3.1 – and doing so at a far lower national level of urbanization and with, by comparison, a tiny big city sector.

SPECULATIONS

How far do the factors, which were earlier suggested might provide some explanation of the American pattern, help us to understand the

Table 3.4 *India: rates of growth of population for the 12 largest cities (one million or more population in 1981), city area and Urban Agglomeration, 1961–71 and 1971–81 (%)*

		Rates of growth	*Rates of growth*	*Ratios of variation*[a,b]	
		1961–71	*1971–81*	*1961–71*	*1971–81*
		1	*2*	*3*	*4*
Calcutta	MC	7.6	4.5	310.5	675.6
	UA	23.6	30.4		
Greater Bombay[b]		43.8	38.0	—	—
Delhi	MC	59.5	48.0	91.7	118.1
	UA	54.6	56.7		
	New Delhi	15.4	−9.9		
Madras	MC	47.1	26.9	133.8	129.7
	UA	63.0	34.9		
Bangalore	C and UDA	35.0	61.1	108.0	124.7
	UA	37.8	76.2		
Hyderabad	MC	43.7	33.3	100.2	122.2
	UA	43.8	40.7		

Ahmedabad	MC	37.9	27.7	117.2	157.0
	UA	44.4	43.5		
Kanpur	MC	31.0	32.7	101.0	99.1
	UA	31.3	32.4		
Pune	MC	41.1	40.5	106.6	93.3
	UA	43.8	37.8		
Nagpur	MC	34.6	40.3	100.6	98.0
	UA	34.8	39.5		
Lucknow	MC	25.8	19.6	93.4	120.9
	UA	24.1	23.7		
Jaipur	M	52.5	57.1	105.1	101.2
	UA	55.2	57.8		

[a] UA/MC etc. × 100. Thus, 100: the growth of both areas is the same.

[b] Greater Bombay is both MC and UA, so there is as yet no separation of island/suburbs or MC/Metropolitan Region.

Abbreviations: M: Municipality; C: Corporation; MC: Municipal Committee or Corporation: UA: Urban Agglomeration; UDA: Urban Development Authority.

Source: Appendix II, 'Population of Urban Agglomerations, Cities and Towns', *ibid.*, pp. 83–215.

Indian? What is the mixture of elements, those unique to each and those common to both, the basis of 'combined and uneven development' (the phrase is Lenin's)?

Almost certainly, differences in the rate of growth of per capita income, some of them related to the location of geographically specific raw materials (farm output, oil petrochemicals, were mentioned in the American southern states), to heavy industrial production or differences in labour costs, play a role, particularly in the last case when we recall that a larger part of the Indian economy than the American is beyond statistical reach. The changed age structure and levels of income capable of supporting a growing proportion of relatively wealthy retired people, a key factor in Florida's rapid population growth, hardly play much role in the Indian scene.

The successive Indian plans have spread key infrastructural facilities over larger spatial areas than before,[16] although the highway system remains poor and power is still notoriously afflicted by shortages. The growth of primary education has spread the availability of labour with some education much further than before. Or, rather, such provisions are available in a wider selection of localities than previously, although it would be absurd to suggest an 'homogenization' of the spatial preconditions of production in India as a whole. The growth of a new generation of modern industry has raised productivity swiftly for a minor part of the industrial labour force, making for enhanced incomes and thus the possibility of great mobility; however, unlike the American case, this still in the main affects public transport networks (so predetermining in part the pattern of residential dispersal) and motor-scooter traffic rather than private cars.

The industrial structure as a whole is a more complicated question. For, under a strict regime of import substitution until quite recently, all sectors of available industry have tended to grow, regardless of their generation of origin and regardless of any specialized role India might play in a world manufacturing system. Thus 'deindustrialization' in employment terms seems an unlikely phenomenon at the present low levels of industrial output, even though the ratios – direct to indirect manufacturing employment, as discussed earlier – will undoubtedly favour the latter as modern output grows. Possibly also the labour employed per unit of production may not increase rapidly in formal sector activities, and capital–labour ratios may tend to move towards the US level for comparable activities.

However, this is misleading precisely because, as is well known, a major part of the Indian economy is only poorly recorded, and we have no very clear sense of the changing relationship between the recorded and unrecorded sectors. Thus, even if the formal sector were to show signs of reproducing the locational patterns found in the USA, we do not know what will happen in the unrecorded sector (or indeed, whether the 'American' locational pattern will not produce in India a disproportionate growth in unrecorded competitive activities). In much of the unrecorded sector, low productivity and low incomes make much commuting impossible, so that those forces which earlier forced a spatial bunching of the labour force in North America and Western Europe continue to operate in India.

Thus, there could be two patterns – the dispersal of high productivity modern industry and later modern large-scale services, and the concentration of low productivity petty manufacturing and trade, where labour mobility is low, industrial linkages high. Insofar as the pricing system favours the first over the second, dispersal will perhaps tend to increase; insofar as the second, through subcontracting or direct production, captures an increasing share of the first, the cities will tend to grow relatively more swiftly. The process could well be dramatically affected by the liberalization of the Indian economy forcing a more specialized role on Indian manufacturing, and thus greatly increasing the competitive strength of labour-intensive activities. It might also be noted that this primitive division of activities (between recorded or formal and unrecorded) is very misleading, and furthermore, does not distinguish the Indian from the American economy as sharply as implied; in the USA, the 'black economy' has received some attention.[17]

Activities which are merely small-scale need not in contemporary circumstances be urban in the traditional sense. Modern technology may relieve the need for physical contact and the physical bunching of the labour force, but this will be true only for prestructured contacts. Unstructured contacts will remain important and require some level of density of particular types of population, even if, in the census, this appears as rural. For example, Highway 101 between San Francisco and San José, Silicon Valley, provides an example of this type of pattern. A journalist reports on the locational advantages of living in the valley:[18]

> In the clubs and restaurants of such places as Sunnyvale, Palo Alto and Mountain View, the budding entrepreneur can, without great difficulty, find advice on how to form a company, recruit managers, optimise marketing strategy, subcontract manufacture and, of course, obtain start-up funds. With a smoothness probably unmatched anywhere else in the world he can optimise his path from employee to employer.

The combination of a dispersed workforce of highly specialized skills, of existing high technology production units, laboratories and research centres, of universities, and a level of available infrastructure of high quality (including an international airport) is still very far from being reproduced in India, although there may be different versions of an imitation in the disposition of 'science parks' etc. India's growing strength in the provision of computer software – at highly competitive rates of labour cost – could perhaps in the future produce a closer economic parallel, even if it is different in spatial distribution.

In sum, then, it would seem that some of the factors underlying dispersal in the USA may also affect part of India's urban system. Yet, the existence of an important unrecorded low-productivity sector of activities suggests that urbanization will still provide a continuing and powerful spatial reflection of economic growth. However, which cities grow may well continue to change, so that as dispersal continues, so small cities might become the main beneficiaries of a growing urban population. Thus the pattern might be construed as one of 'dispersed concentrations'[19] in a limited number of areas, rather than complete dispersal or continuing high concentration; in the Brazilian context, this has been described as an economic archipelago.[20]

PLANNING

From the early efforts at comprehensive physical planning in Britain following the Second World War, through India's experience of Master Plans and regional planning, to the latest efforts in the Ministries of Human Settlements in the Philippines and Mexico (SAHOP, Ministry of Human Settlements in Mexico, 1977–82), the attempts to intervene consciously in the distribution of population in space have not had impressive results.[21] One problem has been the lack of easy criteria by means of which success and failure could be unequivocally attached to given policies. But there has also frequently been a lack of coincidence between what was happening, the problems to be resolved, and the public response. Furthermore, governments frequently tried to resolve issues by spatial means which were not the results of spatial phenomena; the 'urban' was very often a false surrogate. The high tide of demographic hysteria about sheer numbers of people moving made it most difficult to get beyond the crude concept of urbanization – the 'urban explosion' – to the disaggregated picture of changes, let alone detect and try to measure the effect of the different causal factors at stake. The paucity of understanding was too often compensated by heroic aspirations of redrawing the map of the country, aspirations where the aesthetic of the map took priority over either the interests of the inhabitants or common sense.

Territory, outside the doubtful perceptions of geopolitics, has little meaning in society outside the context of the purposes to which it can be put, the activity it supports. Understanding the distribution of people on territory therefore requires us to understand their activity, of which the use of land is only one aspect. The point is not at all novel. Alonso, some time ago, put it in this way:[22]

> . . . population distribution is the territorial aspect of a highly connected and interdependent social system . . . local variations in welfare and productivity are also aspects of this larger system reflected upon geographic space.

Nonetheless, within the realm of physical planning, people have continued to regard the regulation of land as if it were either one of the important causes of variations in welfare and productivity, or one of the main means of remedying problems of welfare – as if the mere concentration of people in one place caused poverty, or their redistribution would cause increased welfare.

Given that planning the distribution of population was supposedly no more than a means to other ends, of which an increase in popular welfare was one of the most important, the link between space and welfare remained singularly ill-explored – as indeed, did the examination of other means to achieve the same welfare results. Professor Richardson enumerates the possible aims of population redistribution polices as:[23]

> interpersonal and interregional equity, national security, political stability and integration, improvement in the quality of life, optimal resource exploitation, and, perhaps, *long-run* economic efficiency.

But insofar as these aims can be identified rigorously enough for effective public action and evaluation, it is not at all clear that they are spatial questions *per se*, nor accessible to remedy through measures designed to redistribute population. Each, in any case, would have to be appraised in terms of alternative methods of achieving the same end before it could be shown that efforts to redistribute population were the most convincing means.

Bertrand Renaud[24] lists the aims of a national settlement strategy, and these also include some which involve population redistribution:

to integrate peripheral regions to increase the size of the domestic market and exploit new resources; to narrow regional disparities; to increase political and social integration; to improve the efficiency of the national urban system, to increase the diffusion mechanism. Similar points apply. Thus, the 'size' of a market is in its important sense not a geographical but an economic concept; extending the spatial extent of a market may be less sensible than increasing the market size in existing areas; regional disparities may or may not matter in terms of welfare – decreases in regional disparities in no way exclude the possibility of increasing interpersonal disparities; political and social integration is scarcely a matter of spatial contiguity, and moving people into backward regions is more likely to cause collision than increased solidarity; finally, increasing the efficiency of the existing urban system has no self-evident relationship to 'diffusing' it, a concept clearer in words than reality.

In sum, as Richardson notes, 'the relationshp between population distribution targets and the broader societal goals that population distribution policies are intended to serve is murky and unclear'.[25] Nonetheless, national urban planning has been inextricably interwoven with policies to redistribute population both between and within regions, but particularly, away from existing large cities. Yet it is strange that the vindication of spatial planning should share in the obscurity of criteria applicable to population redistribution policies, since a more modest set of purposes would appear self-evidently justified. Spatial planning – which may or may not include efforts to alter where people live – is justified by the attempt of public authorities to ease and order the process of economic and social change (territorial distribution being one element in that process); by the attempt to secure some rough coincidence between the demand for workers of particular skills in particular places and the supply; by the effort to secure the co-ordination of the provision of appropriate infrastructural services in particular places at particular times. It is also sometimes a purpose of national planning to seek to enhance increases in territorial productivity by encouraging geographical specialization. Given the sheer scale of public provision in countries today, such efforts would be an elementary part of seeking to ensure smooth change, to minimize losses. They ought to be an element in all national and local planning. But such aims do not seek to impose a given distribution of population territorially, as if such an aim could be determined independently of activity, incomes and productivity; any such exercise could be achieved only by accident.

In almost all countries, developed and developing, 'decentralization' has been for a long period almost the only strategy on offer in terms of territorial planning at the national level. The matching policies at the level of the large city were designed to secure, at least verbally, the reduction, or the discouragement of growth, of existing large cities and the growth of smaller settlements or rural areas.

However, the experience of these policies in less developed countries is that the aims appear to be largely hypocrisy; while ministers wax eloquent, urbanization continues apace. Indeed, a cynic might assume that the purpose of the policies was to prevent planning, to prevent serious efforts to understand and plan the complex disaggregated patterns of activity by pre-empting the field with a utopian abstraction, an intellectual diversion.

Even in the 1960s, evidence was available that the picture was much more complicated than the common wisdom allowed. In the developed countries, it was known that populations were spreading far beyond the boundaries of Metropolitan Regions;[26] yet policy remained proccupied with the task of dispersal, not city decline. In the USA, for example, public authorities continued to behave as if large metropolitan areas were subject to endless population growth until surprisingly recently; the task of planners was to combat 'the discouraging vision of the gargantuan megalopolis' as one public document put it. Congress was persistently urged to curb growth[27] and redistribute people towards more backward regions. Paradoxically, although the measures undertaken were generally considered weak and ineffective,[28] as we have seen, dispersal was taking place.

In the developing countries, perhaps it was more understandable that there should have been concern with the implications of the growth of large cities. But again, quite often that concern was not related to the real processes, comparable to those in developed countries: the dispersal of populations and the absolute or relative decline of inner-city or old city populations.[29] It was as if policy had a life of its own, quite independent of reality. Despite the evidence that big cities did not grow because they were big, that migrants did not cause unemployment, poor water supplies, transport problems, bad housing, policy remained impervious.

If the diagnosis of the problems was wrong, the remedies could not – except by accident – succeed. Furthermore, the instruments chosen to make policy effective were often poorly related to the aims. For example, in India, the control of the geographical distribution of formal sector manufacturing employment was usually identified as a necessary instrument for controlling the distribution of population. Yet, as Mills and Becker[30] have recently shown, manufacturing employment in those cities with the largest share of national manufacturing jobs is both small and declining, the ten largest cities combined have scarcely 6 per cent of national manufacturing employment. Even if this location were – or could be

– controlled (and the problems of control are severe and costly), it would not constitute a means of overall control of the urban population.

Slump, and the problems of high levels of unemployment in the cities of the West, have accomplished what could not otherwise be achieved – a radical reassessment of the purposes of spatial planning. It is still only half accomplished, but nonetheless a plethora of new agencies – in London, for example, the Greater London Enterprise Board, the Greater London Council Manpower Board, the Docklands Development Board; experiments with 'enterprise zones' and now Free Trade Zones – illustrate the *crise de conscience* and the new efforts to come to grips with patterns of activity.[31]

The paradox, however, remains. What the planners aimed to do is coming about, but independently of their efforts. Furthermore, the ultimate problems which population redistribution policies were designed to solve may remain even though dispersal has occurred. Indeed, the problems may be more difficult to deal with simply because of dispersal. Transferring poverty from city to village makes it more difficult to respond. Nonetheless, the opening of new perspectives makes it possible to come a little closer to the central question: under what conditions of economic and social change are labour forces required to concentrate territorially, under what conditions to disperse? It would be as absurd, other things being equal, to seek to prevent dispersal as it was utopian to seek to prevent concentration. The more important target is to protect and enhance welfare whatever the patterns of population distribution.

The process of economic change is not a smooth one of technical adjustment. It arises out of a competitive struggle, even in fully planned systems, a competition which forces all participants, old and new, to change. Thus, the old changes – and indeed may re-establish itself. Parts of formal sector manufacture may expand into areas formerly supplied by petty traditional activities and may do so, in one phase, by increasing the capital intensity of production. But in another, the conditions of the market may entail an increasing share of the market being taken by petty activities once more; a low productivity shoe-making cottage industry may defeat the automated shoe-making plants.

The processes of spatial location may equally produce 'perverse' effects ('perverse' only in terms of our somewhat simple-minded view of trends). In our discussion of trends in the USA, for example, and the growth of the southern population, we might also note that, of the eleven States with a population growth of 20 per cent or more (1970–80), there was one which lay east of the Mississippi river and firmly in the north-east, New Hampshire in New England; of the twelve States with a 10–20 per cent rate of population growth, two more were part of New England – Vermont and Maine. Part of this process of growth was undoubtedly the redistribution of the metropolitan population of the north-east to rural areas, but part appears to be both a revival and stabilization of parts of New England farming (after a very long period of decline), a growth of local small town manufacture (particularly electronic products manufacture) and an inflow of European capital. Or again, some inner-city areas in the north-east are said to be reviving economically under the impact of 'gentrification'.[32] The unrecorded sectors – the black economy – would no doubt change our perceptions of what is happening, particularly where it is said to be strongest, in Italy; perhaps 'deindustrialization' is not as extreme as it appears if industrial activity is moving from the recorded to the unrecorded. Thus, in sum, the useful buzz words – 'deindustrialization', 'deurbanization' – must be treated circumspectly, as suggestive half-truths rather than inexorable trends.

Nonetheless, the city, on the limited evidence presented here, does appear to be arriving at a new functional significance which contrasts with many assumptions. In the past, to oversimplify, the city evolved from a palace-centred or colonizing settlement, to a market-centred, to an industrial or a service settlement. We are partly in the midst of the last transition, partly superseding it. Higher income levels and technical advances make possible continuing centralization of economic and political power without what was, in the past, closely associated with it – physical concentration; spatial dispersion, whether in vast 'urban' regions, dotted with urban complexes, or more generally, appears to be the emerging pattern. The new division of labour supersedes that between town and country. But none of the underlying problems for which the urban and urbanization were surrogate measures necessarily disappear.

However, in poorer less developed countries, particularly in Africa, the physical bunching of the labour force will continue to be the necessary accompaniment of industrialization and accelerated economic growth, and that form will continue to dominate the development of smaller cities. Furthermore – a theme only touched upon here – the integration of the world economy elicits more elaborately specialized spatial divisions of labour, so that settlement sizes and forms in each country become more specific to that specialization, rather than appearing as general phenomena. In the Indian case, this might mean the existing cities – with the newcomers to the category of Class I – becoming increasingly the location for petty and miscellaneous manufacturing and trade (grouped not very helpfully under the term 'informal sector'), while modern large-scale activity is redistributed over far larger areas of inter-city territory. The problems of city planning thus become those of planning *in situ* petty activity, linking the ordering of land to the technical and economic linkages required to make successful different types of small and very small enterprises, rather than with the location of industrial and housing estates. The problems of national spatial planning become those associated with major economic regions encompassing many settlements, rather than seeking to move people and activity across the entire national territory. Urbanization *per se*, as hitherto understood, would not seem to be the key target.

Part II
CLASS

4

On the 'Petty Bourgeoisie' – Marx and the Twentieth Century

'Petty bourgeois' is a cliché term of abuse on the Left. It has a slightly ambiguous connotation. It implies a contrast with 'proletarian', but it can equally be contrasted with 'bourgeois': a term of contempt by those with superior bourgeois standards for those who poorly emulate them. Engels in his more exuberant moments was not averse to employing the second sense.

On the Left, the term presupposes a primitive two-class version of society based upon capital and labour. The material basis for these two classes is assumed to be clear and the ideas appropriate to each class equally clear; the poor petty bourgeois is clear in neither respect, and his ideas are a species of illusion. This poses a problem for Marxists, for the critique of ideological forms becomes weak and moralistic if it is not anchored in the material forces of society, or so it seems. And paradoxically that very moralism is seen as one of the many contradictory attributes of the petty bourgeoisie.

In the study of ideas, Marxism offers powerful insights, but no simple technology to relate them to material forces. And for good reasons. The mass of people are thinking beings, participating in a collective cultural inheritance which consists of ideas in origin perhaps associated with clear-cut material interests, but rarely with whole classes. Once, as it were, 'released', the ideas become part of a common stock, shaped and reshaped, bent to entirely new purposes. The timber is available for all manner of boats. Ideas may have material origins, but once launched, the origins disappear, and indeed the purposes with which the ideas subsequently become associated may be entirely in contradiction to those with which they began. Ideologies are thus not simple reflexes of objective positions, and their various constituents become common property, not for evermore tied to a social origin. The objective structure of society is

Originally published under the same title in *Society and Change* (Calcutta), Vol. III, No. 3, 1983.

difficult enough to identify; how much more so is the changing social function of ideas and ideologies.

This paper seeks to identify how Marx and Engels originally used the term 'petty bourgeoisie', why they attributed certain characteristics to it and what were the political implications. It then suggests what happened to the social strata subsequently in the industrialized countries, and whether the term has use in the Third World. Some speculative connections are made at this point, before drawing some broader conclusions. With such a wide field, important areas are inevitably neglected or treated summarily. The full arguments have been presented in other places and are merely signposted here.

MARX AND ENGELS

Given the heterogeneity of the 'intermediate strata' between capital and labour, it would be wrong to exaggerate the consistency of Marx and Engels in their treatment of the 'petty bourgeoisie'. The centre of their preoccupation was current collective political behaviour – or that seen as representative of collective interests – not social taxonomy. Nonetheless some continuing themes emerge in their treatment of events in France and Germany, countries both engaged only in the early phases of industrialization.

The heart of the social strata concerned was the trader. Engels writes:[1]

> The small trading and shopkeeping class is exceedingly numerous in Germany, in consequence of the stunted development of the large capitalists and manufacturers, as a class, has had in that country. This class, a most important one in every modern body politic, and in all modern revolutions, is still more important in Germany, where during the recent struggles [this was published in 1851], it generally played the decisive part.

The prototype petty bourgeois was the small town trader, merchant, bookseller, journeyman, independent artisan (that is, what is now fashionably referred to as 'the informal sector'), with a vast scatter of allies among the better-off peasantry, even small landlords or landowners, and their landless or small propertied dependants. In addition, there were other constituents, the small-town professionals (lawyers, doctors, school masters, etc.) and the lower functionaries of the State. But at the core were those whose production or activity did not primarily depend upon the extraction of surplus labour from hired workers; they were simultaneously capitalist and labourer, employing themselves. Capitalism would only develop when these two functions were separated in two forces – when the shopkeeper divided himself into merchant capitalist and wage labourer.

It was this dual role which shaped the character of the social stratum.[2]

> Its intermediate position between the class of larger capitalists, traders and manufacturers, the bourgeoisie properly so-called, and the proletariat or industrial class, determines its character. Aspiring to the position of the first, the least adverse turn of fortune hurls the individuals of this class down into the ranks of the second.

The contradictory position of the petty bourgeoisie would be resolved by its destruction as the forces of capital and labour came to dominate society. But the condition for that full development was that local capital conquered the world market; then only could capital establish its rule at home, the precondition for the conquest of power by the working class – 'the industrial bourgeoisie can govern in a country only whose manufacturing industry commands for its produce, the universal market; the limits of the home market are too narrow for its development'.[3] Thus, the condition of national hegemony was international trade, not some growth in the local market.

As in Germany, so in France 'the intermediate classes, the peasants and small tradesmen who are neither bourgeois nor proletarians . . . form the large mass of the nation'.[4] So large were those strata that they tended to dominate the whole society, producing in cultural terms a petty bourgeois aristocracy, a petty bourgeois capitalist class, and a petty bourgeois working class – 'the petty bourgeoisie have at least the consolation in their depressed social and political position of being the standard class of Germany; and of having imparted to all other classes their specific depression and their concern over their existence'.[5] Given this enormous social weight, they tended to play a decisive political role; in Germany, Engels writes in 1850:[6]

> This class of petty tradesmen, the great difference of which we have already several times adverted to, may be considered as the leading class of the insurrection of May 1849.

The political ambivalence of the petty bourgeoisie arose both from its intermediate position, the mixture of rebellious hostility and dependence, but also relative to the State, to those that patronized it. Engels continues:[7]

> In the smaller towns, a military garrison, a county government, a court of law with its followers, form very often the base of its prosperity; withdraw those and down go the shopkeepers, the tailors, the shoe makers, the joiners. Thus, eternally tossed about between the hope of entering the ranks of the wealthier classes, and the fear of being reduced to the state of the proletariat or even paupers; between the hope of promoting their interests by conquering a share in the direction of public affairs and the dread of rousing, by ill-timed opposition, the ire of a Government which disposes of their very existence because it has the power of removing their best customers; possessed of small means, the insecurity of the possession of which is in inverse ratio to the amount; this class is extremely vacillating in its views. Humble or crouchingly submissive under a powerful feudal or monarchical government, it goes to the side of Liberalism when the middle class is in the ascendant . . . but falls back into abject despondency of fear as soon as the class below itself, the proletarians, attempts an independent movement.

The State as buyer and also as employer of lower functionaries was not its only significance. For the internal contradictory character of the intermediate strata required a powerful State to govern them:[8]

> The petty bourgeoisie and the peasantry cannot, therefore, do without a powerful and numerous bureaucracy. They must be kept in leading strings so as to escape the greatest confusion, and not to ruin themselves with hundreds and thousands of lawsuits. But the bureaucracy, which is a necessity for the petty bourgeoisie, very soon becomes an unbearable fetter for the bourgeoisie.

In Marx's time, a particular stratum of the intermediate classes, the intelligentsia, was perhaps not as important as it was to become. 'Intelligentsia' describes a section of the population by the nature of the use of its brain, not relative to a specific function in society; indeed, the use of the brain is compatible with all the collective functions of society. Thus, the term cuts across class analysis; strictly, it does not refer to a social stratum at all. In a society dominated by the preoccupations of the petty bourgeoisie, there will be intellectuals who play the role of expressing its interests, just as other intellectuals express the interests of other classes. In almost all cases, such intellectuals are not part of, nor necessarily drawn from, the classes they aspire to represent. As Marx puts it:[9]

> [One must not] imagine that the democratic representatives are indeed all shopkeepers or enthusiastic supporters of shopkeepers. In their education and individual position, they may be as far apart from them as heaven and earth. What makes them representatives of the petty bourgeoisie is the fact that in their minds they do not get beyond the limits which the latter do not get beyond in life, that they are consequently driven, theoretically, to the same problems and solutions to which material interest and social position drive the latter in practice. This is, in general, the relationship between the *political* and *literary* representatives of a class and the class they represent.

The French socialist, Proudhon, was seen by Marx as one such representative:[10]

> Mr Proudhon is, from top to toe, a philosopher, an economist, of the petty bourgeoisie. In an advanced society and because of his situation, a petty bourgeois becomes a socialist on the one hand, and an economist on the other, i.e. he is dazzled by the magnificence of the upper middle classes and feels compassion for the sufferings of the people. He is at one and the same time, bourgeois and man of the people. In his heart of hearts, he prides himself on his impartiality, on having found the correct balance, allegedly distinct from the happy medium. A petty bourgeois of this kind defies *contradiction*, for contradiction is the very basis of his being. He is nothing but social contradiction in action. He must justify by means of theory what he is in practice.

Proudhon was no more than an extreme example of the problem. The expansion of higher education produced a new stream of, at least initially, rootless young people, 'declassed bourgeois youth', dislocated from a secure social role with nothing but their brains to sell. Their anger, their alienation from established society, provided for a period a regular supply of recruits to revolutionary politics. But their orientation inevitably tended to shift the politics of the party. In the 1870s, Marx deplored[11]

> a whole gang of half mature students and superwise doctors

> who want to give socialism a 'higher, idealist' orientation, that is, to replace its materialist basis (which demands serious objective study from anyone who tries to use it) by modern mythology, with its goddesses of Justice, Freedom, Equality, and Fraternity.

The political danger of the radicalism of the petty bourgeoisie (whatever the different material foundations of the different strata – trading, cultivation, functionaries, professions, rootless 'intelligentsia') was that it diverted the process of revolution to ends other than those which ought to be sought by the proletariat, and did so in order to subordinate the revolution to the protection and enhancement of its own position. The first charge was cowardice:[12]

> The petty bourgeoisie, great in boasting, is very impotent for action and very sly in risking anything . . . the petty bourgeoisie encouraged insurrection by big words and great boasting as to what it was going to do; it was eager to seize upon power as soon as the insurrection, much against its will, had broken out; it used this power to no other purpose but to destroy the effects of the insurrection.

The second was that its arguments served to disguise the basic issues in order to establish its paramount position, to guard society while conceding limited changes, and, incidentally, to promote its own position as mediator:[13]

> The peculiar character of Social Democracy [in France] is epitomised in the fact that democratic–republican institutions are demanded as a means, not of superseding two extremes, capital and wage labour, but of weakening their antagonism and transforming them into harmony. However different the means proposed for the attainment of this end may be, however much it may be embellished with more or less revolutionary notions, the content remains the same. The content is the reformation of society in a democratic way, but a reformation within the bounds of the petty bourgeoisie. Only one must not form the narrow-minded notion that the petty bourgeoisie, on principle, wish to enforce an egoistic class interest. Rather it believes that the *special* conditions of its emancipation are the *general* condition within which alone modern society can be saved.

For the 'proletariat', the petty bourgeois substitutes 'the people':[14]

> the democrat, because he represents the petty bourgeoisie, that is, a *transitional class*, in which the interests of two classes are simultaneously mutually blunted, imagines himself above class antagonism generally. The democrats concede that a privileged class confronts them, but they, along with all the rest of the nation, form the *people*. What they represent is the *people's rights*; what interests them is *the people's interests*. Accordingly, when a struggle is impending, they do not need to examine the interests and positions of different classes. They do not need to weigh their own resources too critically. They have to give the signal and the *people*, with all its inexhaustible resources, will fall upon the *oppressors*. Now, if in practice, their interests prove to be uninteresting and their potency impotence, then either the fault lies with pernicious sophists, who split the *indivisible people* into different hostile camps, or the army was too brutalised . . . In any case, the democrat comes out of the most disgraceful defeat just as immaculate as he was innocent when he went into it.

Conjoining the interests of different social classes in revolutionary struggle poses one set of problems. Seepage of people with petty bourgeois aims (which is not, as we have seen, necessarily the same as people of petty bourgeois origin or occupation) into a workers' party poses another, for it threatens to remove one of the contending forces, or rather convert it into something else. In particular, the struggle, in Marx's view, is likely to be diverted into peaceful and moderate channels:[15]

> Far from desiring to transform the whole of society for the revolutionary proletarians, the democratic petty bourgeoisie strive for a change in social conditions by means of which the existing society will be made as tolerable and comfortable as possible for them . . .
>
> As far as the workers are concerned, it is certain above all that they are to remain wage workers as before; the democratic petty bourgeoisie only desire better wages and a more secure existence for the workers and hope to achieve this through partial employment by the State and through charity measures; in short, hope to bribe the workers by more or less concealed alms and to sap their revolutionary vigour by making their position tolerable for the moment . . .
>
> For us the issue cannot be the alteration of private property but only its annhilation; not the smoothing over of class

> antagonisms but the abolition of classes; not the improvement of the existing society but the foundations of a new one.

Within the workers' party, the petty bourgeois position would be expressed through 'Social Democratic phrases' to conceal their special interests and ensure that the 'definite demands of the proletariat not be brought forward for the sake of beloved peace'. And in the revolution, the working class would wage the struggle, while 'the mass of the petty bourgeoisie will as long as possible remain hesitant, undecided and inactive, and then, as soon as the issue has been decided, will seize the victory for themselves, will call upon the workers to maintain tranquillity and return to work, will guard against so-called excesses and bar the proletariat from the fruits of victory'.[16]

Thus the danger in a society dominated by the complex of 'intermediate strata' included under the label of 'petty bourgeoisie' was severe. It subverted the purposes of the workers' party from revolution to reform, leaving firmly intact the basis of society, the wage system. Indeed, the petty bourgeois aspirants to power required that system to be preserved in order for them to exercise power; without the wage system, not even the authority of the State could be preserved, and lacking the State, the petty bourgeoisie had no vehicle for the operation of power.

Germany and France in the middle years of the last century are no guide to all countries and times, but there are insights for countries which are comparable: that is, where the petty trading and merchant class is important. However, the context is crucial. Classes do not have, as it were, a set political position, but develop a position in interaction with other classes, other threats. If the petty bourgeoisie of mid-nineteenth-century Germany leaned towards radical change against the landed aristocracy, that of the 1920s – ruined farmers and their unemployed sons, traders and small town shopkeepers in Bavaria and elsewhere – provided the basis of the Nazis' rise to power.[17] In a very different context, Ayatollah Khomeini, backed by the force of the Iranian bazaar, an unmistakably petty bourgeois stratum in Marx's terms, overthrew the Shah in the name of Islam. Thus, social positions do not provide the basis for predictable political reflexes; the positions are different forms of accommodation to different balances of class forces.

A final point might be noted. The old petty bourgeoisie was, according to Marx, doomed by the progress of capitalism to disappear; or rather, doomed to disappear as an important social force determining the character of society. But this did not mean the end of the 'intermediate strata':[18]

> In the countries where modern civilization developed, a new petty bourgeoisie was formed, which hovers between the proletariat and bourgeoisie and *continually renews itself* as a supplementary part of bourgeois society.

What the old small owners of capital lose is replenished by different strata, the supervisory employees of capital, hovering between capital and labour even while being employed as labour. Yet other categories of labour developed on a mass scale that were not manual workers – in particular, clerical and sales staff. It seems, although Marx did not develop the argument in detail, as if he foresaw this providing a basis for a proportionate expansion in the 'intermediate strata'. He criticizes Ricardo for forgetting,[19]

> the constantly growing number of the middle classes, those who stand between workmen on the one hand and the capitalist and landlord on the other. The middle classes maintain themselves to an ever-increasing extent directly out of revenue.

It therefore seems that Marx already envisaged that, in the course of capitalism's growth, the mass of the 'intermediate strata' would grow, and the relative proportion of the proletariat to the total population decrease.[20]

In sum, then, a series of social groups – defined relative to separately identified material bases – are included in Marx's original use of the term 'petty bourgeoisie'. The lack of a single structural relationship to the rest of the society suggests that to refer to such groups as a class is inaccurate; they are a series of groups, united in a relatively backward society by their ambivalent hostility to the landed and capitalist classes and to the mass of labour. The faster the pace of accumulation – and, depending upon the coefficients of capital and labour, the wider the social effects of rapid accumulation – the more swiftly is there a relative decline in the old set of groups – small traders, shopkeepers, merchants, better-off peasants – and a relative expansion in the new, the technical and supervisory staffs, functionaries in the State apparatus, and the great mass of clerical staff. Thus, the essential political position derives not simply from the link to small property, but even more from an 'intermediate' position – a structural role which implies at least one other alternative political position to that of capital and labour (insofar as it makes much sense in practice to reduce society simply to these two alternatives).

The issue was not about the status of a clear-cut and distinct quasi-racial social group, a prejudice against those by chance born outside the working class, but about the strategy of 'the abolition of the wage system'. After all, Marx and Engels themselves might just as well have been classified as petty bourgeois, just as Lenin and most of the revolutionary leaders were, since they were from 'intermediate strata' (and many of those with impeccable proletarian origin are unmistakably petty bourgeois in politics). A petty bourgeois origin does not entail a predetermined political position; commitments to other classes are possible, without defeating the proposition that there is a rough coincidence between objectively defined occupational groups and, at given moments of time, particular political views. For much of the period of capitalism, the working class has been generally committed to petty bourgeois politics. This empirical observation does not defeat the theory which is, rather, concerned with necessary tendencies, not simply observable facts.

We cannot pursue the theme in the years after the death of Marx and Engels, but we can note, in passing, Lenin's central preoccupation – indeed, obsession – with the threat posed to the Bolsheviks by the enormous petty bourgeoisie of Tsarist Russia. In particular, the danger of subversion grew extreme in conditions of a low level of struggle by the working class, the danger that the party would be converted to other purposes and thus be quite unable, in conditions of an upsurge of working-class activity, to recruit the mass of workers.[21] In the turbulent conditions of the First World War, the threat was also severe in the society at large:[22]

> The petty bourgeoisie, i.e. the vast mass of the barely awakened population of Russia, is groping blindly in the wake of the bourgeoisie, a captive to nationalist prejudices on the one hand, prodded into the revolution by the unparalleled horror and misery of war, the high cost of living, impoverishment, ruin and starvation, but on the other, glancing *backward* at every step towards the idea of the defence of the fatherland, towards the idea of Russia's State integrity, or towards the idea of small peasant prosperity to be achieved by a victory over Tsarism and over Germany, but without a victory over capitalism.

In the period after the February revolution, the dangers grew even greater. When the Bolshevik leadership in Russia (Lenin being still in exile) gave critical support to the Provisional Government, it was for Lenin guilty of accommodating to the petty bourgeoisie. The Provisional Government's effort to prevent the peasantry seizing land, its urging that they 'avoid excesses' until the official land reform teams could register the land, was similarly a petty bourgeois position, designed to keep all initiative and power in the hands of the State and to stifle popular mass initiative. The dangers that Marx identified, as it were hypothetically, for Lenin were a manifest threat.

THE TWENTIETH CENTURY

In the countries of advanced capitalism, the old petty bourgeoisie did indeed decline although at different speeds in different countries. By the end of the Second World War, it was difficult to identify any specific social influence that still remained. In retrospect, the domination of the Nazis in Germany was rather the last struggle of a declining sector in conditions of extraordinary collapse (that, of course, does not rule out other authoritarian alternatives, only the particular relationship between the Nazis and the old petty bourgeoisie). Postwar attempts were certainly made to revive its political influence on the Right – the Poujadists in France, the National Democratic Party in West Germany, the National Front in Britain – but with no sustained success. What was left became an element within Conservative parties, as illustrious a symbol as the ancient yeomen but far removed from the all-embracing position the petty bourgeoisie held in the middle of the nineteenth century. The material basis of the old petty bourgeoisie could revive – the growth of a black economy and the ubiquitous petty trading and markets currently seen might provide such a basis – but it is difficult to see this being a major influence in society.

The same cannot be said of the functionary and clerical sections of the 'intermediate strata'. We have noted earlier Marx's estimation that these 'middle classes' would expand as capital became increasingly concentrated and the capitalist prised loose of any role in actual production. The process was noted through much of this century.[23] The attrition of the capitalists, while capital continued to grow, and the supersession of their role by giant anonymous companies, banks, trusts, necessarily implied a considerable expansion in the role of the employed intermediate functionaries, from managers to foremen. The sheer concentration of control functions meant the growth of great bureaucracies. The increasing dependence of modern capitalism on technical change and educated labour implied the growth of a major research and education sector. Furthermore, the impact of the inter-war economic crisis as well as two World Wars created large public bureaucracies. After the Second World War the State acquired a whole range of new functions associated with the reproduction of educated labour (this is discussed in the following paper in this book). By the 1950s, forms of State capitalism were powerful elements in virtually all States, advanced or backward.

In Britain between 1911 and 1966, the manual working class increased by some 5 per cent, and 'white-collar' staff by 176 per cent. By the 1960s, this white-collar class consisted of about one-third clerical staff; 16 per cent shop assistants and salesmen; 17 per cent technicians and lower professional staff; and 16 per cent managers and administrators. Since the mid-1960s, the proportion employed in industry has tended to decline relative to services, at the same time as, within industry, white-collar grades have expanded far faster than manual. In the British case, 47.5 per cent of the labour force were engaged in industry in 1961; 42.3 per cent in 1974; and 39.7 per cent in 1978.[24] Between the early 1960s and 1976, there was a net change in the composition of the labour force from manufacturing to 'professional and scientific' of the order of 1.5 million workers – a shift in terms of age, skill and education, and even more dramatically, of gender (since the proportion of women in the newer occupations is much greater than in the older). What has happened in Britain is only a variation in a process affecting all the advanced industrial countries. By the 1970s, in virtually all, the majority of the employed labour force were white-collar.

The change is to some extent a shift in status, but this should not be exaggerated. The new mass activities are often not better paid than the old manual tasks. For example, only 15 per cent of women white-collar workers in 1980 earned more than the average male manual worker.[25] In contrast to the old petty bourgeoisie, the white-collar worker is employed and frequently on a mass scale, is propertyless and waged. Even as the numbers have expanded, the status has declined, and with it has gone increasing recognition of common remedies covering both manual and non-manual workforces. In the period since the Second World War, it has been among white-collar workers that mass trade unions have grown most swiftly, creating new giant trade unions alongside the relative decline of the old manual unions (in Britain, particularly in local government, in welfare services and teaching). It is thus perverse to identify the growth of white-collar occupations as, *per se*, either the 'decline of the working class' or the 'rise of the middle class'; the 'bourgeoisification' of manual occupations is no more significant than the 'proletarianization' of non-manual occupations. Without clear-cut criteria, based upon a theory of the whole society, changes in the composition of the labour force (a process as old as capitalism) have no self-evident political implications. Political attitudes are not simple reflexes of the relations of production, but choices between existing and available political alternatives.

The mass white-collar occupations are not, if we are to retain the clarity of Marx's conception, a new petty bourgeoisie, for the core of that social stratum has, in the advanced industrial world, disappeared along with the material basis that sustained it. The white-collar workers stand in relationship to capital in an identical position to manual workers, regardless of different styles of working life, status, pretensions or income.

The discussion is not helped by the ambiguities of the term 'middle classes'. In terms of subjective consciousness, virtually everybody considers themselves in the middle – from the high officers of State, army and police (objectively part of the ruling class, but still employed functionaries), the high professional managers of private corporations, airline pilots, scientists, Treasury economists, down to much of the working class; on the way we still have the 'lumpen middle class', alienated children of the upper classes surviving as paupers. The term is useless for analysis precisely because it plays such an important subjective role, both aspirant and defensive.

However, the change in the social composition of industrial societies is not the end of the question. In retrospect, we can see that what Marx and Engels identified as 'petty bourgeois politics' and located in the material contradictions of the old petty bourgeoisie, has in fact a much broader connotation. In the twentieth century, we have the paradox of petty bourgeois politics existing without the old petty bourgeoisie. Indeed, petty bourgeois politics is as characteristic of the old manual working class as it is of the new white-collar class, and so it has been throughout much of the history of capitalism. These are the politics of loyal rebellion, of conservative opposition – politics which encapsulate revolt but bind it to no more than marginal reforms of the *status quo*. Such politics are perpetually recreated within class society, regardless of whether the old petty bourgeoisie exists or not, for they are entirely necessary for the survival of established society; revolt is continually recreated by exploitation and subordination, and continually must be harnessed to the maintenance of the existing ruling class. Thus, all electoral politics, every exposure to public gaze of even part of the affairs of the ruling class, must be presented in a 'petty bourgeois' form. Indeed, today, every tin-pot dictator must be a populist of some kind and espouse opposition to poverty and oppression.

Thus, 'petty bourgeois' politics is in danger of coming to cover everything, and therefore nothing, just as 'middle class' comes to cover virtually everybody (except for the freaks of the revolutionary Left!). At the ends of the spectrum, off the stage most of the time, are, at one end, the real operation of power (and even that is rarely expressed by the participants in a naked form even to themselves) and, at the other, revolutionary alternatives, scarcely ever heard except at time of great crisis. There is no necessary relationship between white-collar occupations *per se* and this pervasive atmosphere of apparent compromise.

However, this is not to say that particular people or groups do not play special 'intermediate' roles analogous to some of those in the old petty bourgeoisie – the roles of brokers between the mass and the ruling class. Trade-union leaders are a pre-eminent example of such an intermediate role, as are other leaders of particular groups. Furthermore, the illusion of economic independence that underlay part of the old petty bourgeoisie finds an echo in the claims of the independent professionals – doctors, lawyers, architects (but not teachers). The important characteristic here is not that these professions have an ethic of service – many of the skilled, craft and manual occupations share this – but that, by reason of a particular scarce skill (the scarcity being created by monopoly controls on the supply of such labour) and a quasi-independent role in small companies, the professional illusion of independence is sustained (even though, in practice, most of such professions depend ultimately on the public sector).

The continued existence of class society depends upon the continual recreation of 'third alternatives' that half-capture revolt and divert it to safe channels, that carry the humanity below the inhuman surface of society into some form of relationship with the ruling order. The concepts, radical in the beginning, fade with absorption into the *status quo* and, indeed, become part of the language of the ruling class. Most recently, to be black or to be a woman had radical implications – and, incidentally, like the concept of 'people' cut across the class structure – but is now being absorbed by the ruling orders as part of their own ideological equipment. The alternatives offer, at a given moment, some form of outlet for oppression without challenging the heart of Marx's preoccupation, the wage system, the subordination of the majority to selling their labour power, whether this is labour by hand, by brain or whatever organ is in demand.

LEFT POLITICS

On the margins of the 'intermediate strata', some of the alternatives could include – contrary to Marx's view of the old petty bourgeoisie – a commitment to violence against the State, whether through straight terrorism or armed guerrilla warfare. A commitment to violence does not at all define the difference between political positions. After all, it was Marx who identified the apostle of anarchist violence, Bakunin, as another kind of petty bourgeois alternative, and the rootless intelligentsia endlessly reproduces similar types of case. In what would lie the basis for the characterization of such alternatives as petty bourgeois? That the struggle was not at all to achieve the self-emancipation of the working class, but solely the conquest of State power; that the struggle involved only one national unit, not the emancipation of the world working class? In this sense, those committed to the violent conquest of State power may be no more than 'revolutionary reformists': they seek, by revolutionary means, to capture the State for reformist purposes (reform covering any changes *other than* the abolition of the wage system).

In Marx's time, much of the political argument presupposed a context of Liberalism. In the twentieth century, this is not so; virtually all the forces of radical opposition share the terminology of socialism and, indeed, Marxism. This complicates the task of understanding petty bourgeois ideas, expressed in the concepts of that curiosity, 'Marxism–Leninism'. The activity and writing of Marx and Lenin were structured by the pursuit of a given set of purposes. If the purposes are changed, the language quite easily becomes an 'ideology' in Marx's terms, a system of false consciousness. In this case, Marxism comes to conceal reality and the real purposes at stake. There is nothing in the work of Marx that insulates it from its employment as an ideology; if there were, it would defeat Marx's underlying methodology.

If the terminology persists, the concepts cannot but fail to shift in meaning. One of the points where change is most apparent is in the relationship between practice and the objective analysis of the world (requiring 'hard work' as Marx expressed it earlier), a weakening exhibited in the relative impoverishment of theory. The adjectives come apart from the reality – 'proletariat' comes to apply, not to real workers, but to the party itself, and 'Marxist' comes to apply, not to a given set of purposes (working-class revolution), but to objects that need to be graced with an ideological decoration. We can end up with that loopy misuse of language, a 'Marxist–Leninist State', about as contradictory a concept as could be imagined, since not only did Marx and Lenin demand the 'smashing' of all States (where a State exists, it is evidence of one class suppressing another), but, insofar as Marxism embodies the purpose of revolution and destroying the State, such States invariably suppress it. The use is possible because Marxism has degenerated from a science, historically specific, to a set of abstract universal principles. Indeed, the degeneration returns

Marxism to pre-Marxist methodology – 'ideology' causes practice, and since the principles require little more than learning some eccentric terms, the terminology becomes a form of decoration not of discipline. No doubt ruefully, Marx might have been amused at this further demonstration of the irony of history.

If the objective – measurable – world disappears, so also do classes. Parties swallow up reality, and their attributed labels ('bourgeois', 'proletarian', etc.) become the prime evidence of what classes, millions of people, are doing. The 'proletarian party', far from seeking to lead one class and preserve its independence, seeks in the main to preserve its own independence from all classes. By simple self-declaration, the party becomes the working class. Without a continuing organic relationship to workers, the source of the party becomes simple moral commitment ('ideology') and the link to a magic group of beliefs, 'Marxism–Leninism'. Suddenly there are no material necessities, only revolutionary spirit which can overcome all, and no contradictions which cannot be managed.

Whereas both Marx and Lenin were preoccupied with continually sharpening the expressions of the interests of workers in order to exclude those with other aims, in the modern version 'class alliances' are all and a programme to blur class interests in a common national position. The party's aim is the conquest of State power, not the self-emancipation of the working class – whether through the electoral mechanism for ordinary reformists or through armed struggle for the 'revolutionary reformists'. Just as the weakening of objective analysis (and its relationship to party strategy) implies the voluntarism of the revolutionaries, so also the State must be portrayed as equally voluntarist: the State is supposedly more powerful than the capitalist market.

Since the centre of attention shifts from the capitalist system to the State, from classes to parties, 'politicism' is rife: that is, that party politics is more important than changes in the structure of capital accumulation. Indeed, history is rewritten to correspond to political changes as if the importance of these were self-evidently fundamental, when their importance has to be proved, not assumed. Thus, the world perception of the revolutionaries is conceptually structured to establish their own special role and to exclude the rest of the world, in particular the workers and peasants. Similarly the legitimacy of the party turns not upon its relationship to real workers, upon its capacity to champion working-class demands, but on its ideological lineage and morale.

These features are only part of a distancing of revolutionaries from workers. Not long ago the argument was popular among intellectuals that the role Marx identified for the working class was vindicated in the nineteenth century because they were poor. Now, even if poor, they are privileged, and those who are more impoverished or alienated replace them – the Third World, peasants, students, black people in the United States, women, etc.[26] At different times, there are different heroes in the opportunistic search for a vehicle in which to ride to power (which is not at all to say that the proposed hero does not indeed represent a specific form of oppression). One of the more extreme cases is provided by the decision to call whoever takes your fancy 'proletarian'. Thus, Paul Sweezy's reflections on Chinese experience:[27]

> only 'natural' bearers of values espoused by Marx and Lenin which centre on the imperatives to eliminate all real inequalities (though not, of course, all individual differences) are proletarians who have no privileges or special interests and on whom, therefore, the responsibility falls to carry on the struggle against *all* privileges and special interests.

To the question, from whence derives the singular virtue of the proletarian, and how can we discriminate true from false proletarians, there is no answer; the observer has only his private wisdom, no public criteria.

There is a derivative shift, we might note, once class is separated from structure. Organization assumes a significant independent of its class character. Thus, acts of nationalization or extensions of State power become suddenly 'progressive', regardless of what, if anything, happens to the exploitation of labour. It is this separation which has permitted different socialists to praise figures as diverse as Hitler, Roosevelt, Stalin, Mrs Gandhi in the Emergency, sundry generals and presidents, all suddenly become progressive forces for no better reason than the use of the State. For within the corpus of thought, the State becomes a quasi-neutral force, or, at least in principle, 'non-exploitative'. Thus are the revolutionaries returned to the position of 1914 Social Democracy; the target, the State, cannot be exploitative if the petty bourgeoisie run it, by definition.

If the revolutionaries embrace the State, they embrace also the ideology of the State, nationalism. The collapse of the Marxist tradition into an earlier one, that of Liberal nationalism,[28] is a remarkable one, the more so because it represents just that collapse of a proletarian alternative to a petty bourgeois one. It would take this account too far afield to explore the theme, but even a cursory examination of the views of Marx and Lenin on national struggles would indicate no commitment to an abstract principle, the right of national self-determination, but rather its subordination to the needs of working-class struggle. Engels, more uninhibited than Marx, dismissed those national struggles which he saw as obstructing the struggle for socialism as 'ethnic trash', struggles of 'people without history', rightly doomed to defeat. Lenin in more detail always subordinated the right of national self-determination to the right of the working class to class self-determination – which might imply an *alliance* of the European proletariat with the colonial petty bourgeoisie (the nationalists), but not an identity of aims.

The shift involves a fundamental revision of Marx in all respects. Now 'capital' bifurcates into evil 'foreign' capital or multinationals, and local compradors, all concealing the depredations of 'national capital'. Yet the market is the market, capital is capital, driven to accumulate regardless of the national origin or nationality of the capitalists. The politics of compromise overwhelms the clarity of the original theory.

The combined mixture constitutes something quite other than that outlined by Marx, but insofar as it utilizes his terminology is obliged to blur all the crucial distinctions – confusing popular consultation with majority democratic control; mass support with mass initiative; opposition to bourgeois democracy with rejection of all democracy (thus vindicating the police State as the model of popular freedom); the emancipation of the State and the 'productive forces' with the self-emancipation of the working class; the creation of a new ruling class with the abolition of all classes; workers' welfare with workers' power. Thus, the elasticity of terms is stretched to cover its opposite, to constitute the ideology of State capitalism.[29] The only curiosity is that such a programme should have been extracted from those diametrically opposed to it – Marx and Lenin.

THE HISTORICAL DESCENT

The evolution of this brand of Marxism is a long and complex one. The history of the Soviet Union and of the Communist International is important in seeing clearly the stages of evolution, although the social forces to receive the ideology were not created by that history. In the case of the Soviet Union in the 1920s, we have the first example of a clear-cut collision between two segments of the 'intermediate strata' – between the old petty bourgeoisie, the NEP men and the better-off peasantry, representing 'capitalism', and the new functionary class of the Soviet State, supposedly representing 'socialism'. Echoes of that historic confrontation continue down to comparable collisions in countries of the Third World today. Most of the subsequent battles, however, did not use the ideological expression of the Russian bureaucratic class, Stalinism.

In the evolution of the Comintern, changes in concepts interact with historical experience. The survival of the Red Partisans when the Chinese party was destroyed permitted guerrilla warfare to be substituted for the struggle of workers at the point of production. The exigencies of the threat of Nazi Germany obliged defence of the USSR to be substituted for class internationalism, and the need to retain loyalties in the 'colonial and backward countries' permitted national liberation to be substituted for socialist revolution. The story is too long to be presented here, nor are all the crucial forces clear. There were rarely decisive turning points, only slow evolution by minor adjustments. Take, for example, the 1935 military alliance of the Soviet Union and France (Stalin having declared just prior to the pact that France was 'the most aggressive and militarist of all aggressive and militarist countries in the world', in June 1930 at the 16th Congress of the Communist Party of the Soviet Union). The historian, E. H. Carr, observes:[30]

> It is tempting to dramatize the Franco–Soviet pact . . . as marking an abrupt abandonment of the aim of world revolution inherent in Marxist and Bolshevik doctrine in favour of the diplomacy of defensive alliances . . . But this would be an undue simplification. Faith in imminent revolution in Europe foundered in the German debacle of 1923. Events in China in 1927 showed up the limitations on the aid which Comintern could or would render to revolution in a semi-colonial country. Henceforth, world revolution became an article in a creed ritualistically recited on solemn public occasions, but no longer an item of living faith or a call to action. The place left vacant in the ideology of Comintern was taken by the defence of the Soviet Union . . . The principle of the defence of the USSR was inscribed in the programme of Comintern after the war scare of 1927 at its sixth Congress in 1928; the argument that, since the USSR was the one country where the socialist revolution had been victorious, the prime duty of Communist Parties everywhere was to defend it against the assaults of its enemies became common currency . . . Comintern soon began to sound a note of caution, and impatient revolutionaty enthusiasm became a 'Left' or 'sectarian' deviation . . . What was new in 1934 or 1935 was the recognition that the defence of the USSR could be assured through the support, not of foreign Communist Parties, too weak to overthrow or seriously embarrass their national governments, but of the governments of capitalist countries exposed to the same external menace as

> the USSR, and that the best service which parties could render would be to encourage government to provide that support.

The ideology which emerged from this process of change was complex and, in important respects, ambiguous,[31] but its broad outlines constituted what was called Marxism and what was inherited by the world after the Second World War. The broad 'anti-imperialist front', not the strictly proletarian party of Marx, was the norm in the Third World. It was a front that was either a single organization – but in its programme listed the selected social groups it claimed to represent – or a combination of political parties, each identified as the ambassador of a social force. No criteria were applied to test the link between political formation and the supposed social force. The programme was the place where the supposed separate interests were reconciled – implicitly, the exploited were obliged to concede to the rest for the sake of 'blessed peace', as Marx put it in a different context. The front was not Lenin's united front of the different sections of the working class (Communist, Socialist, Christian Democrat), nor yet his alliance of classes with temporarily coincident interests. Often the enemy was not capital, but foreign capital, and the victory, not the self-emancipation of the working class, but the emancipation of the State, the 'New Democratic State' (in which there was precious little democracy, whether of the bourgeois or the proletarian variety). And in practice, the working class as Marx would have understood it were largely passive bystanders.

There is an interesting paradox of rather more importance than the ideological fantasies of Right and Left. In practice, the period from the early 1930s up to, for much of the world, the 1960s was characterized by strong tendencies to State capitalism in most States. It included States which espoused both right- and left-wing ideologies, a phenomenon which suggests that powerful common material forces were more important in the process than ideological nuances. Nehru, Nasser, Nkrumah, Sukarno, Ben Bella (who, incidentally, created an analogous phrase to the domestic 'Third Force' in the 'Third World', the centre point now, not between capital and labour, but between two dominant States, the USSR and USA) might share a common vision of State-directed capital accumulation, but then so did Chiang Kai-shek in Kuomintang China, and so did the rulers of Mexico and Brazil and sundry others. These forms of partial State capitalism were not sharply distinguished from the behaviour of States in supposedly pure capitalist Europe in the 1930s and 1940s. Just as capital was capital, the State was the State, regardless of ideological eccentricities. In retrospect, it seemed that the world market enforced a behaviour on States in a given historical period that operated quite independently of political aspirations.

THE THIRD WORLD

Many of the countries of the Third World during the process of anti-colonial struggle – or the analogous processes in formally independent countries – were much closer in social structure to mid-nineteenth century Germany and France. Admittedly, the social force of capital was very different, but the dominant social forces were much closer to Marx's petty bourgeoisie than in the industrialized countries. Marx would have felt much more at home there than he would in contemporaneous Europe or North America. Mao noted this in the case of China:[32]

> Chinese society is a society with two small heads and a large body; the proletariat and the big landlords and capitalists are minorities, the broadest group is the middle class.

He continues, in a vein strikingly at variance with those earlier points cited from Marx:

> If the policy of any political party does not look after the interests of the middle class, if the middle class does not gain its proper place, if the middle class does not have freedom of speech, if it does not have clothes to wear, food to eat, work to do, books to read, national affairs cannot be well-managed.

Marx's reaction to a comparable social context was to press for the sharpest clarification of working-class interests, without concession to other social groups (a 'sectarian' attitude in contemporary terms), and to attack directly the 'middle class' as forces seeking to subvert the workers' party. Mao's is the opposite: to seek a form of accommodation with the majority.

There are many fascinating variations on the underlying theme – how an individual leader or party seeks to preserve its independence from any particular class or set of interests by making concessions to all and building a supposed 'alliance'. Gandhi in India provides striking examples of the politics of flirting with all, marrying none; it is only right that now, as presented on the screen, he has become an object of adulation by his natural followers, the middle classes of Europe and the United States (with eight Oscars to prove it!). Gandhi regretted the poor treatment of agricultural labour, of untouchables, of women, but did not oppose the structure of land distribution, the caste system or the organization of genders. He was not a pacifist insofar as he supported the British in the First World War; he was for non-violence, but did not support troops that refused to fire on Indian demonstrators ('A soldier who disobeys an order to fire breaks the oath which he has taken and renders himself guilty of criminal disobedience. I cannot ask soldiers to disobey; for when I am in power, I shall in all likelihood make use of those same soldiers. I should be afraid they might do the same when I am in power'.)[33]

One of the few threads of continuity in Gandhi's constant attempt to prevent spontaneous mass initiative is the continuing fear that the mass of Indians, once in movement, might both settle the issue of the British Raj and deprive him of his position of mastery. But building a movement without being captured by specific class demands poses severe problems. This is not a problem for the leadership for their interest is in directly inheriting power; they are therefore 'nationalist', embracing the ideology of the State (or in this case, an aspirant State after the removal of the British). But the masses do not inherit power. Nationalism is thus a weak basis for mass mobilization if kept in isolation from specific class interests. For example, take the case of Congress in Orissa in the 1930s; Bailey in his account notes that Congress made a poor showing until a local Congress leader identified the destruction of British imperialism as including the end of the structure of local interests which supported the British, the landlords and the Rajahs.[34] A comparable observation might be made during the Vietnamese war with the United States. Although the National Liberation Front was explicitly a class coalition, the heart of its agrarian programme was land reform (and the Saigon State was firmly based on the Roman Catholic landlords, so nothing was to be gained by making concessions to them). The land reform programme was a powerful factor in cementing the loyalty of the mass of Buddhist peasants for whom US domination was directly felt only as the domination of Catholic landlords. Indeed, the US Government early recognized the basic problem, and many advisers urged land reform; it was not practicable, however, since it would have involved the destruction of its local supporters, the Saigon State, and replacement by direct American – and thus, colonial – rule.

The pattern by which Gandhi and the Congress High Command wove together a complex of half-conceded, half-denied, social concessions to create a movement capable of bringing Congress to power without the risk of losing control, of revolution, is a subject still only partially explored. In the case of the Chinese Communist Party, the matter is easier, partly because the party was unusually explicit in its aims and tactics. Within the 'United Front Policies' of the 1935 Seventh Comintern Congress, the Party returned to the aim of securing a political alliance with the ruling Kuomintang, the basis for the Bloc of Four Classes that were to oppose imperialism in general, and the Japanese in particular. The Party made important concessions in order to give some semblance of reality to this alliance, including the abandonment of land reform.[35] However, in striking contrast to the situation in India, the Party possessed its own territory and its own armed forces; thus, its independence was never in doubt. The peculiar conditions of China with a weak central State, barely able to curb the warlords let alone a Japanese invasion, made possible the 'liberated areas' (something that would have been impossible in the British India of the time). However, concessions to win the support of 'patriotic landlords and enlightened gentry' and 'patriotic capitalists',[36] inevitably jeopardized support from those who were victims of these social groups. The Party settled on seeking to persuade landlords to concede reductions in rent, for otherwise 'the masses in the newly liberated areas will not be able to tell which of the two parties, the Communist Party or the Kuomintang, is good and which is bad'.[37]

In the autumn of 1947, for reasons which are still not entirely clear, the Party leadership made a radical but temporary departure from this line by urging the peasants to seize the land directly, by urging spontaneous mass initiative. By December, the change was being denounced as a serious error, as 'Left excesses'. Mao wrote:[38]

> there has been an erroneous emphasis on 'doing everything as the masses want it done', and an accommodation to wrong views existing among the masses, one sidedly proposing a poor peasant–farm labourer line . . . that the democratic government should listen only to the workers, poor peasants and farm labourers, while no mention at all was made of the middle peasants, the independent craftsmen, the national bourgeoisie and the intellectuals

Henceforth, the Party line was that:[39]

> Spontaneous struggle by the peasants must be firmly prevented in agrarian reform . . . Pending the arrival of an agrarian reform team, no official action is permitted, and only political, publicity and preparatory work is permitted.

Compare this with Lenin's attack on the agrarian policy of the Provisional Government in 1917 (that the peasants should await the arrival of government teams to draw up land reforms and determine redistribution). Already in 1905, he had made the point:[40]

> There is only one way to make the agrarian reform which is unavoidable in present day Russia, play a revolutionary role: it must be effected on the revolutionary initiative of the peasants themselves, despite the landlords and the bureaucracy, and despite the State.

The difference is not simply one of time and place. Lenin aimed to 'smash' the Tsarist State as the first step in smashing all States; Mao aimed to inherit the Kuomintang State and strengthen it. Lenin aimed to mobilize a class, the urban industrial working class, and a temporary ally, the peasantry; Mao had no need to do either since his armies were the ultimate basis of his strength. Whereas Lenin urged:[41]

> the proletariat must organise and arm *all* the poor, exploited sections of the population in order that they *themselves* should take the organs of State power directly into their own hands.

Mao's instruction was:[42]

> Do not be in a hurry to organise the people of the city to struggle for democratic reforms and improvements in livelihood. These matters can be properly handled in the light of local conditions only when the municipal administration is in good working order, public feeling has become calm, surveys have been made.

Like Gandhi, Mao did not, except in rhetorical terms, trust popular initiative in the process of the revolution. 'Once the masses are aroused, they become blind.'

CONCLUSION

It is the mark of Marxism as false consciousness that it has no historical specificity; the point of historical time, the balance of local class forces, the underlying unique configuration of economic activity, all disappear in a set of general abstract principles or slogans. Gandhi is even more different from Mao than British India was from Kuomintang China. Indeed, it might seem unreasonable to draw even the slight comparison made here. Yet the most striking correspondence between the two societies has not yet been indicated – the lack, not of a proletariat, but of a proletarian political alternative. In China, that alternative briefly existed and was destroyed in the terrible débâcle of 1927. In the much more stable and conservative context of British India, any working-class alternative was colonized within Congress and its allies, what Mao might have recognized as a clear example of a 'Four Class Bloc'. In both countries, it was not the absence of numbers, for the working class in absolute size was possibly larger in both countries than in 1917 Russia, and was probably comparable in relative weight in the politically decisive areas of the country. Also in both countries the capitalist class was weak and, as in Tsarist Russia, with very shallow roots in the wider society.

In the end, the material forces are only one side of the coin, a necessary but not a sufficient condition for specific political alternatives. The two Communist Parties took their positions in the first instance from a ruling State, from Stalinism, identified earlier as the most clear-cut expression of the interests of the bureaucratic 'intermediate strata'.

But the two cases provide an entry point to the radical political changes in the Third World in the period since the Second World War, whether achieved through the peaceful or violent overthrow of colonial powers, or in the violent overthrow of existing independent regimes (as in Cuba, Nicaragua, Iran, etc.). In broad ideology if not behaviour, the new forces show striking similarities. How, in Marxist terms, are they to be characterized? They can scarcely be proletarian in Marx's terms since in all cases they took place without the serious participation, let alone the leadership, of the local working class, and certainly not beneath the banner of its pre-eminent interests. At most, workers received, in Marx's terms, 'alms' for their good behaviour. On the other hand, if these are bourgeois revolutions, nowhere did they establish the unrestricted power of private capital as bourgeois revolutions were supposed to do. They are, by this primitive classification, neither fish nor fowl.

To invent a third category, 'petty bourgeois revolutions', would be to enter further absurdities. Thus, Marx observes in a famous statement:[43]

> No social order ever perishes before all the productive forces for which there is room in it have developed: and new higher relations of production never appear before the material conditions of their existence have matured in the womb of the old society itself.

To sustain the new category, we would have to assume that a more advanced form of the productive forces, the petty bourgeois one, was struggling to emerge from the old society before the conquest of political power. The argument falls apart. The regimes that came to power did so apparently without a pre-existing material base, but with an aspiration to create more advanced productive forces.

The paradox can be resolved if we widen the canvas and accept that the real empirical world consists of more than two alternatives. Marx's comment fits the first bourgeois revolutions – pre-eminently in Britain and France – if we assume that 'revolution' in Marx's historical sense is not a single act of transfer of political power at one moment of time, but a long-drawn-out epoch involving many political collisions along the way as different sections of the bourgeoisie slowly expanded their economic role and social significance. That model might fit Britain from the Civil War to the Reform Act of 1832, a period of nearly two hundred years.

Thus, not every radical or violent change in the political and social order is a 'revolution' in this specific sense (that is, indicating the emergence of a new form of material production). Taking merely political changes as the prime evidence of changes in the society is thus quite wrong. Whether or not the change reflects a fundamental one in the society at large needs to be proved from evidence independently of the political change (of course, political leaders always like to describe their advent to power as a fundamental change, as a revolution, but we have no need to be guided by their subjective judgement).

Secondly, countries do not go through paths of development in isolation from each other; there is 'combined and uneven development', as Lenin put it. Once the first bourgeois revolutions had occurred, they forced a different pattern of development on all who came later. In Marx's sense, possibly Germany and Japan were the last to go through that process, and in both cases, it was an 'unsatisfactory' one by Marx's criteria; the destination turned out to be not the bourgeois republic, but Nazi Germany and the militarist Japan of the 1930s. In those two countries, in that period, the private capitalist class could not establish its unrestricted rule (a factor not unrelated to other external events, namely the world recession). Thereafter, private capitalist classes have never succeeded in establishing their complete domination of society; they have always required a powerful State, which, in some cases, has displaced them altogether.

The post-1945 revolutions have had different targets. They are dedicated to modernization (education systems, highways, industry, etc.), to accelerated capital accumulation as the basis of a national power capable of defending national independence against the domination, encroachment or influence of foreign powers. None even raised the question central to Marx's concerns, 'the abolition of the wage system', but, on the contrary, are dedicated to establishing the conditions for the growth of the wage system.

The old order overthrown was not, in economic terms, exhausted by the internal dynamic of capital accumulation, but rather by external threats. The revolutions are thus responses to the growth and changing stucture of world capitalism, defensive reactions; not the expression of past economic changes, but aspirations for the future. A mechanical Marxist view, assuming the primacy of national boundaries, would thus always be led to describe such changes as 'premature', since the national society was not 'ripe'. This would be a myopic view, for the revolutions are predicated on the basis of the growth of world productive forces, not necessarily local ones. This was indeed Marx's position in encouraging the Narodniks of Russia even though the material conditions there were thought inappropriate for a bourgeois revolution; it was also Lenin's position on the Russian revolution.

However, none of the regimes encouraged private capitalism; accumulation was, at least initially, firmly in the hands of the State. As we have noted, the tendency was much more general than simply left-wing regimes, which implies a considerable change in the nature of contemporary private capital. The alternatives appeared to be either domination by foreign companies or economic autarchy, which in turn severely reduced the dynamic of local monopoly capital to transform society. All deduced the same conclusion: only the State, urged on by its competition with other States, could provide the local drive to accumulation in such circumstances.[44] In the short term, the statistical evidence vindicates the inference; in the longer term, the State itself reproduces all the irrationalities of the private system, the chaos of the market, in bureaucracy, waste, extravagance, and war. The reformist alternative – State capitalism – is today everywhere crumbling in the face of the strength of world capitalism.

In sum, then, the concept of the bourgeois revolution does not fit the modern changes, in terms either of the prior changes in society or of the programme of the revolutionaries. They are a response to the creation of a single world capitalist economy, not to some prior stages of development in one country. They are paradoxical, for, on the one hand, the subjective intention is to emancipate the country from foreign domination, while, on the other, the objective function within the world system is to establish the appropriate conditions for accumulation and the wage system, a long way indeed from Marx's self-emancipation of the majority.

The straitjacket of the two-class methodology is likewise at fault.

For brief moments, capital may face labour on a political plane, but most of the time, it does not. Those moments are the rare occasions of proletarian revolution. For the rest, it is other intermediate issues which occupy the stage; no doubt they refract issues at the extremities, but only at a tangent. We can note in passing that the effect of the two-class model is to exonerate the 'intermediate strata', for if there is only capital and labour, the intermediate strata can wriggle through as proletarian, and thus be the heirs to the apostolic succession of 'Marx-Engels-Lenin-Stalin-Mao' or whatever.

It is rare for whole classes, or a significant part of them, to attain a collective perception of their existence. The alignment of the objective position of workers in society with their subjective self-perception requires not merely the crude truncheon of crisis, but also the existence of a political alternative, a party endlessly expressing that identity and linking it to a coherent tradition. No generation can, as it were, spontaneously invent that tradition any more than humanity can spontaneously invent the sum of culture out of its particular experience. We can blunder empirically and by accident into some of the right conclusions but, given that society is awash with other apparently attractive alternatives, even this is difficult; by the time the lessons have been learned, it is too late to act.

Given the virtually universal redefinition of Marxism – a revisionism far more extensive and thoroughgoing than anything conceived by Bernstein and his followers – is Marx's central idea, the self-emancipation of the majority achieved through the abolition of the wage system, entirely utopian? To decide that it is would be a premature judgement. The evolution of world capitalism has by no means ended, even though its final crisis has frequently been announced on the Left. The phase of the world system in which the State dominated accumulation – was seen as the 'progressive' force of history – is already, I think, coming to a close.[45] The inherited notions of the Left which are the product of that phase are coming to be seen not merely as historically limited, but as reactionary (harking back to an earlier national phase of accumulation). They have no relationship whatsoever to Marx's programme. This represents a severe intellectual crisis for the Left, both in its form of Third World nationalism and autarchic nationalism in the industrialized countries. The integration of the system proceeds apace, integration in an essentially private market system (even if some of the 'private' owners happen to be States) superseding the powers of local States and therefore the political target of the Left. We can already begin to see the emergence of an appropriate world social structure, with, at its base, a world working class, technically integrated but subjectively parcelled out to different States.

In an important sense, the world is catching up with Marx's outline of the tendencies of capitalism rather than superseding it. He himself was certainly guilty of underestimating the potential of the system, of seeing revolution in a shorter-term perspective than his own theory implied, and that is a cautionary note for us. In the long term, the hundred years since his death will be seen as a very short period; few will remember all the deviations and false starts along the way.

5

The International Migration of Labour

The rise of modern imperialism is also the rise of the modern State. The manifestation of the power of the State is in the first instance its tight control of one patch of very clearly defined territory and the population trapped within its boundaries. The imposition of this pattern on humanity by the first group of modern States, those of Europe, produced a defensive reaction by the ruling classes of the rest of the world. They in turn were obliged to establish the same type of tight control over whatever territories could be appropriated. The pattern which emerged is reminiscent of the enclosure movement in Britain: the appropriation of common lands by private owners to the point where all territory within Britain was officially parcelled up among a category of 'owners'. The process both within the territory of any given State and internationally eliminated all 'free lands' and all free men and women: all who do not officially belong to one or other local ruling class (and can, in principle, acquire a valid passport to prove that they actually exist).

By now almost all inhabitable territory in the world has been demarcated, and humanity corralled within licensed national pens. Indeed, the division is so all-embracing that its sheer novelty is no longer apparent; most people cannot conceive of a world not divided into national patches, not dominated by baronial fiefs.

The development of the internal control of States over the respective territories and populations – the increased 'nationalization' of the globe – is the other side of the coin to increased 'internationalization'. For what is meant by internationalization is interaction between increasingly defined national patches. The growth of the one necessarily presupposes the increase in the other.

Now, each national patch is almost equally related in economic terms to every other one – a condition in sharp contrast to the

Originally published as 'The New Untouchables: the international migration of labour' in *International Socialism* 8 (new series) (London), Spring 1980, pp. 37–63.

imperatives of political or military interaction where geographical proximity is of primary significance. This interaction ensures increased synchronization of the world system, or rather, its increased subordination to the dominant centres of world power. Yet such subordination should not conceal the necessary parallel process of 'internal colonization', the attempt by particular States to subordinate all areas within their control to a single centre, usually the capital city.

Thus, the obverse of increased nationalization of the areas of the world is increased interdependence of the national patches. It is a contradictory process, for the interests of individual States are in collision with the imperatives of a world economy, with capital accumulation on a world scale. The State's primary interest is in retaining and extending its territorial control, not assisting the development of an international economic order outside its control. In a slump, the contradiction emerges so sharply that the accumulation is sacrificed to the maintenance of the power of the State, of the local ruling class, over its inhabitants.

The 'internationalization' of labour is one element in these processes. Throughout the history of capitalism, workers have moved in search of work, or been driven to work, in areas other than those where they were raised. This common phenomenon, however, becomes remarkable only when national boundaries are laid down and become of sufficient importance to impede, block or shape the international movement of workers. That is, political controls are imposed in the attempt to break a movement impelled by the operation of a world labour market. To put it another way, growth in the world system prompts the ruling classes of growing and dominant economies to despatch raiding parties to capture part of the labour force belonging to a weaker ruling class. Then the passport and visa, with the whole complex of subsidiary controls, become an instrument for the control and direction of the marginal labour force.[1]

Whether the system is expanding or contracting determines the precise form of the contradiction between the interests of the State and those of the world economy. In expansion, the world labour market acts like acid upon territorial controls, other things being equal. Either ruling classes are obliged to dismantle trade, finance and labour movement controls, or black markets in each area threaten the structures of control: 'liberalization' is the product, rather than – as is frequently claimed – the cause of expansion. Nonetheless, although in the 1950s and 1960s many labour-importing countries liberalized entry procedures, the essential formal controls were retained, and with the onset of contraction, strengthened. Protectionism in trade was matched by a protectionism in labour, and both exaggerate the severity of contraction.

The unprecedented expansion in the world economy after 1948 was a highly uneven process, producing disproportionate growth at certain key points in the advanced capitalist countries as well as in particular regions in the backward countries. This disproportionate growth was reflected in an increased concentration of the demand for labour. The two most important centres of the world system, the core zones of the American and European economies, attracted a sustained flow of workers from abroad. But many other smaller centres, at various times, also attracted inflows – in the 1970s, the Middle Eastern oil-producing States, South Africa, Ghana, Nigeria, Ivory Coast, Venezuela, Singapore, etc. The legal movement was accompanied to a greater or lesser extent, depending upon the restrictions in force and the powers of the local State to enforce them, by both a black market in labour, illegal migration, and the 'unscheduled' movements of refugees – for example, the large-scale movements in Africa, the flight of Cubans, Argentinians, Cambodians, Vietnamese, Bengalis, and most recently, Afghanis.

The concept of a crude undifferentiated 'labour' is quite inadequate to understand the process of official worker movement. Those who move tend to be in the most active age groups, eighteen to thirty-five years of age, and in terms of ability and skills, to be above the average for the sending area. The jobs they move to are restricted, although they range across the spectrum from temporary seasonal work to permanent highly skilled jobs (for example, doctors). Each stratum of occupations has a separate dynamic.

For relatively unskilled workers, the areas of recruitment have often been geographically close – Eire for Britain, the Mediterranean countries for Germany and France, Mexico and Central America for the United States. But it is also true that European labour demand stretches far into West Africa, to Turkey and Iran, British demand to India, Malaysia and the Philippines, and American to Korea, Taiwan and the Philippines on the opposite side of the Pacific. Territorially, each national labour market expands and contracts geographically with the rhythms of growth. There are also countries now which supply unskilled or semi-skilled labour globally; for example, the Philippines. As the level of skill in demand rises, so the extent of the catchment area expands, until a world labour market operates, as for example with doctors.

Where labour-exporting countries are geographically close to the place where labour demand is increasing rapidly and the controls on movement are weak, the emigration of workers can be proportionally very large. North Yemen, adjacent to Saudi Arabia, has some 44 per cent of its adult labour force working abroad. Lesotho supplies to

South Africa some 21 per cent of its domestic labour force; Algeria and Tunisia at one time had between 11 and 12 per cent of their workers abroad. In the heyday of movement, emigration amounted to 70 per cent of the increase in Portugal's labour force, and, before 1962, to over 100 per cent of Eire's.

Since emigrants are not drawn uniformly from a country as a whole but from particular districts, these national figures conceal the much greater effect on particular sending districts. For example, Indian migration to Britain is drawn from one medium-sized State, Gujerat, and a small State, Punjab, and within Punjab, largely from one district, Jullundur; Indian migration to the Gulf is drawn mainly from another small State, Kerala, while the largest State in India, Uttar Pradesh (with a population of around 100 million) provides few emigrants.

The movement is not just one way. Most countries export and import labour at the same time. Greece, with over two million workers abroad, imports workers from Egypt and Pakistan. Jordan, a major supplier of Palestinian labour to the oil-producing countries, uses labour also from Egypt and Pakistan. Sicilians move to North Italy and Germany, leaving their harvests to be collected by Senegalese. Mexicans move north for the harvest in the United States, while Guatemalans enter Southern Mexico for the harvest there. The United States and Britain supply highly skilled labour to the Middle East. The movement of labour is thus an exchange of skills, a continual redistribution of a margin of each national labour force in response to changes in the geography of capital accumulation.

THE PRICE OF LABOUR POWER

The orthodox explanations of worker movement usually turn on the 'overproduction' of labour in some countries (the backward) and a 'scarcity' of labour in others.[2] But there is never a 'scarcity' of labour, only a scarcity of workers willing to sell their labour at a given price. In so-called 'population surplus' countries, there is rarely a real surplus; for example, in both India and China, a good harvest produces full employment, a 'labour scarcity' and rising agricultural day labourers' wages. The problem is employing people at an adequate wage all the year round; but so far as the system is concerned, the existing labour force is only the 'right size' for producing the existing output.

In the advanced capitalist countries, a number of factors have reduced the physical availability of labour power, the number of labour hours on offer per year, in the postwar period: a decline in the birth rate (reflected fifteen years later in the new entrants to the labour force); a decrease in the number of hours worked per week; an increase in the holidays per year; an increase in the number of years of full-time education, or the conversion of apprenticeships to part-time education; earlier retirement, and, perhaps, the continued process of the decasualization of the labour force.[3] On the other hand, there are factors working in the opposite direction – the end of the National Service in Britain or the draft in the United States, the remarkable increase in the number of women entering paid employment, immigration and temporary workers entering work from abroad; at certain times, the considerable increase in part-time work by the pensioned (off-setting the earlier retirement); the expansion in second and third jobs ('moonlighting'). How are we to explain these different changes, and the creation of specific 'labour scarcities'?

The price of labour power is determined by what Marx calls the socially necessary costs of maintaining and reproducing labour power; by 'reproduction', we mean, not the biological creation of a baby, but the process of creating an adult worker from the age of 0 to, say, between 12 and 15 years of age. Marx's statement is applicable collectively, not necessarily individually – that is, the return to the working class for its labour power is determined by the costs of maintaining the working class and reproducing it. What is determined here is the value of labour power; actual collective wages may, to a greater or lesser degree, diverge from value but will ultimately remain in some definite relationship to value.

What determines the 'socially necessary costs'? There are obviously many factors, but one of the most important for modern capitalism is the need to attain a given level of productivity by the labour force. Defining what is 'necessary' is obviously difficult, for the productivity of labour is a function not simply of the more obvious training and educational inputs, the quality of diet ensuring consistent concentration and discipline, the quality of housing ensuring the worker does not spend much of his or her attention worrying or seeking a roof, the condition of the worker's family, parents and children, so that he or she is 'free' to work fully, etc. There are factors relating to the possible exhausting or psychologically debilitating results of work – and an adequate level of recreation and leisure, and the facilities to pursue these, etc. Which of these elements are necessary, which optional extras?

In some backward countries, levels of productivity in particular plants can be pushed up to roughly the same level as those pertaining to an advanced economy, even though the labour force in the plant does not receive wages remotely comparable to similar workers in an advanced country, not does he or she have access to anything matching the services available there. Does this mean the wages received and services available in advanced capitalism are not necessary? It does not. For while particular plants may emulate the same level of productivity, the society as a whole cannot; it can utilize a particular range of technical innovations, but it cannot generalize them, nor itself innovate.

Average labour productivity in the advanced capitalist countries has increased enormously over the past century. There has been a substantial but much smaller increase in the absolute level of real wages required to sustain the worker at these rising levels of average productivity. If we took the return to labour as a whole which, today, is much more than simply the wage, we could divide it into two elements: (i) the cost of maintaining the workers at a given level of productivity; and (ii) the cost of reproducing the workers' children so that, when they enter the labour force, they can attain a given level of productivity. While the first element has increased considerably over the past century, the increase is dwarfed by the growth in the second element. Leaving aside the family-borne cost of rearing, the growth in the public sector inputs – through the expansion in educational, housing, welfare and medical services – has been very considerable, particularly in the postwar period (in practice, of course, it is exceedingly difficult to separate 'maintenance' and 'reproduction' in looking at the public sector services, and to separate these elements from the costs of the control and supervision of the population).

To deal with the average for a class is misleading. For much of the history of capitalism, the bottom third of the workforce has not been paid enough to meet the costs of reproduction at the average level of productivity then prevailing. Some sections of the workforce have not been paid sufficient to meet the bare minimum costs of reproduction (the infant mortality rate, like the rate of deaths to women in childbirth, is a partial index of this). And at certain times, the wages of the lowest categories of labour have been insufficient even to maintain the worker, a factor producing increasing levels of malnutrition and, during epidemics, a very high death rate.

So far as the world labour force is concerned, this situation has not changed very much. For example, a recent study of Calcutta small firms shows that if we assume the going day labourer's wage rate is the minimum subsistence and reproduction price of labour power, then both small capitalists and the family labour employed in their firms receive returns which are some 41 per cent below what they should be; they are, as it were, 'committing suicide' by working.[4]

Thus, the labour force is a highly differentiated object. If we could imagine a national capitalism as an unchanging entity – output and employment, both absolutely and relatively, remaining constant – then the hierarchy of skill grades would persist indefinitely. Reproduction would consist in replacing a set number of workers of given skill by exactly the same number with the same skills. If reproduction costs were entirely borne from the wage paid out to the worker through the family, then household incomes would form a hierarchy exactly corresponding to the hierarchy of skills and the hierarchy of productivities. Each skill stratum of workers would reproduce its successors in the stratum at the average costs of reproduction of labour at the level of productivity appropriate to the stratum. Of course, instability would arise at the base of the hierarchy if the price of labour power there was too low to ensure the reproduction of the numbers required. Nonetheless the main idea of a stable pyramid in which maintenance and reproduction expenditures are proportional to the size and productivity of each stratum is the important element. In practice, there are no stable strata; the essence of capitalism is change, the continuous transformation of relationships and productivities so that the literacy of today is the illiteracy of tomorrow.

THE PUBLIC SECTOR

The only purpose of the abstract exercise at the end of the last section is to allow us to identify more clearly what happens when the State intervenes to meet a major part of reproduction costs directly. Then the link between the wage received by the worker, the productivity on which we assume the wage is based, and the outlays incurred by the worker's family to meet reproduction costs is broken. Variations in productivity and wages are no longer directly reflected in variations in family expenditure on reproduction.

By necessity, the State must now set some average minimum standard for the provision of its services to ensure the proper reproduction of the labour force. Leaving aside social and political factors, it can only do so in relationship to some notional average level of productivity for the labour force as a whole. Even if it endeavoured to tailor its services to a more complex structure of productivities, since there is no guarantee that a given worker would work at the trade for which he or she had been raised – and in conditions of rapid change, the trade itself may have disappeared altogether by the time the child enters the labour force – setting an average minimum standard is the sole method available. Alternatively, the State could identify a special category of people for high productivity jobs and concentrate reproduction expenditure here. To a greater or lesser extent, in reality this does happen in particular services (for example, education), but there are political constraints on how far such a discriminatory system can be generalized.

The State assumes this role for a variety of reasons, one of which is that the speed of change and the nature of the skills required mean that the skills can only be transferred collectively, on a standardized basis. As capitalism develops, parents become increasingly poor instruments for transferring skills required in the future.

A powerful factor in determining what average the State chooses is competition. States compete with each other – indeed, the State is the single most important agency of competition in the world system. A factor identified as important in the State's ability to compete is the quality of its labour force. Public welfare programmes in Britain begin with an official report on the quality of troops recruited for the Boer War; that is, the ability of the British State to compete in military terms with its nearest rivals was jeopardized by the poor physical quality of its young men.[5] In modern times, the output of graduates or toolmakers in the United States or the Soviet Union, as proportions of the labour force of those countries, become standards for all lesser powers. The argument was explicit in the British Labour Party's propaganda for the 1964 general election, and provided the justification for the Wilson government's programme to expand higher education rapidly. Thus, the level of labour productivity on the basis of which a programme for higher educational expansion was based was not the actual level of 1964, but an aspired level – the level thought to be necessary to keep up with or overtake the leading industrial powers of the world. Of course, the *intention* of the State is not the same thing as the actual performance; the new British universities may have been intended to produce engineering graduates, but in fact, produced many more sociologists! Nor does the fact that the State had the intention mean that what it proposed is correct; it can and does make major errors of judgement.

The potential for mistakes when the State endeavours to establish a minimum requirement for reproduction costs is enormous. Such errors are compounded by the conflicts and rivalries rife within the public sector itself, by the competition for funds. For example, educational standards are not simply the product of a cool appraisal of what is required to meet certain levels of productivity (that is difficult enough); they are weapons by which, for example, the Ministry of Education endeavours to capture a larger share of finance and defeat rival agencies. There are pressure groups pressing on all sides: building contractors for hospital construction, universities for expanding higher education, MPs seeking favour for their constituencies, for their brothers and mates. Bribes and threats bend decisions to paradoxical conclusions. And beyond the narrow circle of power, from time to time, the class struggle itself reshapes government priorities.

In periods of growth and relative optimism, the State gambles by setting standards at high levels, even though, on strict calculations, this is not justified relative to the needs of the system at that time. In fact, the decisions may be errors even though expansion continues. In a number of backward countries, decisions to expand higher education in order to expand economic growth have merely produced an excess of graduates and the problem of educated unemployment.

But there are other problems which arise. First, State intervention in this field imposes a rigidity upon the system which renders it much more inflexible when expansion changes into contraction. Expenditure on reproduction could, when the family was the primary spender, be varied with fluctuations in economic activity; wage cuts were reflected in a decline in family nutrition, for example. But public expenditure is an issue of public debate and public employment, issues discussed in conditions of a competitive political party system where, for example, demands for more housing are weapons in the battle to win elections. Large changes in public expenditure to stabilize the profit rate under the pressures of slump cannot be secured speedily without economic disaster, nor without political challenge. There are other rigidities in particular sectors; for example, if workers hang on to their houses when local unemployment rises, even though jobs are available in other areas where housing is not.

Second, the State's assumption of an *average* standard for the whole labour force is, from the viewpoint of the interests of the system, enormously wasteful. Advanced capitalist economies exhibit great unevenness of development. Parts of the economy operate at levels of labour productivity far below the average. It follows that the bottom strata of the workforce are 'over-educated' or physically 'over-maintained' for their role in the economy. This contradiction receives subjective expression in the unwillingness of workers, trained to work at an approximation to the average level of productivity, to work for wages well below the average. The price of labour power in the sectors where there are vacancies is below the rate of return which is appropriate to the costs of reproduction of the unemployed. For the unemployed to work at such a price would permanently jeopardize the chance of their ever working at the appropriate price. Thus, in the Greater London Council area in 1979, with the unemployment total standing at 130,000, there were severe labour shortages in London Transport, in the clothing, timber, metal goods, and electrical engineering trades, not to mention in the case of school canteen supervisors.

Third, the State institutes regulations to prevent the employment of minors, in part to protect the quality of the subsequently available adult labour force. This in turn reduces the contribution of child labour to household income, thus weakening the economic incentive to families to have children. The introduction of pensions for the aged removes another element in that incentive – that is, reduces the need to have a sufficient number of children to support the worker's old age. The results of this, in conjunction with the introduction of birth control techniques, have been a decline in average family size – and, in due course, a decline in the number of new entrants to the labour force (this decline has been partly compensated by an increase in the survival rate of children, a decline in infant mortality). There is a further factor, however, in the decline in family size. The intervention of the State produces not only standardization of the publicly borne reproduction costs. The costs have been further increased by the transformation of household activity since the Second World War. The capital intensity of household activity has been advanced very rapidly, enormously boosting the productivity of household labour at the same time as considerably increasing the costs of the family unit. It appears that adult male wages have not increased commensurately with this process, so that today, the adult wage male wage cannot, as it was supposed to do in the nineteenth century, cover the costs of a wife and two children. Two adult wages now appear to be necessary to meet family-based reproduction and maintenance costs. One result of this process has been the expulsion of housewives from the home to pursue paid – albeit very low paid – employment. It should be noted in passing that the family can be no wiser than the State in assessing what is a socially necessary level of costs; parents perforce must, like the State, gamble. 'Keeping up with the Joneses' is thus not an eccentricity, but a primary mechanism of capitalist competition relative to the household.

In practice, the system heavily qualifies its commitment to an average standard for all. The labour supply to low paid worker sectors is identified by using special social criteria, by instituting a kind of 'caste identified' labour supply – certain occupations are reserved as temporary, for 'amateur workers' – the aged, school students (for example, newspaper delivery, Saturday morning shop assistants, etc.), students on vacation or looking for work, housewives. As is well known, there are whole strata of 'women's jobs'. In the United States, a special category exists of 'native immigrants', that is, those who are by all ordinary legal criteria fully natives, but are treated as if they were not: blacks, Puerto Ricans, Chicanos, etc. However, the more sustained the process is to reproduce the whole population to a particular average level of competence, the more such groups resist the typecast employment, preferring to remain unemployed rather than jeopardize their long-term job prospects. Nor is this preference simply a function of the availability of social security support for the unemployed. Educated unemployment in Calcutta illustrates that people will fight to the bitter end to prevent their occupational downgrading, preferring starvation to indignity.

SECTORS OF 'LABOUR SCARCITY'

What types of employment are affected by a general upgrading of the labour force? The factors at stake are not simply questions of the price of labour power if by that we mean the take-home pay. It is rather the price of labour power relative to the intensity and conditions of work (which includes the danger, the physical hardship, the cleanliness, the noise, the tedium of work, the provision for paid holidays, the hours and shifts, the health and safety conditions, how good local facilities – housing, medical services, schools, creches, etc. – are, and so on). Industries with old plants and poor conditions exist everywhere, and survive because the overall costs of upgrading (as opposed to simply investing in a new machine) are higher than the expected rate of profit. Parts of the textile industry and plants in the old areas of engineering exemplify some of these factors.

There are other activities where price competition is severe and the workers poorly organized because of the structural conditions at work. Take, for example, catering, hotels and restaurants. If we assume for the sake of argument that in 1979 Britain, the Supplementary Benefit rate of £55.90 per week for a couple with two children represented a benchmark for the 'maintenance and reproduction' costs, a worker would have to earn £61.75 in gross earnings to reach this level. The lowest grade of non-service hotel workers at that time received a weekly minimum rate of £40.40, rising to £42.80 (with, for London workers, an allowance of £2.40). Younger workers, employed on a seasonal basis, could expect £36 for a six-day, 40-hour week in London (out of London young cleaners might expect £27.30). There are between half and three-quarters of a million workers in this activity, 63 per cent of them full-time, with average gross earnings in 1978 of £59.60 per week (or 8.5 per cent below the 'socially necessary' level).

In construction and agriculture, seasonal work produces short-term demands for labour which cannot be met if the workforce is being simultaneously upgraded. In construction, as in the coalmines in Belgium and West Germany, the key factor is less the price of labour power alone, and more its relationship to the danger and hardship of the work.

At its base, the labour market fades away into outworkers: people, usually housewives, working at home at rates where there is no pretence at all to meet even the lowest maintenance wages, let alone an element for family reproduction. There are estimated to be a quarter of a million home workers in Britain. In Nelson in Lancashire, some 6,000 mainly Asian women sew ribbons and bows for the textile trades at rates equivalent to 10p per hour. Garment workers on a rate of 9 to 35p per garment can expect weekly pay of £20 to £25. Nineteenth-century conditions continue to flourish in modern capitalism.

MIGRATION

When the system grew rapidly, masses of native workers were drawn into sectors where the price of labour power was relatively higher, sectors we have identified – somewhat oversimply – as those of higher productivity. Thus, agricultural workers in France, Germany, the United States and Japan moved in the 1950s and 1960s into urban industrial and service jobs. In the sectors vacated, equipment was substituted for labour on a considerable scale but without eliminating labour scarcities. It is here that labour demand was created for workers from abroad.

Immigrant labour has been reproduced at costs below the average for the destination country. It was therefore subjectively willing, at least initially, to work for wages well below the average, or work at average wages in conditions inferior to the average. The picture is more complicated than this because, in many cases, the immigrant worker was drawn from that minority in the backward country which had been reproduced at costs well above the local average. The wages on offer to the worker in his or her home country were fixed relative to the local average level of productivity, but were below those appropriate for his or her costs of reproduction, as assessed by the open world market. Thus, the excesses of the rivalries between States – the underproduction of 'low productivity labour' in the advanced, and the overproduction of 'high productivity labour' in the backward – receive some partial equilibration by the international movement of workers.

There are also important socio-psychological factors at work. Workers who grow up in a particular social environment tend to absorb the defensive ethics developed by preceding generations to protect themselves from the ravages of capital. There are jobs they will not do, paces or hours or conditions of work they will not accept, moves from one locality to another that they will not make for the sort of wages and terms on offer. A worker torn out of this environment is much more appropriate to the needs of capital, much more ruthlessly driven to earn at whatever the wages on offer are. Such a worker is less able to support himself or herself during unemployment by borrowing from local networks of relatives and friends, and less likely to have reserves on which to fall back in hard times, less likely to have possessions that can be sold or pawned. Such workers are likely to be much more responsive to differences in wages – regardless of conditions – and, lacking local social ties, much more geographically mobile in response to changes in the labour market. This – as well as overt discrimination – is a factor in the general picture of immigrants working longer hours, working more night shifts, doing more piece-work, with a higher rate of job changing and of geographical mobility than native workers. It is also a factor in explaining what seems to be a more extreme mismatch between the qualifications of immigrant workers and the jobs they actually do. If the natives refuse to be downgraded even if this means the misery of long-term unemployment, the immigrants start in grades well below what the natives, with the same qualifications, would accept (of course, it is also true that at least at first foreign workers are more uninformed about what is locally considered reasonable, what alternatives exist, etc.; they may also be consoled by the fact that a poor job in an advanced country often offers better returns and conditions than a good job in a backward country). Some employers recognize this factor: migrants make the best workers; and they always try to recruit new immigrants since those who have lived for some time in the country are likely to have become 'spoiled', i.e. conform to local working class standards.

MOVEABLE JOBS

The import of labour is necessary where the price of labour power is too low to induce a sufficient number of workers to work in 'immoveable' jobs: that is, jobs which cannot, at least in the short term, be relocated abroad. For example, local coal mines cannot be mined abroad, nor can local dustbins be emptied, local houses built, and local soils cultivated abroad, although, in almost all cases, alternative supplies from abroad can be found. There is, however, no permanently fixed boundary between moveable and immoveable jobs; changes in comparative wage costs, in technology and so on can radically shift the boundaries.

Capital can gain access to labour power at prices well below those governing in its home territory where jobs are moveable. Parts of manufacturing (for example, in the recent past, labour-intensive links in textiles, electronic components, television sets, etc.), some agricultural tasks, tourism, conform to this. States, recognizing the dangers implicit in the dispersion of activity, sometimes impose regulations to prevent jobs moving; the US Government, for example, does not permit US aircraft manufacture to move (but does permit imports). Export processing zones in South Korea, Malaysia, Brazil, the Caribbean, etc. have attracted industrial activities from the advanced countries, at the same time as these countries have exported labour. On Mexico's northern border In-Bond plants have been permitted, set up by US companies to manufacture consumer goods with raw materials and equipment imported from the States and Mexican labour; the output is exported back to the United States. The In-Bond plant areas have thus been expropriated by the US labour market. At the same time, US nationals have started horticultural farms in northern Mexico to produce foodstuffs for the US market. Finally, Mexico is a major exporter of labour to the USA for farmwork and employment in textiles and services.

There are other examples of this kind, although not on such a large scale. Thus, India exports labour to the Gulf States, and Saudi Arabia finances vegetable farming in the Indian State of Andhra Pradesh, the produce being flown to Riyadh.

Firms with equipment and productivity standards derived from the advanced capitalist countries are able to transplant activities as isolated colonies to backward countries, providing the political context is right. Capital in the backward countries can then emulate the activity. But while productivity in the plants can be sustained at high levels, the general social average remains low. The workers in such plants are, as it were, 'home-based emigrants'.

THE THEORETICAL SIGNIFICANCE

Access to foreign workers makes possible the continued growth of certain national capitals for three main reasons. Firstly it allows more workers to be utilized by a given capital stock: the small farmer in the Punjab produces much more surplus value when he is imported to work in a foundry in Wolverhampton, and in doing so he is benefiting the capitalist class as a whole.

Secondly, the costs of reproduction of such labour are, as we have seen, less than those of the average labour in the advanced countries. Utilizing it enables the capitalist to increase the proportion of the working day that goes in surplus to him rather than in the maintenance of the worker. Ideally then, from the point of view of profit maximization, the native workers would be expelled to permit the lower-cost immigrants to take the jobs. The absurdity of this idea illustrates clearly why the State cannot, in slump, pursue directly the accumulation of capital; on the contrary, it must sacrifice accumulation to social stability. The State consists of people, linked by social bonds to the rest of the population. Attempts to expel the natives would involve the State in political self-destruction. On the contrary, the State must do the opposite, stressing the inviolable rights of the natives in order to direct blame at the foreigners.

Finally, apart from the effect of the import of labour on the long-run decline in the profit rate, it constitutes a net subsidy from the capital of one country to that of another. The sending country bears the cost of reproduction of the worker from its domestic product; the destination country receives adult labour power without the costs that would be needed to raise and train the worker. The higher the skill level, the greater the subsidy involved in the transfer. The subsidy is between national capitals (it could also be called 'theft'), between countries. It does not necessarily benefit any individual employer who may employ the immigrant worker at the same rates as native labour. How far the destination country in fact is able to realize the full value of the subsidy varies, in particular with the terms of entry. Immigrants who settle and establish families, who draw on local public 'maintenance' services (including ultimately old age pensions) will, in time, reduce the net subsidy. The subsidy is maximized for single adult workers on temporary contracts without any right to participate in local reproduction and maintenance services.

RUSSIA AND JAPAN

The framework presented here does not have the same application to all movements of workers internationally. For example, in the oil-producing States of the Middle East, some of the relationships are reversed. Backward Saudi Arabia imports labour from more advanced Egypt, as well as from Europe and the United States (but it also imports labour from more backward North Yemen). Reproduction costs for an important part of the Egyptian labour force were certainly much higher than those in Saudi Arabia at the beginning of the migratory movement. The 'raiding operation' is much more extreme – the loss to Egypt is the same as it would be in emigration to an advanced country, but the gain to Saudi Arabia is much greater.

The Soviet Union has a very highly educated labour force but poor levels of labour productivity. Does this refute the general argument presented here? First, a high level of reproduction costs is a necessary but not a sufficient condition for attaining high levels of productivity. There are many other factors at stake in productivity, including the volume and quality of equipment available to the workforce, the organization of the capitalists (in this case, the State bureaucracy) and so on. Second, as the earlier discussion noted, the components of the conditions required for sustaining high productivity are very varied and cannot simply be reduced to education; they include adequate and easily available housing conditions, recreational facilities, and perhaps a given measure of 'social freedom', all elements notoriously poor in the Soviet Union. High educational levels alone would not make up for the generalized poor quality of existence for the average Russian worker.

The case of Japan is an interesting one. First, its public services are much inferior to other advanced capitalist countries, but the levels of productivity attained in its leading industries are well in advance of its nearest rivals. Second, its rates of economic growth have been spectacularly high without this generating the sort of specific demands for labour which impel immigration. There is virtually no immigration to Japan, although there is a significant minority of Korean immigrants in the country (left over from the Second World War and the partition of Korea, formerly a Japanese imperial possession).

Japan has reached the position of an advanced capitalist country very recently. Far from exhibiting labour scarcities, as recently as the early 1960s the government was endeavouring to increase Japanese emigration by subsidizing migrants to leave. In the mid-1950s, some 15,000 emigrated each year under agreements between the Japanese Government and those of Brazil, Bolivia, Paraguay and Argentina, as well as those who moved to the United States (much as the Netherlands Government encouraged emigration up to the mid-1950s in the belief that the country had too many workers). In the last half of the 1950s, 75,000 departed; in the first half of the 1960s, 43,000; in the second half, 25,000 (there are said to be now 630,000 people 'of Japanese origin' in the States, 760,000 in Brazil). Second, the reserves of agricultural labour in Japan have remained intact until relatively recently as can be seen in this comparative table:

Percentage of the labour force in the primary sector

	1960	1970	1975
Japan	33	20	12.5
United States	—	4	3.8
France	22	14	10.8
West Germany	—	8	6.6
USSR	42	26	—
United Kingdom	—	3	2.5

(– = *not available*)

Thirdly, Japan is alone among the advanced capitalist countries in having a decrease in female participation rates as income has risen (from 50.1 per cent in 1963 to 47.1 per cent in 1973). This suggests that Japan has not exhausted its domestic labour reserves to the point where women's employment begins to increase. The poor level of public services also tends to keep a higher proportion of women at home; home-based reproduction services must replace those of the State. Even today, in many companies women are still expected to retire at the age of 40, or, in some cases, on marriage, indicating that employers are not under pressure to keep women at work.

There are other indications of 'relative labour abundance'. Most workers still retire at 55 (although pensions are not payable until the age of 60). There is still a low rate of turnover in the large-scale sector – employers are not bidding against each other for scarce skills. To some extent, the decline in labour hours available has not matched the other advanced capitalist countries – between 1960 and 1974, West German hours worked per week in manufacturing declined by 20 per cent (from 48.8 to 39.1), Japan's by 5 per cent (from 45.7 to 43.3 hours).

Japan's economy is, in comparison with its rivals, a fractured one – between a bloc of very high productivity modern industries of enormous scale, and a fluctuating mass of small enterprises, many of them subcontractors to the large firms, with relatively low productivity, low pay, little security of work and poor conditions. The high growth of the leading companies is purchased at the cost of the small enterprises.

In general, Japanese growth is achieved by a high concentration on certain key sectors, not by attempting to generalize performance on all fronts. The increase in reproduction costs required to support the advanced sector is not spread through society and there is much heavier reliance on the family (but not, of course, in education). The low level of public intervention in the provision of maintenance and reproduction services is thus much more characteristic of a backward economy than an advanced. There is no supplementary benefits system, unemployment pay is very low. Hospital and medical services are notoriously bad for the majority. There are few homes for the invalided or elderly. Housing is very poor and extraordinarily expensive; a 1978 survey showed that a quarter of households lived in tiny one-room flats; a quarter of households had no bathroom; 10 per cent no running water; and two-thirds were not connected to the sewerage system. Parks are rare (London has 22.8 square metres of park per head of the population, Tokyo 2), as are libraries and museums.

In sum then, Japan is still arriving at the situation where the State is obliged to seek to guarantee a minimum reproduction standard for the whole labour force. The obligation is also affected by the political context; the class struggle in Japan has never reached the point of forcing standardization as happened in, for example, Britain immediately after the Second World War. The State of Japan has also no doubt delayed embarking upon this transformation as it observes the gambles undertaken in other advanced capitalist countries and their effect on gross investment[6] and thus the overall rate of economic growth.

Low public expenditure in Japan becomes another factor of competition in conditions of slump. The other advanced capitalist countries on the one hand press Japan to raise its public spending; on the other, they are tempted to try to sacrifice reproduction expenditure and lower their own rates of spending to the Japanese level. Meanwhile, South Korea and Taiwan seek to emulate the Japanese trajectory of growth, to Tokyo's alarm.

There is a final factor worth noting in connection with 'moveable' jobs. Japan's investment abroad – unlike other advanced capitalist countries – is mainly in backward countries. In particular, Japanese companies have invested heavily in certain sectors of production in South Korea, Taiwan, Malaysia, etc. (in textiles, electronics, etc.). To some extent it may have widened its low-priced labour pool to a greater extent than its rivals.

There are an enormous number of unanswered questions in examining the relationship between reproduction costs, labour productivity and immigration. But at least on a superficial level the Japanese case does not seem to defeat the main argument.

THE FUNCTIONS OF IMMIGRATION IN PRIMARILY DESTINATION COUNTRIES

When world capitalism expanded, migration to the core zones of the system made possible the performance of low productivity jobs important for the national economies concerned. Perhaps, without the remaining structures of protection, many of those jobs would have been 'exported', or reshuffling of occupations would have made possible high growth without immigration. Be that as it may, the degree to which immigration was necessary depended upon the size of existing labour reserves (in agriculture, in home labour, etc.) and the rate and pattern of growth of the particular national economy concerned.

Native labour moved upwards to jobs, the return to which more closely related to the appropriate return to average levels of productivity. Once immigrant workers had been drawn in, they were able to follow native labour, depending upon how freely they were permitted to change jobs and sectors – out of construction, agriculture, mining, to former native strongholds, metal manufacturing and assembly. This in turn created new vacancies where they had formerly worked, necessitating new immigration. By now the foreign-born are roughly 6 to 7 per cent of the population in most West European countries (the remarkably low figure for Britain – 3.3 per cent – is a mark of the poor growth rate here); and possibly 9 to 10 per cent of the local labour force (but 18.4 per cent of the Swiss population). Between a fifth and a third of the labour force in the metal trades in Switzerland, Holland and Germany are immigrant workers.[7]

The situation in the United States is more complicated since it has the largest minority of 'native immigrants' (black people, Puerto Ricans, Chicanos, etc.). In the case of black people, there has been a sustained movement over a long period out of southern agriculture to metal manufacturing and steel production in the old industrial centres of the north and north-east. Later, the expanding new industries of the west coast, and now the south (aircraft, electronics, science-based industries, etc.) have attracted white skilled workers from the north and north-east. Currently, the expansion of southern industry is for the first time since the Civil War attracting net black immigration. The possibility of immigrant labour moving up the hierarchy cannot be separated from the movement of 'native immigrants'.

Seasonal migration by agricultural workers is important in parts of Europe – for example, the movement of casual labour from southern Spain to southern France.[8] It is also important in the United States.

The only contract labour system for foreign workers still remaining there brings Caribbean workers to Florida's apple orchards each year. Elsewhere, illegal seasonal workers from Mexico plug the gaps left by the upgrading of the American labour force. In this case, not only does the farmer not meet annual reproduction costs since the work is paid only in the season of employment, he does not pay annual maintenance costs. In the case of illegal migrants, the farmer can pay wages below the legal minimum by using the threat, if the worker does not accept this, of denouncing him or her to the police and immigration service. Real returns to the workers can scarcely be much above what they might expect to earn in Mexican agriculture – if jobs were available. It is hardly surprising that there are too few native Americans willing to work for such pay even when there are high rates of official unemployment in the district concerned. Texan farmers, in trying to strengthen their case to the government against the imposition of fines on employers taking on illegal immigrants, advertised 4,000 farm-hand jobs at the minimum legal hourly rate (then $2.20 per hour). They received only 300 applications from workers with legal status.

In Europe, it has often been argued that, in the absence of strict border controls, the flow of immigrants varies with the level of unemployment in the destination country – as unemployment rises, immigration falls. But this affects only legal movement. There are no useful figures on illegal movement. In the United States, it is argued that illegal migration has increased during the current phase of stagnation since 1974. This could represent a substitution of cheap labour for more expensive native workers. Or it could reflect changes in the structure of the labour market – a sharp contraction in the core metal-using industries, without an equivalent decline in labour-intensive agriculture, and possibly even an expansion in catering and restaurants (which could result from a big increase in tourism, for example). The same could be happening in Europe in the illegal sectors.

This illustrates that the demand for cheap labour power does not disappear in slump. On the contrary, it can increase. The British Government has pursued policies of deliberate discrimination against black people in the name of its immigration policies, in defiance of the needs of the British economy, but it has made consistent concessions to permit the entry of European workers on work permits. Some 120,000 permits were issued in 1978. Any increase in foreign tourism increases the pressure of the restaurants and catering trades on the government to permit the import of labour. Nonetheless in November 1979 the government tightened the regulations to reduce work permits as part of its attempt to bludgeon native workers into accepting low paid jobs.[9]

The French Government has recently cut residence permits for foreign workers from ten to three years, and now to one, affecting between half and one million North and West African workers. This was supposedly done to increase the job opportunities for the native unemployed. Yet a recent official report calculates that for every 150,000 foreign workers sacked, only 13,000 jobs become available for native workers. Indeed, we could go further and infer that, since French workers will not accept the wages on offer for most of these 13,000 jobs, important tasks in the economy will not be performed and one possible result will be an increase in native unemployment in other sectors dependent upon the performance of these tasks. The government's policy has little at all to do with unemployment; it is designed to lower public expenditure by reducing the cost of maintaining the unemployed by expelling immigrants from the country.

Immigrants provide a target in slump, a measure of flexibility made necessary precisely because of the rigidity of structure of modern capitalism. The expulsion of immigrants is a substitute for increasing the level of unemployment more dramatically,[10] even though it is deleterious to the economy. Between 1974 and 1977, the number of foreign workers in West Germany fell by 19 per cent, and in France by 16 per cent. Or, take the example of the British merchant fleet between 1976 and 1979. Carrying capacity fell by 20 per cent; the number of British officers fell by 5 per cent, and of British ratings, hardly at all. The number of non-British ratings fell by 20 per cent. Given the difference in wages between British and non-British ratings, this change must have raised labour costs per unit of freight carried; thus, the employers purchased the loyalty of British ratings at the cost of a decline in their capacity to compete internationally.

The function of immigrant labour depends on an accepted level of social discrimination; the exclusion of immigrants from the same rights as the natives is accepted by the natives without protest. It is this which makes possible the harassment of foreign workers by the State. Whether it is the obscene persecution at Heathrow airport, the manhunts in Texas or the border States, or the French police checking everyone with dark skins on the Metro, the aim is the same – to keep open the division between native and foreigner.

In the Middle East, these mechanisms are often more advanced. In Saudi Arabia, the regulations governing the mass of immigrant workers include a ban on strikes; employers are, in theory at least, fined for employing illegal immigrants; immigrants have no right to change their jobs without a passport check (drivers on intercity buses are supposed to check passenger passports). To add terror to the regulations, there are periodic mass expulsions; for example, 30,000 people called by the government 'Pakistanis' were expelled from the country *en masse* in March 1978. In the United Arab Emirates, under the July 1977 regulations, the government assumed the right to deport any foreign worker who disobeyed the orders of his or her employer, tried to organize a work stoppage, damaged production, assaulted an employer or representative, or committed any other serious misdemeanour.

The aim of such regulations appears to be to force the solidarity of the native population by the continual demonstration of the 'disprivilege' of the foreigner. Such demonstrations are particularly required when economic contraction is continually reminding the poorest natives of their own misfortunes. Thus the panoply of intimidatory controls has nothing to do with the specific characteristics of the foreign worker concerned, but rather is related to the need to secure the loyalty of the natives. The argument that immigrants are the cause of the native response is of the same logic as blaming the poor for their poverty, the unemployed for being jobless, and so on.

Controls can work in a slump provided there is sufficient police power. But they do so with paradoxical results. First, they have negative effects for native employment (tending to raise native unemployment rates, and force natives into poorer paid work) and for the economy as a whole, leaving aside the waste involved in employing a bureaucracy and police force to implement the regulations. But secondly, regulations drastically reduce just that flexibility which is one of the main advantages of immigrant labour to capitalism. For example, in West Germany in the 1960s, 60 per cent of Italian workers stayed for under two years, returning to Italy after that time. If tight border controls are introduced, foreign workers will not return to Italy for fear of not regaining re-entry to Germany – they are forced into permanent settlement, exile. And it then becomes politically difficult to expel them. Similarly, if the United States succeeded in controlling the Rio Grande border with Mexico, it would no doubt curb seasonal migration but increase the numbers permanently resident in the United States.

Singapore, being a very small territory with a powerful State, has apparently succeeded in operating tight controls. The city is an industrialized economy, based upon a mass of cheap labour (but the State maintains possibly the most advanced system of publicly provided reproduction and maintenance services in Asia, restricted to natives). Every expansion in the economy produces a shortage of labour in certain sectors – construction, ship repair (for men), textiles and electronics (for women). Immigrant labour fills the gaps, but under tight control; employers are permitted to recruit abroad, but remain responsible for their labour force. The State, with the close collaboration of the trade unions, ensures control to hold immigrant wages down, to prevent the labour market operating. Immigrants are used as the lever to keep down wages in general in the city for the mass of workers. Foreign workers are permitted to enter in the first instance for six months in construction; others, many of them young women, may not change jobs for three years, hold trade union office, marry or have children; they have no right to public housing, medical services or schools; those that ultimately secure permission to marry do so only on condition of signing a bond to accept sterilization after the birth of their second child. The penalty for disobeying the rules is expulsion.

These regulations apply to those entering the city on work vouchers (granted to those earning below 750 Singapore dollars per month). They do not apply to the highly skilled, professional or business classes who are granted employment vouchers (for those earning 750 Singapore dollars or more). In 1979, the government announced a new policy to reduce or eliminate the island's dependence on immigrant labour, by trying to force an increase in the capital intensity of production (that is, substituting equipment for labour by changing the industrial mix of the city's output). Companies utilizing a great deal of labour are expected to leave the island, locating in the countries from which immigrants are drawn (the government is also trying to locate labour-intensive industry on the Indonesian island of Batam). To achieve this aim, it has proposed increasing wages for three years by 7 per cent. In fact this is a very small increase to achieve such a change; the Singapore Manufacturers' Association estimate the wage bill for its members at between 8 and 15 per cent of total costs, so the increase will add only between 1.6 and 3 per cent to costs. Of course, consistent with its record, even this small increase is not to be paid to the workers (lest 'they get used to high wages') but paid into the government Provident Fund. The payments can be stopped if the Singapore leadership decides the policy is in fact jeopardizing the economy.

In other countries which are expanding, the controls are much weaker. In the Middle East, governments have moved from accepting general immigration to, at least officially, tolerating only temporary project-related entries (and the employer in the project is required to remove the labour force from the country at the end of the project). But the labour market continues to operate. Workers escape from the project or take second jobs. In mid-1978, 5,000 Indians working for Engineering Projects of India went on strike when the company, under government pressure, tried to prevent moonlighting. EPI asked the Ministry of the Interior to deport 250 of its workers, and made a small pay increase to the rest.

In summary, then, foreign workers are necessary when the system grows to compensate for the deficiencies of national planning (whether the planning is declared or not), to straddle the contradiction between the development of the State and the growth of capital. In slump, they are also necessary, but this economic function is subsidiary to their social role: they are the anvil upon which the loyalty of the natives to the existing State can be forged.

THE EFFECTS OF EMIGRATION ON PRIMARILY SENDING COUNTRIES

If a State exports workers, labour power, on a significant scale in competition with other States, then the world labour market would begin to exercise an influence over the domestic production of labour, as the world market guides the domestic production of any other commodity. The more developed the export of labour, the more an exporting State would seek to control the lease or sale of labour power (to become a labour contractor or supervisory agent for labour contractors), to standardize its quality and tailor it to the specific vacancies abroad. To maximize its profits, it would need to minimize the costs of reproduction, ultimately to convert the economy to a manufacturing plant for breeding and raising workers. This might be done directly, or through the medium of the family, with State incentives and services being directed to induce the family to produce and train the numbers required (the family would then become, as it were, a private firm under the supervision of the State). It follows that such a State would have relinquished any ambition to create a diversified national economy in favour of filling one specialized niche in the world system.

At the moment, States 'pillage' their domestic labour forces – or permit them to be pillaged by other States – without paying attention to sustaining future supplies, much as capitalism ransacked pre-capitalist sectors in the early phases of its growth. But exporting States do seek to control emigration, to ensure certain levels of pay and remittances, and to supervise their nationals abroad to prevent conflicts which might jeopardize their competitive position. In particular, in East and South Asia, prices are partly set in relationship to competing States in the provision of labour to multinational employers for construction work in the Middle East or merchant seamen's jobs.

What are some of the immediate crude effects of large scale emigration for work? Some of them can be listed as follows. Firstly emigration is drawn from particular districts, so that an important first effect is localized depopulation – as in parts of Eire, northern Portugal, Algeria, Lesotho, North Yemen, etc. Those leaving are workers in the most active age group 15 to 35, and often among the most skilled. Thus, the domestic labour force is stripped of its most decisive elements. Sometimes, emigration draws heavily on one sex, producing a sex imbalance, which has maximum effects on those in the reproductive age groups, reflected in a decline in the marriage and birth rates. Thus, not only is the present generation stripped, the next generation is jeopardized.

Secondly, the resulting shortage of skills can produce considerable labour scarcities in particular trades, and wage inflation. It is reported, for example, that the daily wage rate for masons in Pakistan used to be 15 rupees, but by 1979, under the impact of emigration of building craftsmen to the Middle East as well as a local house-building boom financed from the remittances of workers abroad, the daily rate was 40 rupees. In North Yemen, large-scale emigration has generated such wage inflation that now child labour can work as drivers at high wages. While this is good for low paid workers, it is catastrophic for local ruling classes with any ambition to speed capital accumulation. More generally it indicates a tendency for emigration to draw wages in the sending country up towards the level in the destination country, to create a single price for an international labour market.

A sequence of events in South Korea also illustrates this. In March 1977, Korean workers were involved in a three-day riot at a Hyundai project in Saudi Arabia. President Park of South Korea intervened to raise the minimum pay level to (US)$240 per month. This in turn almost certainly encouraged more workers, particularly drivers, to opt for work in the Middle East. In May 1978, Park was obliged to raise the pay of Pusan bus drivers by 70 per cent to discourage emigration, but without success since shortly afterwards he imposed a temporary ban on the recruitment of drivers for work abroad.

Thirdly, for some exporting countries, remittances from their nationals working abroad have become very important as sources of foreign earnings. Take three countries exporting labour to the rest of Europe:

Remittances as a percentage of export earnings

	1970	1973	1974
Greece	54	58	35
Portugal	55	62	50
Turkey	46	90	94

These cases are not as extreme as North Yemen which is said to be able to import one hundred times more than it exports.

Having workers abroad firmly yokes the growth of local incomes to growth in the centres of world production abroad. Contraction in the world system similarly has reverse effects. For example, the virtual end of European recruitment of Turkish workers – as well as a flourishing black market in remittance payments to Turkey – was a powerful element in the severity of the economic crisis in Turkey. Official remittances peaked at (US)$1.42 billion in 1974, and fell to $0.98 billion in 1978 (unofficial payments 1973–8 are put at just over $2 billion). The pressure from the Turkish Government to be admitted to the European Community and the EEC provisions for the free movement of labour are a measure of the despair of the Turkish ruling class – only by leasing its labour for exploitation by foreign capital can it retain its hold on Turkey.

Fourthly, while in theory remittances make possible industrial imports to accelerate domestic growth, in practice States have to offer incentives to persuade their nationals to return part of their earnings through the official markets. That means that the exchange rate must either give special advantages to those wishing to return remittances or the currency must be permitted to float so that any advantage in operating on the black market is removed. Such measures make it extremely difficult to control national finance in the interests of capital accumulation. Furthermore, since workers abroad can buy foreign consumer goods, they will do so abroad unless they can buy such goods at home at the same price – thus, incentives to repatriate earnings include the 'liberalization' of the import of consumer goods. This further reduces the chances of building national industry on an import-substitution basis.

Finally, in general, emigrants regard home as merely home, not somewhere where they can use their foreign earnings to set themselves up as small capitalists (an illusory aim, given the relatively small earnings they individually make). Thus, remittances converted into local currency are used to buy land for housebuilding, to build houses and buy consumer goods. One result is, as noted earlier, inflation in the construction industries. In sum, the districts of emigration become dormitory suburbs or country cottages of workplaces abroad, places where foreign earnings are consumed, not where productive activities are improved.

These elements indicate some of the pressures on world labour demand that restructure labour-exporting countries, making even more difficult any independent strategy for national economic development. In practice, States react pragmatically, adjusting policy step by step without being conscious of the overall drift until it is too late to reverse the process. Their preoccupations are directed more at supervising the return of remittances.

The power of the State over nationals outside its frontiers is limited. At most, it can withhold the renewal of passports, seize property left behind or punish relatives. But abroad, no international policy yet exists to trace recalcitrants in the way, at least in principle, stolen goods can be traced. Usually, documentation is its sole power, which explains in part efforts made to enforce the necessity to travel with documents, to eliminate the possibility of undocumented movement.

Other measures are taken to strengthen control. Where local companies employ local labour on contracts abroad – as happens with Korean, Turkish or Greek construction companies in the Middle East, or Mexican construction companies in Venezuela – controls can be tight. The state can penalize the company. In turn the company handles the transport (and keeps the return ticket until the worker is instructed to return), housing, feeding and supervision of the worker. The South Koreans stiffen this control by appointing, in charge of each gang of workers, a volunteer craftsman demobilized from the army for the purpose of supervision.

Such controls require local capital to be developed enough to act as employer. For the Philippines, this it not usually the case. The government has therefore moved towards leasing labour in groups to foreign employers. Hirers of labour are required to sign a contract with the government guaranteeing certain conditions and accepting an obligation to return a certain proportion of foreign earnings to the Manila agent directly (that is, not through the worker).

Regulations on remittances vary widely, as does the power to enforce them. South Korea demands remission of 80 per cent of foreign earnings. India requires, in theory, 10 per cent. Filipino workers abroad are required to return 40 per cent of earnings, and 70 per cent if they are seamen. Pakistan demands that 20 per cent of the earnings of professional and technical staff be paid to the State as tax, but it has little or no power to enforce this.

The People's Republic of China has recently entered the market by permitting provincial governments to offer Chinese labour to foreign employers for work abroad. Guangdong province has recently published details of its proposals in Hong Kong. It offers 'unlimited numbers' of workers, aged 18 to 35, to work a 48 hour week, with three days holiday per year. The government promises that its workers will be 'diligent and obedient to the employers' reasonable instructions and work assignments'. Workers will receive free board and travel; they will be given 10 per cent of their total earnings (which should be between £69 and £104 weekly) as pocket money while abroad, and 10 per cent on the termination of the contract, the rest presumably accruing to the Guangdong or Chinese Governments.

Perhaps the Chinese are copying the Philippines Government which has developed a marketing strategy for what is known as 'the export of warm bodies'. The Overseas Development Board of the Ministry of Labour circulates glossy brochures to multinational companies proclaiming the superior character (and very low cost) of this 'prized living export', 'the best bargain in the world labour market'. The government lays out its terms and promises, on signature of the contract, to 'package and deliver workers to various worksites round the world'.

In conclusion, then, the national organization of the sale of labour power is, at the government level, already quite effective. Private labour contractors tout their wares round the globe and have done so for much of the history of capitalism, but State organization – with a close eye on the balance of payments – is relatively new. If the process were to persist, sooner or later States would have to intervene in the reproduction process to ensure continued supplies and proper maintenance.

CONCLUSION

International migrants are a particular stratum of the world working class, embodying the contradiction between a world economy and its national political and social organization. Relative to the national ideologies which dominate the world, they should not exist at all. Endeavouring to eliminate them, regardless of the damage thereby inflicted upon the world economic system, is part of the self-destructive drive of capitalism in crisis: the growth of world production is sacrificed to the maintenance of class rule.

The legal migrant is still a person. Although frequently oppressed, recognized immigrants are still in an infinitely superior position to those who dare to move without a licence: the illegal migrant and the mass of refugees. Since these people belong to no ruling class, any barbarity may be inflicted upon them. They can be treated as cruelly as those lost peoples encompassed by the expanding modern national State: the Red Indians, the aborigines, the nomads.[11]

The ruling classes of the destination countries seek to stabilize their national power at the cost of the world system, at the same time as borrowing or stealing the labour forces of more backward ruling classes. There is a strikingly vivid model for a different method of achieving similar results. South Africa reclassified the majority of its natives as foreigners, nationals of a set of hastily run up independent States, the Bantustans. To do this, the distinction between 'labourer' and 'labour power' was vital, as the Minister of Mining explained in 1965: 'They (black workers) are only supplying a commodity, the commodity of labour . . . it is labour we are importing and not labourers'.[12] Apartheid, insofar as its aims in the field of labour were actually achieved, secured the purpose of offloading the costs of the reproduction of black labour to the Bantustans while retaining access to the labour power of adult workers. It also prevented black workers seeking to emulate the reproduction costs of white South Africa. Its viability depended upon being able to maintain a divided economy, between a majority low productivity sector and a minority high productivity sector. It has analogies with Japan. Insofar as this structural condition is superseded, apartheid comes to act as a powerful constraint on the growth of South African capitalism.

No issue today so sharply differentiates internationalists and national reformists as that of the international migration of workers. The issue at stake is a challenge to the very existence of the national State and its prerogatives in the control of a territory and the inhabitants. Much of the politics of the Left is concerned with gaining control of the State and accelerating the growth of its power over its inhabitants, not with abolishing the State. Deploring the ill treatment of immigrants is seen, not as an attack on the powers of the State, but as an argument for ending all immigration. Demands for a 'humane immigration policy' rival the fantasies of 'send the capital to the countries from which the immigrants come, not immigrants to the countries where capital exists'. If the Left had power to direct capital to new locations, it has the power to abolish capital. In the United States, it is part of the Left which stresses that illegal immigrants menace only the oppressed but native groups – blacks, Puerto Ricans, women – and that, to protect these groups, illegals should be expelled. Yet to permit the expulsion of illegal immigrants is to take one step nearer to the expulsion of immigrants, which in turn is a step closer to the expulsion of selected sections of natives. That way madness lies. Accepting the right of the State to control immigration is accepting its right to exist, the right of the ruling class to exist as a ruling class, the right to exploit, the 'right' to a world of barbarism.

In South Africa, the white trade unions allied with the State for immediate gains to a minority of workers at the expense of the majority. In the US it is the AFL–CIO which campaign more consistently for the rounding up and expulsion of illegal Mexican workers; they 'permit' US business to locate across the southern border to use cheap Mexican labour, but refuse to allow them to recruit Mexican workers and establish parity of wages on both sides of the frontier (a demand which would of course bring them into direct collision with the interests not only of US business but also of the Mexican ruling class, also dependent upon cheap labour). It is the British TUC which continually presses for an end to the issue of work permits, an aim which, if achieved, would rob the TUC leadership of the opportunity of banquets in expensive London hotels. While it is the labour movement which leads the attack on foreign workers, employers may sleep quietly in their beds: whatever the secondary quarrels, the unions accept 'the national interest', the employers' interest, that this is the best of all possible worlds.

6

Newly Emergent Bourgeoisies?

'The capitalist system, once a mighty engine of economic development, has turned into a no less formidable hurdle to human development', Paul Baran, *The Political Economy of Growth* (Monthly Review Press, New York, 1957, p. 249).

CAPITALISM AND DEVELOPMENT

Baran's judgement on the potential of capitalism to produce the economic development of what were then called the underdeveloped countries, was surprisingly widely shared in the 1950s, the formative period for what became known as development studies. The case was two-edged. On the one hand, the world capitalist order made development through orthodox methods either impossible or only exceptionally possible. On the other hand, the domestic underdeveloped economy, the social structure, the culture or sheer brute material scarcity made it virtually impossible to create a dynamic domestic capitalist class.

In Latin America, Raúl Prebisch developed a critique of the world economic order[1] which seemed to show that countries dependent upon the export of primary commodities were condemned to a long-term deterioration in their terms of trade, so that it became impossible to import the manufactured goods upon which the economy depended except where they could be paid for in gold. Long-term impoverishment was bound to follow. The case had many historical precedessors and proved enormously influential as the theory of unequal exchange[2] – whether the inequality lay in straight robbery of the poor by the rich countries, in an 'accident' of the structure, or in a systematic phenomenon whereby the exports of

Originally published under the same title as Working Paper 28 of the Centre for Urban Studies and Urban Planning, University of Hong Kong, November 1987.

what Prebisch called the 'periphery' were consistently undervalued while those of the 'centres' (the developed countries) were overvalued. Free trade, it seemed, always favoured the more developed trade partner. Why this was so involved different arguments, but these usually turned upon the political capacity of the developed to form a monopoly selling position while the multiplicity of competitors among the less developed rendered this impossible.[3] (The implausibility of this case led in some hands to a revision: it was the monopoly control of the supply of labour by Western trade unions which kept industrial export prices high.) Less clearly worked out cases implied that the great concentrations of what were to become known as multinational or transnational corporations, allied to the small group of dominant States, controlled the entire world economy and would use this monopoly position to stifle all rivals.

The other side of the case was that modern economic backwardness had peculiarities which prevented any repetition of the capitalist development of Europe and North America in the less developed countries. Local private capital would always be overshadowed by the giant companies of the developed countries, and would be unable to compete and remain restricted to the role of importer of goods manufactured by foreigners (the concept of 'comprador capitalist' was important here). Others suggested that the interests of capitalists in less developed countries were, unlike the situation in Europe, too closely interwoven with 'feudal' forces, the landlords, or with short-term commercial speculators; capital accumulation would always be sacrificed to expanded land ownership or short-term gains, production to consumption. The nature of the economic framework in any case militated against the rapid expansion of private production: the income level was too low and the market therefore too small to allow efficient scales of production, and subsidized production would only narrow the market further; skills were too primitive, and resources lacking to improve them; cultures, religions, ideologies and psychologies militated against the energetic pursuit of profit. In sum, private capitalists had become not merely unable to undertake national economic development, but a positive obstacle to that process, consuming – indeed, squandering – scarce resources. In the grubby trader there was no longer any trace of the Promethean and Puritan spirit to transform the world. As Baran put it:[4]

> a political and social coalition of wealthy compradors, powerful monopolists and large landowners dedicated to the defence of the existing feudal, mercantile order . . . has nothing to hope for from the rise of industrial capitalism, which would dislodge it from its position of privilege and power.

The only way out of this impasse was for economic development to be undertaken by the State. The government could control the economic forces transmitted by world capitalism – imports, fluctuating prices, flows of currency, foreign investment – and protect the domestic economy. It could overcome the domestic inertia or lack of drive by itself assuming the primary role in capital accumulation (whether this was undertaken directly by the public sector, or the government used the private sector or forms of joint venture). There would be no need to rely upon the market, notorious for its 'anarchy', duplication and waste. Nor were the resources lacking to support this process. Unlimited supplies of cheap labour was one base for State-directed accumulation, independent of profit motivations. If the State reordered the domestic economy, it could then maximize the public take – from the profits of business, from general taxation, and from progressive direct taxation. Baran had no doubt that in India 15 per cent of the national income could be invested without reducing mass consumption, since 25 per cent was already absorbed by 'unproductive strata'.[5] With State-directed investment, industrialization could break the stranglehold of unequal exchange, and do so with improved popular consumption and equity.

The case for the exhaustion of the historical role of capital and the necessity for State initiative had a much older ancestry than contemporary development studies. The predominance of the economic role of the State characterizes all early phases of economic development, even that of the British, and such a role inclines the conventional wisdom to dismiss the petty short-term greed of capitalists as irrelevant to the historical process of transformation. However, there are more explicit arguments on this question, particularly in the first instance on the Left.

The common opinion of Marxists in the more backward areas of Europe at the turn of the century was that capitalism had failed there and must of necessity fail. The bourgeoisie, as a result, would never attain sufficient social power to risk overthrowing the old 'feudal' order and establishing the political and social framework for capitalism. Unlike the situation in Western Europe where capital emerged on a small scale, with powerful local roots spread throughout the countries concerned, capitalism in Eastern Europe had been imported by absentee foreign capitalists; a significant working class had thus been created without a socially rooted and significant capitalist class. In such circumstances, capital would always be more afraid of workers than aristocrats. The first Manifesto of the Russian Social Democrat Party identified this as the reason why the working class in Russia would, paradoxically, have to lead the bourgeois revolution in the face of the possible opposition of the bourgeoisie:[6]

> The farther east one goes in Europe, the weaker, meaner and more cowardly in the political sense becomes the bourgeoisie, and the greater the cultural and political tasks which fall to the lot of the proletariat. On its strong shoulders, the Russian working class must and will carry the work of conquering political liberty.

In fact, the Social Democrats – both Menshevik and Bolshevik – were wrong in the early phases of the 1905 revolution. At least some important employers in St Petersburg even went so far as to pay their workers to join the anti-Tsarist demonstrations. However, in the chaos of 1917, they were right; business was far too fearful of the Bolsheviks to risk radical opposition to the Tsar. The *smychka*, the alliance of workers and peasants, was required to do what the bourgeoisie refused to do.

Communists remained committed to the twin propositions that capital could not develop what were known as the 'backward and colonial countries', and that, therefore, there could be no bourgeois-led anti-colonial struggle. Just as Russia's capitalists were seen as wedded to the Tsar by their fear of worker rebellion, so their equivalents in the colonies were entirely dependent upon the colonizers, the imperial State. In the scenario, a shadowy role was allowed for a 'national bourgeoisie' in an anti-imperialist coalition, provided that this was firmly led by the 'workers and peasants' (which, in practice, invariably meant the Communist Party). But in essence capital was comprador. National liberation, a kind of bourgeois revolution, would have to be undertaken by non-bourgeois forces. It followed that the post-revolutionary order would have no direct interest in creating a private capitalist economy.

The case was, in essence, very influential far beyond the ranks of the Communist International. It was partly strengthened by a parallel intellectual evolution in the heartlands of world capitalism, Europe and North America. For some, not necessarily on the Left, the First World War seemed the necessary outcome of private capitalist competition allied to the interests of the State. The Great Depression of the interwar years seemed again to demonstrate the failure of capitalism, the impossibility of an ordered and progressive private market economy. The 1930s were a period of fashionable State capitalism, founded upon a quasi-corporatist tripartite federation of the State, capital and labour, in which the State, by reason of its monopoly of the legitimate use of physical force, its control of the economic borders (so determining the degree of domestic competition from imports), and its privileged access to the surplus generated in the economy, was overwhelmingly the dominant partner.[7]

In the expansion of Germany's war machine, private business was bullied, badgered and bribed, parts of it expropriated or just shut down; there was little question of businessmen accepting any definition of the national interest which diverged from that dictated by the *Führer*. Roosevelt's New Deal was nowhere near as dictatorial as this, but State initiative assumed such unprecedented forms that there were those who saw the Federal Government as virtually socialist. In Britain, successive Conservative governments had more limited autonomy than that of the Third Reich, but they did seek to form the corporatist alliance of the State and the largest monopolistic or oligopolistic businesses to control markets, not ensure competition, in order to establish an economically protected empire and controlled currency zone.[8] Other spirits went further. In 1938, Keynes, an enthusiastic supporter of the corporatist ideal,[9] could propose, astonishingly, the 'euthanasia of the rentier'.[10] Harold Macmillan, a rising backbencher, argued in 1938 for the nationalization of all basic and food industries as a condition for the survival of capitalism.[11] Indeed, in the 1945 general election, the Westminster Conservative Association produced a cheap edition of Macmillan's *The Middle Way* to support the charge that Labour had stolen its programme from the Conservatives, but had weakened its radicalism.

The world system seemed then to consist of a set of warring empires, dominated by a group of extraordinarily powerful States, each with its own discrete segment of national capital and its groups of monetary associates – Sterling, Franc, Dollar, Reichsmark and Yen spheres of influence. Bukharin's vision of a world consisting of competing State capitalisms seemed entirely vindicated.[12] The Second World War only served to confirm the picture, for each belligerent State assumed the role of a board of directors of a single national conglomerate, a war-making machine, the needs of which superseded most individual and private rights. Even long after the war, when extraordinary and unexpected prosperity had transformed the developed countries (and much of the old empires had been dissolved), the theorists of modern capitalism still accorded the decisive economic role to the State, not the market.[13]

It was hardly surprising that this experience coloured postwar perceptions of the problems of economic development, particularly given the far weaker role of private capital in the newly independent countries. Both on the Left and the Right, it seemed, the State in developing countries was the decisive economic agent. In terms of maximizing both capital accumulation and popular welfare, it appeared that no reliance could be placed for long on private businessmen. The private sector was something to be directed in the interests of the State, to be induced to act and to be milked for funds.

Nationalization was the punishment for the unruly. The high officers of the State, dedicated to a vision of the future of the nation and the dignity of the people, had no reason to regard businessmen as anything more than short-sighted, immoral, greedy, a barely tolerated minority whose very survival depended upon the goodwill of government.

The paradox in the original case, however, was that, insofar as the State was successful in forcing economic development, it accelerated the growth of a private capitalist class (that is, assuming the public sector had not entirely swallowed the private), which in turn would come to limit, challenge or dominate the State itself. The index of such a 'maturation of capitalism' might be thought to be the intervention of businessmen directly in politics. For it is almost inevitable that government would resist the limitations on its actions that the rise of a new capitalist class would imply; there is unlikely to be a smooth covert evolution from one type of State to another, so that the role of businessmen and of parties directly supporting their interests has to be overt, entering the public arena to contest for State power. In certain circumstances, this might imply revolution but revolution to establish a mature capitalist order, not abolish it. Once firmly in place, businessmen could return to their basic concern of the pursuit of profit, leaving the political class to run the state within a framework which would defend and advance the interests of capital (as well as doing all the other things States are required to undertake).

NEW DEPARTURES

These thoughts arise in part in reflecting on the widening ramifications of Mrs Aquino's accession to power in the Philippines. It is almost as if the yellow shirts have become a rallying banner for a similar coalition of forces in many countries, all now reaching the stage where the old State apparently needs to be reformed by the discipline of business-led forces. The Manila movement mobilized students, the poor, the educated middle class and, of most interest here, the major part of Filipino private business (except the narrow circle of President Marcos's 'cronies').

This was a similar coalition to that which in June 1987 shook to its foundations the South Korean Government (the Korean movement invoked the Filipino example as its inspiration). During the demonstrations throughout the spring of that year, journalists noted the apparent shutdown of the Seoul downtown area as young businessmen, bankers, brokers, managers and other office staff stopped work to join the cheering crowds. In a country where car ownership was still restricted to the better-off, motor cavalcades were organized to hoot defiance at President Chun. The demands of the marchers seemed to echo those of the 1830 movement in Britain to widen the franchise and many other such movements in nineteenth-century Europe against the arbitrary and corrupt absolutist State (misidentified in much socialist literature as 'feudalism').

The rebelliousness of Korean business was in striking contrast to its complete subordination to government in the quarter of a century of very rapid economic growth after 1955. The removal of the Japanese imperial order (which included the capitalist class of colonial Korea), the postwar radical land reform measures, and the chaos of the Korean War seemed temporarily to remove all major social forces in the country, giving the State an unprecedented autonomy. Many observers have noted this peculiar dominance of the State, and the complete dependence of private business upon government, particularly during the regime of General Park.[14] Not only was business overwhelmingly dominated by the State, the State owned and directed a major part of the economy. One commentator regarded the government's ownership of the banking system as decisive; 'No State outside the socialist bloc ever came near this measure of control over the economy's investible resources'.[15]

However, there were signs of increasing restlessness among businessmen over this close public tutelage even before the murder of Park in 1979. There seems to have been growing opposition to the State's appropriation of such a large share of national investment and its use in prodigious capital projects of doubtful value (particularly in the heavy industry drive of the 1970s) to the neglect of the basic retooling of the textile industry, a key exporter:[16] to the arbitrary discrimination on the part of government officials, the judiciary and tax systems, towards favouritism and corruption. The Fifth Plan (1982–6) even went so far as to make some half recognition of this discontent when it diagnosed the slump of 1979–80 as due to 'Excessive Government intervention in the private sector . . . [discouraging] private initiative and efficiency of investment which are vital to growth in a market economy'. A Minister subsequently summarized one of the key elements in the government's account as the 'maturation' of Korean capital: 'The economy is already too big to be managed in the old way by heavy-handed Government bureaucrats'.[17]

Going a little way to meet the criticisms was one thing, but instituting effective reforms was quite another. Despite some important measures, the Korean Government did not decisively change its mode of operation. In the immediate aftermath of the 1980 crisis, companies resisted on an unprecedented scale measures ordered by the government to rationalize selected industries and to release land hoards to improve company liquidity. In 1987, Hyundai, the largest business group in the country, was so indiscreet as to express publicly its fury at the government's action in first awarding an important contract to build a power station to one of the Hyundai companies and then cancelling it in favour of a rival firm.

The leading opposition party, the Reunification Democratic Party, developed a programme to summarize the core demands of the coalition. The Party was for continued high growth but with income redistribution, freeing of business and banking from government ownership and control (or, as the programme put it, breaking the 'economically privileged structure of government and big business'), decentralization and more social spending. The public sector should be fully privatized and government controls ended, in particular, controls on business borrowing abroad.

Workers apparently played a very minor role in the spring 1987 events. Nonetheless, the Reunification Democratic Party felt it important to propose that workers should be guaranteed the right to form national trade unions (under President Chun, only plant unions were permitted, and the Korean Federation of Trade Unions was forbidden to assist its affiliates in dispute) and that there should be an end to the 'low wage policy' (but with firm opposition to 'excessive wage demands'). By mid-July the government had not enforced the law after thirty new unions had been set up without following the legal procedure. However, in the following two months there was an astonishing outbreak of worker rebellion, affecting some 1,600 companies in all the major sectors. All these many strikes were illegal, but the government, no doubt fearful of inciting further opposition, refrained from enforcing the law. Perhaps it also felt that the expression of such pent-up feelings might be its ally in dealing with business, frightening private capital back into accepting State direction as a lesser evil than worker militancy (so perhaps confirming the Bolshevik thesis mentioned earlier). The Labour Minister expressed the need to intervene to prevent 'chaos', the two leaders of the opposition and the Federation of Korean Industry urged restraint lest the export drive be affected (and the military use the pretext of labour unrest as they did in 1960 and 1980 to seize power again). However, it seemed that many of the larger businesses accepted the Reunification Democratic Party case (or even themselves proposed it) that Korea ought to move away from a low wage to a high productivity economy, and might also have accepted the importance of worker representation in independent trade unions in making this transition. But there was possibly a sizeable sector of small and poor Korean companies whose very survival depended upon maintaining low wages and keeping out independent unions. The crisis thus sharply divided the business class rather than strengthen the position of the government.

The outcome of the Korean events is less relevant to the theme of this paper than the demonstration of the emergence of a much more independent business class, with its own views on the operation of the State. Other Newly Industrializing Countries may well be exhibiting similar features. How far, for example, is Taiwan's more controlled democratization and privatization programme the result of the 'maturation' of the business class? Certainly, the role of business is said to have been decisive in the restoration of civilian and representative government in Uruguay, Argentina and Brazil. Within Brazil, the key debate among businessmen concerned those who favoured the continuation of the old model of public sector-dominated protectionism (with secure business dependence) and those who were anxious to liberalize and become part of the world market. The key to this debate, it should be noted, was not external influences (multinational corporations, Western governments, the International Monetary Fund, the World Bank, etc.) but the maturation of a section of Brazilian business, eager to become multinational itself. Paradoxically, the section of capital most resistant to liberalization finds itself allied to the Brazilian Left on a simple basis of economic nationalism. The issue of public sector corruption was no less important than in Korea, particularly since the press discovered the 'Maharajas', public officials receiving extraordinarily high salaries. (In the key case for the campaign, a São Paulo traffic police officer is said to have received (US)$203,755 a year, the leader of a group of nineteen top earners in official posts.) However, the Panama case more closely paralleled some of the events in Korea.

South Korea was by no means alone in invoking the name of Mrs Aquino. Events in the Philippines were one of the inspirations in the movement against military dictatorship in Panama (that is, before the US military intervention). Not long after the spring events in Seoul, a similar movement constituted itself on the other side of the Pacific. The Panama Chamber of Commerce and the National Council of Private Enterprise were important in initiating a Civic Crusade (a coalition of 107 business, Church and professional organizations) to oust the *de facto* dictator, General Manuel Antonio Noriega. In July, the Crusade was able to shut down most of the business operations in the country for two days. Panama is an important offshore banking centre (there are 125 foreign banks in the country, with a combined asset value said to be of the order of $39 billion). The government ordered the banks not to close, but the bankworkers settled the issue by staying away from work. The Canal workers also struck in support of the 'democracy movement', but the two largest trade union federations withheld support. Again there were motorcades hooting defiance, on this occasion every lunchtime, and office workers showered the streets from their downtown office blocks with white streamers. Six thousand, mainly middle class, women had a saucepan banging session in July (shades of Chile just before the fall of Allende), and organized a large march through the capital in late August. In the same month, the government raided the Chamber of Commerce, alleging that its members were guilty of subversion, and arrest warrants were issued for the five Crusade leaders, including the President of the Chamber of Commerce, Sr Aurelio Barria.

As in the Philippines, the role of the United States was important. There had been growing alarm in Washington at the allegations against General Noriega of murdering the previous dictator, Torrijos, of torturing his opponents and of corruption. In late June, the US Senate called for the general's resignation as chief of the armed forces, and in late July, Washington suspended civil and military aid to the country. The hostility expressed in the United States allowed General Noriega to accuse the democracy movement of being a CIA front organization, orchestrated from Washington and dedicated to treason on behalf of American imperialism (or more specifically, dedicated to reversing the treaty which would transfer the Canal to Panamanian hands in the year 2000). The governing party, the Revolutionary Democratic Party, loyally organized its supporters – or at least, civil servants were given a day's leave – to stone the US embassy and petrol bomb the Bank of America. For a short time, Noriega appealed for support to Nicaragua, and the then President, Daniel Ortega, flew to Panama to pledge the solidarity of the Sandinistas. This bizarre episode was overtaken by cooler tempers quite swiftly.

The events in Panama were a striking illustration of the overt intervention of private business in politics. Of course, these are not the only occasions in which this has been apparent in recent years. Business was very active in the overthrow of Allende's regime in Chile. In South Africa, the opposition of much of business to apartheid[18] was decisive in the crisis of the late 1980s, an opposition symbolized in the deliberate flouting of the law when a group of important businessmen visited Lusaka for discussions with the then banned African National Congress leadership (a visit presumably made public as a deliberate indication of the alienation of businessmen from current government policy). Business was also an important element in the Sandinista movement against Nicaragua's dictator, Somoza: indeed, the Sandinistas, although organized as a military formation for the civil war, in social composition were not strikingly different from Mrs Aquino's support. Of course, business reactions were not exactly the same in each case; they range from the active initiative of businessmen (as in Panama) to opportunistically backing the winning movement in time to ensure survival (as happened in Iran, with the overthrow of the Shah).

Mexico is very different from both South Korea and Panama. It is a very large country, rich in natural resources and with a powerful manufacturing economy. It has experienced a rapidly growing economy – 6 to 7 per cent per year – for many of the past forty years, and that economy is now about the tenth largest in the non-Communist world. However, there is one similarity with Korea, the size of the public sector and the dominance of the State.

Throughout much of the growth, relations between private business and the single political party which overwhelmingly dominates the country, the Party of Institutionalized Revolution (PRI), have been unexceptionable. While the PRI has preserved a slightly Leftish image, based upn a strong economic nationalism, it has nonetheless consulted, collaborated with and supported business, all the while assuming the dominant role. The PRI, a quasi-corporatist federation of three elements, the official trade unions, the official peasant associations and 'popular forces' (mainly, the intelligentsia and the middle classes), has always provided direct access for important businessmen to senior government officials, so there was not much need to pursue a suggestion once mooted, to make business a fourth section within the party.

However, in the 1970s, this situation began to change. A group of very important businessmen, the Monterrey group (taking their name from the important northern manufacturing centre), became well known as sharp critics of the government. The President between 1970 and 1976, Luis Echeverria, cultivated a style of populist rhetoric which included attacks on the 'reactionary private sector', with hints of its treasonable relationship to the United States, but he still continued to consult with a group of the largest businessmen on a weekly basis and with apparent cordiality. The Monterrey group criticized government policy from an economically liberal position and also argued that the President's Leftish phraseology encouraged terrorism; there were a number of guerrilla activities in the early 1970s, and in one, Eugenio Garza Sada, a leading Monterrey industrialist, was murdered. At the end of his period in office Echeverria also encouraged peasant seizures of large farms in the north, and in the economic crisis of the mid-1970s, a substantial expansion of public sector activity to compensate for a decline in private investment and capital flight. Some of these issues sharpened the Monterrey critique, and many of the business organizations elected leaderships from the group.

The next President, Lopez Portillo (1976–82), had the good fortune to preside over a country which discovered that it had major oil reserves at a time of rising oil prices. The ensuing boom, unprecedented in its speed, swept away much of the business reservations, or, at least, induced acquiescence. Yet it was in this period that the State, the immediate recipient of the oil revenue (or the public borrowings that took place on the basis of expected oil revenue), vastly expanded the scale of its operations. In the 1970s as a whole, public investment grew by 20 per cent a year (1972–81).

The process of growth culminated in the spectacular collapse of 1982 amid a major flight of capital and an unprecedented scale of cumulative external debt.[19] A demoralized President attacked 'usurers' and traitors and, with no consultation even with a majority of his Cabinet, nationalized the domestic banks. In fact, the measure underpinned the private external debts with sovereign authority, but in the confused and dispiriting conditions of the time, the President could not forebear to make the act of expropriation appear as an heroic nationalist and even socialist measure, a blow in the class war. Bank nationalization brought into the public sector a mass of manufacturing companies that were owned in part or whole by the banks.

Bank nationalization, along with the severe crisis in the economy and the need for sustained retrenchment, brought to a head a mass of discontents in the business community. The new President, De la Madrid (1982–8) indicated to business opinion his disapproval of the nationalization measure and ordered the sale of a third of the shares in banks and all bank-owned companies. He promised that there would be no extension of the public sector and, later, that there would be radical privatization of whatever existing assets could be sold. Indeed, in his 1985 Presidential Address he attributed part of the crisis to the excessive growth of public activities (echoing the South Korean governmental self-criticism):

> excessive proliferation of public enterprise has weakened the State by upsetting its financial balance and by limiting its ability to fulfil adequately its primary responsibilities.

The President also held out the prospect of a new order, an elimination of corruption and the institution of public accountability. Furthermore, he promised that, in contrast to the past, the PRI would not seek to manipulate elections and would respect the victories of opposition parties. This seems to have produced a significant movement, particularly in the north, of businessmen and money into a leading opposition party, the Party of National Action (PAN). The party had traditionally stood for a conservative, nationalist and corporatist position, not unlike that held in the past by certain Christian Democratic parties, with a strong emphasis upon the importance of the role of the State. However, in recent years, the party has been divided between the traditional position and a completely free enterprise programme of economic liberalism, *neopanismo*. A similar transformation can be seen in the French Gaullists and the British Conservatives.

Important businessmen emerged as PAN candidates in northern local and State elections. In doing so, they risked the displeasure of a very powerful government with great resources to penalize their business activities. The same is true of subsidiary campaigns financed by business (for example, to establish Church schools). In at least one case, the government forced the resignation of a leading businessman from the board of directors of a major business group because of his public support for PAN.

The government was particularly nervous of opposition as the economic crisis affected popular living standards. Officially, unemployment more than doubled (to 18 per cent) as the total labour force expanded by 3.8 per cent annually, and real wages possibly fell by up to half as the government followed a programme of radically cutting subsidies on staple foods and transport.

Neither objective circumstances nor public assurances assuaged the frustrations of northern business. There was much talk of the PRI's uncontrollable drive towards State capitalism, towards totalitarianism, orchestrated by an international socialist conspiracy. The mildly conservative politics of the PRI seemed very remote from this fantasy. It was especially unkind, given all the favours shown to business over many years, as well as the public sympathy demonstrated by President De la Madrid.

What made the collisions between northern business and the government so extreme was the elections. After initially accepting the loss of any important cities to PAN in the early years of De la Madrid's presidential period, the PRI resorted to unprecedented doctoring of the elections to prevent it increasing its vote. In 1985 and 1986 this led to serious rioting in the north and great discredit to the government. The left-wing parties were unable at this time to utilize popular discontents to expand. However, in time for the next Presidential election, a radical faction in PRI united with the left-wing parties to provide a new and much stronger Left nationalist opposition under a former important PRI leader (and son of the most famous President this century), Cuauhtémoc Cárdenas. It is possible that this radically shifted the perceptions of businessmen to counting their blessings rather than embarrassing the government. In any case, the following PRI President, Carlos Salinas de Gortari, made major efforts to privatize the public sector, liberalize the economy and open up major opportunities for business.

THE MATURATION OF CAPITAL

Is it possible to say that these different examples reflect not merely the irritability with government induced by unfavourable circumstances in the world economy, but rather the 'maturation of capital'? What that phrase implies is that the social weight of private capital has reached the point where its role in society requires redefinition, where its relationship to the State has to be re-identified. This is not simply a matter of the relative size of capital after an extended period of rapid economic growth. It also relates to the composition of output, an increasingly sophisticated and skill-intensive product. An economy dominated by the production of, for example, crude raw materials is susceptible to the direction of an interventionist State in a way that is not so for an economy producing a diverse, complex and continuously changing manufactured output. The more sophisticated the output, the less the capacity of a single national agency to plan its growth and change, to foster innovation, to be sensitive to the appropriate imports required to sustain a changing output, to ensure a pattern of skills constantly readjusted to the changing demand for labour. In fact, this hypothesis about the changing nature of output is only half-true, for when we introduce historical time, it becomes clear that the production of raw materials has also been transformed by new technologies to become no less sophisticated. Merle Lipton[20] in her study of South African capital shows how the increasing capital intensity of farming necessitated increasingly advanced and diverse skills in the black labour force. To attain the appropriate levels of productivity, such workers had to be settled with their families in reasonably secure living conditions. The white farmers, for so long dependent upon unskilled migrant labour, came to press the government to provide rural schools and housing for their now much smaller, more skilled and settled workforce.

'Maturity of capital' as seen in terms of the composition of output relates also to the nature of markets. Production for the home market, protected against imports, permits monopoly pricing and poor quality. Capital can be seen as mature when it operates primarily in a world market (even if a major part of its output happens to be sold in that part of the world market which is at home). With domestic slump, exports can become the means to ensure the survival of capital, provided the government is supportive. Being supportive means at least maintaining the exchange rate at a level which ensures that exporting is profitable, allowing the import of the cheapest inputs to exports in order to retain a competitive edge, maintaining the quality of the infrastructure, ensuring that power and transport are good and available at the right time and place and that the educational system produces the right skills in the workforce, and not wasting resources on 'irrelevant' projects. Of course, if local production is so inefficient that it can never be exported, the only demand on the State is to keep out imports. But in the Newly Industrializing Countries, substantial opportunities continue, even in a situation of world stagnation, to expand exports, provided the State plays its part. It is, of course, misleading to speak of business as a whole since these issues affect different sectors and firms to different degrees; some must retain protection to survive, some must gain access to a world market to grow.

Slump and stagnation add a painful urgency to some of these questions, and perhaps that is part of the explanation for the coincidence of business oppositions in a number of countries. The opportunities for business survival today, however, are quite different from those in the Great Depression of the interwar period. Then, States attempted to organize protected enclaves to exclude foreign competition. Today, the movement towards economic liberalism seems only to go from strength to strength (despite sporadic efforts to introduce elements of protectionism in the developed countries). The difference reflects, I believe, a degree of economic integration in the system which has now passed beyond the stage at which the more powerful governments could reverse it at acceptable cost.[21] To protect, for many governments, is now suicidal; more is to be lost than gained (this does not necessarily apply to all countries equally, especially the poorest).

With the benefit of hindsight, it is now possible to see how curious it was that national capitalist classes could no longer play their supposed historical role, and the State must act for them. For the State-induced process of accelerated capital accumulation was just what was required to create an expansive capitalist class. The problems of analysis were increased by a somewhat mythological account of European economic history that failed to note how late in capitalist development was the emergence of a bourgeois republic, how dominant, protectionist and corrupt was the State which preceded the bourgeois republic, and what a diversity of cases were abstracted in the theory.

We can now see that all cases of economic development required a phase of State domination and initiative, of which protection is usually an important part. For import substitution organizes a transfer of resources from consumer to selected monopoly accumulators, a system of unequal exchange far more profound than the trade relationships between centres and peripheries. This forced accumulation is the precondition for sustained economic development. In countries where the State could not achieve the degree of autonomy sufficient to institute such a process (for example, under colonialism), accumulation was inevitably very slow and vulnerable.

However, the State is a social institution, a coalition of interests deriving from past practices. It is not simply a set of arrangements that can be changed at will. What has been set up to speed development in one phase becomes, in another, a restriction on development, the beneficiaries of the old fight to prevent change to the new. Then the old State must be reformed or overthrown. With the maturation of capital, the enemy is not 'feudalism' but the old State, whether the corrupt particularist absolute monarchy of the eighteenth century or the hyper-entrepreneurial dictatorship of General Chun.

The reshaping of the State may or may not involve establishing representative democracy. Where businessmen – or their political champions – cannot subvert the government from within, they may be obliged to collaborate with a mass of discontents, a coalition of interests and demands. Thus, the breadth of interest called up by the refusal of the State to accommodate a mature capitalist class, with its threat of revolution, is more likely to produce universal suffrage than piecemeal reforms. The resistance of the State – as shown here in different forms in Korea, Panama and Mexico – makes it increasingly difficult to avoid a violent confrontation.

However, a division within the ruling order between the old State and business opens up much wider possibilities of change. In particular, in both Korea and the Philippines, new labour movements are emerging in the wake of new capitalist classes. Like capital, the social weight of the labour force has also grown substantially. Today, the largest concentrations of the world's industrial working class are probably in developing countries – in São Paulo, Mexico City, Shanghai, Calcutta, Seoul, etc. In at least some of the movements towards democracy, workers have played a role, but nowhere as an independent force. It is perhaps for this reason that the Bolshevik and Comintern estimate – that capital would never contest for political power against the old order for fear of inciting a worker revolution – proved wrong. The workers of South Korea appear mainly concerned with improved pay and conditions, and the right to form independent unions, not the conquest of the State.

If the thesis outlined here is correct, we can expect further collisions as business classes reach the stage of seeking to redirect the role of the old State. Even with relative stagnation in the world economy at large, many Newly Industrializing Countries are continuing to sustain expansion. Despite all the fears, that process seems likely to continue for the foreseeable future, and as it does, so does capital accumulation and the creation of capitalists. While it is far from a perfect index, one measure of this growth might be the projected value of the assets of the thirty-three leading less developed countires traded on the equity markets. This is expected to multiply five or six fold by the year 2000, reaching a combined total value of between $500 billion and $800 billion. (By way of comparison, the current value of the assets traded on Europe's combined stock exchanges is about $500 billion.) That represents a lot of capitalists colliding with a lot of States.

III
TRADE

7

Theories of Unequal Exchange

There are a number of variations on the theme that, in conditions of free trade between different geographical areas (two countries, two groups of countries, or town and country), there is a systematic bias for the economically more advanced to gain disproportionately or exclusively relative to the more backward partner. In Marx's scornful reproach of classical economics in 1848:

> If the free traders cannot understand how one nation can grow rich at the expense of another, we need not wonder, since the same gentlemen also refuse to understand how, within one country, one class can enrich itself at the expense of another.

The idea that the more advanced invariably exploit the more backward is an ancient idea, and a powerful thread in the earliest mercantile school of economic thought. Thus, in the late sixteenth century, one of the mercantilist thinkers of more backward England reflected on the export of English raw wool to, and the import of finished woollen goods from, more advanced Europe.[1]

> What grossness be we of, that see it and suffer such continual spoil to be made of our goods and treasures . . . They must make us pay at the end for our stuff again . . . whereas with working the same within our Realm, our own men should be set on work at the charge of the strangers.

In essence, it was thought, international trade was a mechanism for pumping money out of England into the hands of foreigners. The case was the first justification for using the State to limit imports in order to force the pace of growth of domestic manufacturing: what in

Originally published under the same title in *International Socialism* 33 (London), Autumn 1986, pp. 111–22.

the twentieth century became known as 'import-substitution industrialization'. Of course, in terms of the pure theory of capitalism, such an approach was absurd – the capitalist is or ought to be concerned with the profit rate whatever the phase of production concerned, and it might well be that the rate of return on the sale of raw wool is higher than that on the manufacture of woollen goods. Where the mercantilist case makes sense is not in the abstractions of world capital, but in the struggle of a more backward national capitalist class to close the gap with the more advanced.

The case thus emerges as part and parcel of the development of national capitalism in contest with more advanced national capitalisms. Many regimes in the eighteenth and nineteenth centuries experimented with import controls to force domestic capital accumulation. They did so without much theorization, let alone a theory of unequal exchange. However, there were two now much neglected theorists – Alexander Hamilton (in the backward United States) and Friedrich List (in the backward states of Germany).[2] There was also theorization in the backward states of Eastern Europe in the interwar period of the present century, part of a nationalist corporatist case of grain exporters against the economic domination of Germany. The Rumanian economist, Mihail Manoïlesco, described free trade and the international division of labour as an intellectual swindle to conceal how the rich countries robbed the poor:[3]

> Just as Marx's theory leads us to understand the social phenomena of the capitalist world and especially that of exploitation by *classes*, this theory of international exchange makes us understand the inequality *between peoples* and relations of exploiter and exploited that connect them.

* * *

There was a different thread of speculation about cities. Marx and Engels in their account of primitive accumulation, show how cities – or towns – drain resources out of the countryside. Indeed, Marx placed heavy stress on the economic relations between urban and rural:[4]

> The foundation of every division of labour that is well developed and brought about by the exchange of commodities is the demarcation between town and country. It may be said that the whole economic history of society is summed up in the movement of this antithesis.

Or again:[5]

> The greatest division of material and mental labour is the separation of town and country. The antagonism of town and country begins with the transition from barbarism to civilisation, from tribe to state, from locality to nation, and runs through the whole history of civilisation to the present day.

By what means did the urban take resources from the rural? Through direct appropriation – the king or State taxed the peasantry, and often obliged it to perform unpaid services, service in the armed forces, etc. Rural migrants swelled the urban labour force without the towns being responsible for meeting the costs of the reproduction of these workers (a continuous net transfer of resources from one to the other). And in the market, the few urban buyers of agricultural output could force down the prices for the many competitive sellers of produce, while the few urban sellers of urban manufactured goods could hold prices high. Similar mechanisms operated in the European empires between the colonies and the metropolitan power. The British, to the very end, had an item in their accounts with India called 'Treasure'. Note that the transfers did not arise from the free operation of the market, a most rare phenomenon in the reality of capitalism, but from monopoly manipulation of the market, the use of pure power outside the market and from straight robbery.

In Soviet Russia, Preobazhensky,[6] the leading economic thinker of the Left opposition in the 1920s, turned this account of the economic history of capitalism into a strategy for the country's development. He argued, with foolhardy bravery given the emerging power of Stalin, that the rural areas of Russia should be treated, within certain limits, as colonies of the urban industrial centres, the private peasantry as colonized labour of the State sector. By manipulating prices – using the State's monopoly of the supply of manufactured goods, and its dominant position as buyer of agricultural produce – accumulation in the hands of the State industrial sector could be accelerated. Again, it should be noted, this is not 'unequal exchange' in a free market, but the deliberate use of monopoly power to force a redistribution of the surplus in favour of one of the trading partners. Subsequently, Stalin appeared to copy the Preobazhensky case in a much more ruthless form, including the barbarism of collectivization, but in fact the Stalinist regime appears to have relied for accumulation on the exploitation of urban labour first and foremost rather than ransacking agriculture. (Although the disastrous effects of collectivization continued for many years, this was not matched by a substantial transfer of resources from rural to urban.)

THEORY OF TRADE

Speculation concerning the trade relationships between urban and rural, between producers of manufactured and of agricultural goods, within one country was inevitably paralleled by theories concerning relationships between exporters of manufactured and of agricultural goods in different countries. At the same time as Manoïlesco was formulating his case, a not dissimilar one was being developed in another country that was a major exporter of agricultural produce, Argentina. Raúl Prebisch, doyen of what later became development economics (as well as inspiration of the Economic Commission for Latin America, CEPAL, and, later, first chief of the United Nations Conference on Trade and Development, UNCTAD), began with two problems.

Firstly, between 1929 and 1933, the period of the Great Depression in the world system, the prices of Latin American exports declined disastrously, resulting in a 60 per cent fall in the region's export earnings. Yet, simultaneously, the prices of Latin America's manufactured imports did not fall: the squeeze was devastating.

Secondly, in the late 1940s, it seemed on the basis of various studies that raw material prices in world trade were tending to decline in the long term when compared to the prices of manufactured goods. Latin American exporters would therefore have to increase the volume of their raw material exports continually in order to earn the same revenue and thus be in a position to purchase the same quantity of manufactured imports.

Prebisch[7] offered different kinds of explanation for these phenomena, of which two were most influential. His first account turned upon the replacement of Britain by the United States as a dominant power in the world economy. In the nineteenth century, he argued, because of its size, Britain had imported most of its raw materials and exported capital to those areas of the world that produced raw materials; thus as the British economy grew, it simultaneously stimulated the growth of its trade partners – each end of the trade relationship grew in step with the other. However, the United States was a continental economy, rich in its own raw material resources and thus with a low propensity to import. As the US economy grew, its imports did not (at that time) expand on the same scale, and profitable opportunities within the United States tended to restrict the export of capital. Thus, the replacement of Britain by the United States introduced a severely negative force in the world system, reflected in the long-term deterioration in the terms of trade between manufactured and agricultural exporters which was in turn demonstrated in the drain of gold out of the rest of the world and into Fort Knox. The same case incidentally emerged in Europe in the late 1940s to explain what was seen as the permanent disequilibrium between the North American and European economies.[8]

The first case was an historically contingent one: it turned on the accidental characteristics of Britain and the United States. The second form of explanation was much more general. The prices of manufactured exports did not decline in a world slump, Prebisch argued, because the industrialized countries were able to hold them up, whereas the more backward countries could not sustain the prices of their raw material exports since there were many of them competing. Because of this powerful monopoly element, the benefits of technical progress which ought to have lowered the prices of manufactured exports did not do so; all the gain accrued to the sellers, none to the buyers (obversely, all the benefits of technical progress in the production of raw materials accrued to the buyers, not to the sellers). Thus, again, the monopoly position in one side of the trade relationship produced an unequal exchange.

Historically, the idea of a monopoly by the governments of the industrialized countries (the 'Centre' or 'Centres' as Prebisch now called them, merging the vital distinction between capital and the States) over the supply of manufactured goods to the less developed (or 'periphery') never seemed very plausible. Perhaps this was a reason for the radical revision of the case that came later: the prices of manufactured exports stayed high, it was now said, because the trade unions in Europe and North America were able to prevent wages and employment falling in a slump. Thus, the monopoly element was not in control of the supply of goods, but control of the supply of labour to produce the goods. The terms of trade were now determined by the class struggle. The weak or non-existent trade unions in the periphery, impotent to control a vast supply of low waged workers, could not hold the price of labour time in a slump. In sum, the gain to labour in the industrial countries was the direct loss to labour in the backward countries.

There were other explanations of unequal exchanges. Incomes were low in the backward countries, the market correspondingly small, so no economies of scale in production were possible and manufactured output could not compete with the Centres.[9] Hans Singer proposed that the long-term deterioration in the terms of trade occurred because of 'Engels Law', the proposition that raw material inputs to production declined as manufacturing output expanded (because of economies in the production process).[10] Arthur Lewis argued that the wages in backward countries were determined by a low level of subsistence costs there, so that workers in exporting sectors were, by world standards, underpaid; this artificially low price of labour produced surpluses that were transferred through foreign trade or profits to high wage countries where the foreign owners of the enterprises lived.[11]

All these cases were advanced by political reformists (as was Prebisch). The critique did not necessarily add up to a demand for radical political change. Prebisch's case supported an argument that the Latin American countries should seek to break out of their role in a specialized international division of labour by industrializing. Thus, they would claw back the benefits currently accruing to the Centres, equalizing trade relationships. To protect themselves against competition from the much more advanced manufacturing of the industrialized countries, their governments should control imports and support industrialization programmes. Later when the benefits of these changes seemed to have been exhausted, he argued for larger markets so that more elaborate economies of scale became possible (the background to the proposal for a Latin American Free Trade Area and other regional trading pacts), and for a direct assault upon the unfavourable conditions of international trade (through UNCTAD).

There was a different school of thinkers, the revolutionary nationalists, who took off from where Prebisch stopped, and expressed their case in Marxist terminology – for example, Paul Baran,[12] Samir Amin,[13] Arghiri Emmanuel,[14] and André Gunder Frank.[15]

The most clearly elaborated case was that presented by Emmanuel. The problem, he said, lay not with different types of commodities (raw materials or manufactured goods) but different classes of economy (backward and advanced). Even if the advanced exported raw materials and the backward manufactured goods, the price differences would stay the same, for the problem was a function of the distribution of wealth and power, not of type of goods.

Emmanuel took his starting point in the work of Ricardo, a classical economist writing immediately prior to Marx. Ricardo assumed that capital and labour were immobile between countries, so that the means to equalize prices in the system could be achieved not by moving capital or labour between countries, but by moving goods, international trade. Now the third factor of production, land, was even more immobile, and this allowed the landowners to divert a disproportionate share of the national surplus away from the other two factors. The landowners used the State to prevent imports, so keeping the prices of domestic agricultural produce high: the most immobile factor was thus able to operate a quasi-monopoly.

From the third quarter of the nineteenth century, Emmanuel says, capital became increasingly mobile, while land became a very marginal element in the composition of productive factors. Immobile labour, however, increasingly constituted itself, as land had been, as a monopoly. Control of the supply of workers allowed trade unions to determine wages and employment, to squeeze capital. By contrast, in the backward countries, labour remained disorganized and weak.

There was thus a fundamental asymmetry in the system – in one area, high wages and low profits; in the other, low wages and high profits, with international companies establishing a world profit rate between them. In the end, a few hours of labour in an industrialized country were rewarded with an income, says Emmanuel, thirty times as great as the reward to many hours of labour in a backward country. If living labour of the same skill was of equal value everywhere – as it ought to be under the labour theory of value – and labour was the sole source of value in goods produced, then the trade relationship between backward and advanced countries was a clear case of unequal exchange. That relationship, for Emmanuel, constituted the exploitation of the first by the second, the expropriation of the surplus value created by the proletariat of the backward countries by the workers of the advanced.

The case presented by Emmanuel was fascinating, worked out in great detail in its theoretical presentation but with surprisingly little empirical material. It was very influential, offering a theoretical rationale to the gut feeling of many Third World left-wing intellectuals who saw the contrast between the standard of living of workers in the industrialized countries and the horrifying poverty in the backward.

* * *

The critical observations on the theories of unequal exchange fall into two groups – contingent factors and theoretical observations.

Contingent factors.

In practice, there was no long-term deterioration in the terms of trade between backward and advanced, raw materials and manufactured goods. Deterioration there was in the bundle of goods exported in 1870 (both raw materials and manufactured goods) compared to the present, but the composition of the bundle had changed radically. There were considerable fluctuations, but not a trend – as the rapid rise and later decline in the real price of one raw material, oil, has shown. Furthermore, by today, the industrial countries export more raw materials than the less developed, and over half the exports of the less developed are manufactured goods. The old Prebisch diagnosis has disappeared.

Emmanuel does not distinguish between the mobility of financial capital and the relative immobility of productive capital. Today, there is almost 'perfect capital mobility' internationally among the industrialized countries, but factories can only with some difficulty be shipped round the globe. The distinction is important in understanding the different relationships of capital to the State, and so the plausibility of seeing a single entity, the Centre, where the interests of capital and the State are the same. If capital is more mobile, the immobility of labour is of declining importance – and in any case, labour is increasingly mobile (although on nothing like the scale of capital).

If, as Emmanuel suggests, the heart of unequal exchange arises from an immobile factor squeezing a mobile one, how is it that Emmanuel does not notice a more powerful immobile factor than labour, the State (a point made by Michael Kidron).[16] We would expect taxes to be more important than wages on this score.

It is also strange that capital does not as a whole go to the backward countries if that is where the profits are highest. That this has not happened suggests either that capital is not as mobile as Emmanuel thinks (it is required to remain *in situ* in the industrialized countries) or that business does not pursue profit maximization. In practice, the evidence suggests that today neither labour nor the State can prevent the mobility of finance capital, so that it is not at all clear why capital does not move. A second perverse outcome of the Emmanuel model is that unequal exchange can presumably be reversed if the State in the backward countries raises wages to the level of the advanced countries – the inequality is rectified immediately.

History has partly overtaken the case also, for Emmanuel does not explain how Japan and the Newly Industrializing Countries were able to beat the trend and move from raw materials to manufactured exports. Furthermore, with declining real wages and over 30 million unemployed in the industrialized countries in the mid-1980s, the case for the trade unions holding a monopoly of the supply of labour looks as silly as it ought always to have looked outside the editorial columns of *The Daily Telegraph*.

Theoretical points.

Emmanuel claimed to be a Marxist (Prebisch did not, even though the two cases have similarities), yet unlike Marx, he identifies trade, the sphere of circulation, as the mechanism of exploitation, not the relations of production. For Marx, the theory of value is not a function of the market but of the distribution of socially necessary labour time between branches of production and the requirements for the reproduction of the system.

Furthermore, for Emmanuel, wages are a freely self-determining element in the system, capable of overcoming market deterioration and defeating the theory of value (for according to him, wages in the industrial countries are far in excess of the socially necessary labour time required to reproduce the worker). For Marx, there are no independent variables – all are determined by, and in turn shape, the relations of production and the productive forces. Wages are among the most constrained elements in the system precisely because of their relationship to the generation of surplus value. For Emmanuel, not only can workers determine their own wages, which in turn determines prices; all other factors of production are omitted. This feature prevents Emmanuel seeing that the difference between advanced and backward countries is not in the politics of monopoly, but the scale of productive forces, the radically different organic compositions of capital, producing enormous differences in the productivity of labour (and so the price of goods). The problem of economic backwardness is not simply one of oppression by the dominant states, but of brute material scarcity, itself the product of different processes of accumulation not simply of exchange relationships.

There is an interesting cluster of issues here. For Emmanuel speaks of the industrialized countries 'exploiting' the backward as if this were the same as the exploitation of labour by capital. Capital and labour form a single production system, but it is quite unclear what single *production* (as opposed to trading) system two territorial areas could constitute. There are many forms by which resources can be appropriated by the more powerful, but they do not constitute exploitation in the Marxist sense – although, insofar as they imply unreasonable treatment, they may constitute exploitation in the popular sense. It is very difficult to see what the argument is if we take one whole country as capital, and one as labour – and transfers of wealth between them (even, as Marx describes it in the earlier citation, growing rich at the expense of another) do not show exploitation in the Marxist sense. Of course, the blurring of the distinction is very common; consider the speech of an Italian delegate, Graziadei, at the Second Congress of the Comintern:[17]

> Comrade Lenin poses the question in the following way: just as in every nation there are exploiters and exploited, so too in international relations there are nations that are exploited by other nations.

This is only a step away from the purely nationalist division of the world into 'proletarian' and 'bourgeois' nations,[18] the spirit of which would have been entirely comprehensible to Manoïlesco, but not to Marx. But one would not expect a scientific work by an author so steeped in Marx to perpetuate the muddle, a particularly significant one for the division between Marxism and nationalism.

Furthermore, even if we could say in a rigorous sense that the rich countries exploit the poor, this would still not constitute robbery or a relationship without net advantage to the exploited. The collapse of Marxist categories into populist nationalism produces the elimination of the contradictory nature of reality. Marx is careful in his formulation of this:[19]

> the circumstances that on the one hand, the daily subsistence of labour power costs only half a day's work, while on the other hand, the very same labour power can work during a whole day . . . is, without doubt, a piece of good luck for the buyer, but by no means an injury to the seller.

In sum then, while dominant States do indeed use their dominant position to attempt to transfer resources to themselves, employing brute force, political power, elements of monopoly, against weaker States, it is a dangerous theoretical confusion to call this 'exploitation' as if it were the same as the relationship of capital to labour. Emmanuel treats countries as homogeneous social classes.

In a similar fashion he omits serious attention to differences in the productivity of labour, relating these both to the very great differences in the prior accumulation of capital and the socially necessary costs of the reproduction of labour. Other things being equal, the higher the productivity of labour, the higher the income paid to the worker (since his or her reproduction costs are higher) and *the more exploited he or she is* – that is, the greater the proportion of the worker's output is appropriated by the employer. Kidron has convincingly demonstrated that, in the Marxist sense, British workers are more exploited than Indian.[20] The lower the productivity of labour, the more miserable and impoverished the worker, and the less the possibility that he or she can be very exploited. It follows from this that it remains true that the heart of the world system for the generation of surplus value remains that part of the working class which is most productive, located in the industrialized countries.

For Emmanuel, it seems, the Western working class has abolished itself, and is no longer exploited, for it has joined the bourgeoisie (a popular, middle-class prejudice of the 1960s in the First World, faithfully played back by the intellectuals of the Third World). It follows, although Emmanuel would not dare to voice such heresy, that the ruling classes of the Third World have joined the proletariat!

Nations and classes merge, and the State becomes, as in Stalinism, the primary instrument of the class struggle, alias the struggle to defend national independence.

The working class of the industrial countries, by becoming the bourgeoisie, come to exploit the masses of the backward countries. High wages in one area are possible only on the basis of low wages in the other. Underlying this idea is, it should be noted, the idea of a fixed wage fund. The real struggle is within the world working class: to appropriate the largest share of the fund. Indeed, capital begins to emerge as a neutral victim of this struggle, a picture much loved by Western conservatives. Trade unions may squabble, they say, but the total wage fund cannot be increased – only redistribution can take place from the weak to the strong.

Marx is turned on his head, for now the Western proletariat exploits the world. This is the authentic expression of the revolutionary nationalism of the rising bourgeoisie of the Third World, asserting the primacy of nationalist conflict between stronger and weaker ruling classes over world class struggle. It has the subsidiary purpose of providing a case to close borders to imports, so that the State can exploit a monopoly position (whether in alliance with local private capital or not) to force the pace of primitive accumulation. Once accomplished, the rulers return to the world market, quite unblushing at all the old nationalist rhetoric.

Far from a theory of unequal exchange being necessary for any theory of imperialism, the substitution of countries (or rather, States) for classes, destroys the theory of imperialism. For changes in the relationships between countries can accomplish the entire programme of social transformation. The heart of the theory of imperialism, the domination of the world system by a disproportionately powerful group of States, hitherto the homeland for the largest part of world capital, remains valid. But it does not mean static relationships between the geographical parts of the system, nor that all manufacturing will remain in the industrial countries (a point noted long ago by Lenin, following M. N. Roy). The world is divided still into spheres of influence of major powers, but it is not divided by different blocks of national capital. It is an over-politicized view to see no more than national entities, a view appropriate to Third World nationalism, but one which omits the dynamic force in the system, the world market.

8

The End of Economic Nationalism and the Emergence of a New World Order

INTRODUCTION

The now voluminous literature on South Korea's remarkable trajectory of growth[1] has been mainly preoccupied with identifying the domestic factors which account for development. This allows us to compare the pattern of growth with the other three 'Little Tigers' in East and South-East Asia (Taiwan, Hong Kong and Singapore) or with less developed countries in general. The differences between the Four are now well recognized: State direction in three; foreign capital domination in one (Singapore); free trade in two (Hong Kong, Singapore); dependence on small private enterprise in two (Taiwan, Hong Kong); agricultural procurements in one (Korea) and so on. They do not tell us a great deal about growth other than that *several* formulas are consistent with export-led industrialization. Nor is there reason to believe that the common features of the four by any means exhaust the possibilities. Indeed, the pioneers make it easier for those following them to separate the necessary from the extraneous features.

Starting the Korean growth process was also slightly accidental, and its management less clear in direction than subsequent rationalization often implies. The Korean State, as Bhagwati and Krueger put it, 'intervened as much and as "chaotically" on the side of export promotion as others have done on the side of import substitution'. The indisputable successes in achieving such a swift transition cannot therefore be attributed to 'the presence of a neoclassical efficiency allocation mechanism'.[2] In the heavy industrial and chemical programme of the 1970s, this is clear, for the Korean

Originally presented as a paper 'The key to Korean development: Economic nationalism or world economy?' for a colloquium on Specificity of development in East Asia, at the Center for Social Theory and Comparative History, University of California at Los Angeles, 5 June 1989.

State selected and created comparative advantages. Despite the heavy losses and reduction in shipbuilding and heavy machinery manufacture, nonetheless by 1986, 56 per cent of Korea's exports consisted of heavy and chemical industry products. Now Korea, like the other three of the four, is approaching an early maturity marked by labour shortages[3] and capitofxports.[4]

If the discussion of the causes of Korean development is restricted to domestic factors, the account has a misleadingly timeless quality (fully appropriate, of course, to economic theory): as if export-induced growth were always and everywhere equally possible, provided the government gets 'right' its policy stance and prices. This is certainly the message of many of the historians of Korea's growth; for example, Ian Little observes of the four that 'the success is almost entirely due to good policies and the ability of the people – scarcely at all to favourable circumstances or a good start'.[5] Such views give great comfort and moral support to the governments and economists concerned.

Too often, however, the reply has been restricted to disputing the enumeration or weighting of domestic factors – to indicate (rightly), for the two larger economies, the predominant role of the State in fixing domestic markets and external prices, particularly in ensuring the underpricing of labour (so that, far from approaching optimal allocation, the Korean labour force possibly subsidized the consumption of the rest of the world). The most that is acknowledged is that the two larger States were clients of the United States and, for some, this is the key force in growth (even though other US clients have not had the same growth experience). However, this approach tends to repeat the timeless character of the original thesis, and also take for granted the primacy of the national framework – and governmental relations – in explaining growth. Perversely, this nullifies one of the strengths of dependency[6] and world systems theory, its emphasis upon the external context of world capitalism.

The Prince missing from these versions of *Hamlet* is the changing structure, scale and composition of world demand. This is the other half of an explanation. It indicates why this pattern of growth, led by manufactured exports, did not occur before a particular historical moment. When that moment arrived, it became possible for the first time to mobilize in the service of world capital at least part of the vast mass of cheap labour in the less developed countries, and thereby change the capital–labour ratio with important implications for the future of capitalism and the development of technology. Thus, if this argument is correct, the significance of Korean development is far greater than the fate of that particular country, for it marks a turning point in the system as a whole, and one which will take a very long time to work itself out. The turning point could not have been easily anticipated, and it is this factor which gives much greater sense to import-substitution strategies of industrialization in the 1950s than appears to many observers today.

The exploration of this theme in this paper provides us with an entry point to considering broader issues of the type of world capitalism emerging and the prospects for economic development.

A WORLD PROCESS

The changes taking place between the 1950s and the 1980s in South Korea were by no means restricted either to that country or the three other 'Little Tigers'. Concentrating on the one case or the four obscures the fact that these were only the most extreme versions of a much wider process, affecting the majority of less developed countries to a greater or lesser extent, whether or not the governments concerned consciously tried to exploit the process or not. Indeed, the precipitation of growth in the 1960s seems to some extent much cruder and simpler in purely economic terms than is often assumed: where the structure of current output and pricing (including the exchange rate) were appropriate, then it became possible to enter the learning process that, with luck and persistence, produced the quality and flexibility required to exploit a particular niche in the world demand for manufactured goods. Of course, few countries were socially and politically equipped to undertake the initial process: and it is here that some of the main obstacles to development occur. Furthermore, there were a host of failures. In addition, noting the beginnings of the process is to say nothing about the very different conditions of the 1980s (which will be discussed later), nor about the desirability of the process and the scale of hardships involved in economic growth.

In an earlier analysis of the 27 developing countries exporting goods worth $1 billion or more in 1980[7] – countries including some 54 per cent of the world's population – it could be seen that virtually all had experienced rates of growth of exports well ahead of the rate of increase of world trade. Furthermore, for all 27 countries, the increase in manufactured exports was much faster than the increase in exports as a whole. To the four Little Tigers, we should add some other high performers – Israel (where manufactured exports increased from 62 per cent in 1960 to 82 per cent in 1980), Yugoslavia (from 38 to 73 per cent), and Portugal (54 to 72 per cent). Finally, in all cases, the skill intensity of manufactured exports increased if we take as a surrogate of this exports of 'machinery and transport equipment' (which on average increased from 2 to 10 per cent). For the nine leading countries, this category increased from 4 to 23 per cent. This was the picture in 1980 when South Korea's exports were put at $19 billion, whereas now they are said to be approaching $70 billion. In sum, up to 1980, what happened in Korea and the other three was only an extreme version of what has been happening to most exporting developing countries.

There are important qualifications. First is the great inequality in participation between countries. Second, the relative role of exports varies in part with the size of the country (a large country is able to internalize the manufacture of a greater proportion of the goods it requires); the smaller a country, the more dramatic the rates of increase and changes in composition of exports. Third, the size of the manufactured exports of the 27 countries are still far below that of the developed countries; even combining the 27, their total manufactured exports in 1980 were only equal to 91 per cent of those of the United States or 10 per cent larger than Japan's. Furthermore, the total exports of the 27 in 'machinery and transport equipment' were equal to 38 per cent of the United States or West Germany, 47 per cent of Japan, 82 per cent of Britain. The leading developing country in this respect, Singapore, exported in 1980 only just over one third as much as Belgium (but was approaching two-thirds by 1986).

If we expand the picture to include all developing countries (and include the first four years of the 1980s), the relative growth rates of manufactured exports by different regions are as follows:

	Low-income Africa	Latin America & Caribbean	Europe, Mid. E, North Africa	Middle Income	All LDCs
1967–73	5.5	17.1	9.0	15.1	12.4
1974–79	15.0	10.2	5.2	12.8	11.3
1980–84	−12.7	9.7	12.6	10.1	11.2

The categories of trade conceal important changes of content. For example, the limits on garment imports to the developed countries under the quota system imposed from the late 1950s and subsequently embodied in the successive versions of the Multi-Fibre Arrangement have forced exporters to increase the value of the same quantity of goods (or relocate production to a country which has not yet filled its quota). This makes room for newcomers to export low valued garments. Even so, the leading countries have tried to hang on to their garment exports for as long as possible. In the case of South Korea and Taiwan, it has taken the sharp appreciation in their currencies to reduce garment exports. Taiwan's currency has appreciated by 40 per cent in three years, and at last textile and garment exports fell by 10 per cent in 1988 (toys and sportswear, −8.2 per cent; footwear, −7.9 per cent). Newcomers have been able to take over the markets of the four, as the four originally took over Japan's markets. The newcomers include China, Indonesia, Malaysia, Thailand, Sri Lanka and, most recently, Mauritius (where a quarter of the capital involved is officially reported to be from Hong Kong).

Table 8.1 brings the story up to 1986. It covers two groups of countries – the 18 with the poorest record in terms of growth of gross domestic product in the 1980s, and the 21 which experienced a GDP rate of growth of 4 per cent or more (listed according to per capita income). Eleven of the 18 had negative rates of growth of exports. However, of the 17 where the information was available, 13 had experienced long-term growth (1965–86) in the share of manufactured goods in exports, some of them remarkably so (for example, Haiti, the Philippines, Uruguay, Trinidad and Tobago). Twelve had increased the share of machinery and transport equipment. Countries with negative GDP growth rates are not necessarily the worst-off (for that, the list would have had to include Ethiopia and Sudan which just missed inclusion by having positive growth rates – 0.8 and 0.3 per cent respectively), but it is still remarkable that the same changes in structure of exports can be seen here, despite the grave severity of the crisis afflicting these countries.

The 21 fast growers include some of the largest countries – China, India, Pakistan – in the low-income group. Only two had a negative rate of growth of exports, and some had particularly high rates – China, Thailand, Cameroon, Turkey, Mauritius, Malaysia, South Korea, Hong Kong. Of the 20 for which data were available, 14 showed a marked shift to manufactured exports, and 12 to an increase in exports of machinery and transport equipment.

In sum, then, despite the poor rate of growth of world trade in the 1980s and the growth of protectionism in the developed countries, the rates of growth of a significant number of developing countries continued to be high. The most important cases here are the striking improvement for China, and, to a much lesser extent, India, together raising the rate of growth of GDP for the low-income group from 4.8 (1965–80) to 7.5 (1980–86). The period covers a sharp contraction in the world system – with rising oil prices, for a time an appreciating dollar, high international interest rates (both affecting cumulative debts) and a collapse of raw material export prices.

Table 8.1 *Low and high growth in developing countries 1980–86*

	1. Rate of change GDP	*2. Rate of change exports %*	*3. Manuf. Exports (%mach. and tpt)*	
			1965	*1986*
Negative growth rates:				
Low-income				
Mozambique	−9.0%	—	2% (0)	—(—)
Madagascar	−0.1	−3.7	5 (1)	12 (2)
Togo	−1.1	−6.6	5 (1)	20 (1)
Niger	−2.6	−13.4	5 (1)	3 (1)
Zambia	−0.1	−2.1	0 (0)	3 (1)
Haiti	−0.7	+3.4	25 (2)	63 (10)
Lower-middle income				
Liberia	−1.3	−2.0	4 (1)	1 (0)
Philippines	−1.0	−1.7	6 (0)	61 (6)
Bolivia	−3.0	0.0	4 (0)	2 (0)
Nigeria	−3.2	−6.0	2 (0)	1 (0)
Côte d'Ivoire	−0.3	+3.5	5 (1)	9 (2)
El Salvador	−1.0	−6.3	17 (1)	23 (2)
Guatemala	−1.2	−2.5	14 (1)	32 (2)
Peru	−0.4	+0.1	1 (0)	23 (3)
Upper-middle income				
Uruguay	−2.6	+0.9	5 (0)	42 (2)
Argentina	−0.8	+1.5	6 (1)	22 (6)
Venezuela	−0.9	−1.4	2 (0)	9 (3)
Trinidad & Tobago	−6.3	−8.1	7 (0)	31 (9)
High growth rates (4% or more)				
Low-income				
Burma	4.9	−0.2	0 (0)	13 (9)
Somalia	4.9	−7.9	14 (4)	1 (0)
India	4.9	+3.8	49 (1)	62 (10)
PR China	10.5	11.7	46 (3)	64 (16)
Pakistan	6.7	6.2	36 (1)	68 (3)
Sri Lanka	4.9	6.4	1 (0)	41 (2)
Lower-middle income				
Yemen AR	4.3	1.9	0 (0)	—(—)
Egypt	4.7	7.4	20 (0)	13 (0)
Thailand	4.8	9.2	4 (0)	42 (9)
Botswana	11.9	—	—	—
Cameroon	8.2	13.8	5 (3)	6 (1)

Table 8.1 continued

	1. *Rate of change GDP*	2. *Rate of change exports %*	3. *Manuf. Exports (%mach. and tpt)* 1965	1986
Congo PR	5.1	5.4	63 (2)	19 (1)
Turkey	4.9	19.9	2 (0)	56 (5)
Mauritius	4.4	10.4	0 (0)	41 (2)
Jordan	5.1	5.7	18 (11)	59 (10)
Upper-middle income				
Malaysia	4.8	10.2	6 (2)	36 (26)
S. Korea	8.2	13.2	59 (3)	91 (33)
Algeria	4.4	0.9	4 (2)	2 (0)
Oman	5.7	6.7	0 (0)	1 (0)
Hong Kong	6.0	10.7	87 (6)	92 (21)
Singapore	5.3	6.1	35 (11)	68 (38)

Columns: 1. Annual rate of increase of GDP, 1980–86. 2. Annual rate of increase in exports, 1980–86. 3. and 4. Manufacturing exports, 1965 and 1986, with the proportion of exports provided by machinery and transport equipment in brackets.

Source: World Bank, *World Development Report 1988*, Tables 2, 11 and 12.

Thus, there has been real growth. Nor is this simply in shares of trade. There has been significant growth in the productive forces, as can be seen in Table 8.2 for the selection of countries with the highest rates of growth of manufacturing. The fragility of this, however, is indicated in the much less consistent performance in investment: seven of the eighteen countries experienced negative rates of growth. The figures show a growth in the potential for improving the conditions of people, but *not* necessarily an improvement in conditions. As a salutary reminder of the contradictory nature of growth, Table 8.3 lists all the countries which experienced a decline in per capita food production in the 1980s. In Zambia, a 1987 UNICEF study at Lusaka University hospital shows that, of the 433 children admitted there in a one-week period, 60 per cent of the more than one hundred who died were suffering from malnutrition. Thus, the growth of capital and the growth of consumption need not go together at all.

Slow growth in the world system conceals a considerable heterogeneity, but it does not rule out changing shares of world trade and production. The greater the disaggregation of the figures –

Table 8.2 *Growth of manufacturing, selected developing countries 1980–86*

	1. Rate of growth of manuf.	*2. Proportion manuf. in GDP*	*3. Gross dom. investment*
Low-income			
Burma	5.8	10	−2.8
Burundi	6.9	10	5.0
Benin	4.6	4	−15.5
India	8.2	19	4.6
China	12.6	34	19.3
Pakistan	9.3	17	7.5
Lesotho	16.1	13	—
Sri Lanka	5.6	15	−4.9
Lower-middle income			
Indonesia	7.7	14	3.7
Yemen AR	16.5	7	−12.9
Thailand	5.2	21	0.8
Botswana	6.2	6	−6.9
Turkey	8.0	25	5.1
Tunisia	6.5	15	−1.8
Mauritius	7.8	23	11.7
Jordan	4.9	14	−5.8
Upper-middle income			
Malaysia	5.8	—	0.8
South Korea	9.8	30	9.6
More Developed (average)	2.3	23	1.7

1. Annual rate of growth of value added in manufacturing, all less developed with a rate of 4.5 per cent or more, 1980–1986. 2. Manufacturing as a proportion of GDP, 1986. 3. Gross domestic investment, rate per annum, 1980–86.

Source: Ibid., Tables 2, 3 and 4.

Table 8.3 *Average index of food production per capita (1979/81=100) – in order of GNP per capita*

Ethiopia	87	Haiti	96	Cameroon	94
Bangladesh	98	Lesotho	82	Guatemala	97
Malawi	90	Sierra L.	97	Congo PR	93
Mozambique	85	Mauritania	88	Colombia	96
Madagascar	98	Afghanistan	99	Costa Rica	92
Burundi	98	Guinea	93	Syria	94
Tanzania	92	Liberia	99	S. Africa	83
Togo	91	Yemen PDR	89	Mexico	97
Niger	85	Philippines	94	Panama	98
Somalia	98	Bolivia	93	Argentina	99
C. African R.	94	Zimbabwe	92	Venezuela	93
Rwanda	87	Papua NG	99	Gabon	98
Kenya	87	Honduras	86	Trinidad	92
Zambia	96	Nicaragua	76	Singapore	97
Sri Lanka	85	El Salvador	90	Iran	99
Sudan	96	Botswana	76		

Source: Ibid., Table 7.

by country, region or locality on the one hand, by sector, subsector and individual commodity, on the other – the greater the divergence from the aggregate performance. Textiles and garments as a general category had long stagnated in the 1950s when the Four Little Tigers turned the manufacture of garments into the means to high growth; while developed country consumption increased by 3 per cent, developing country exports increased by 20 per cent per year. Indeed, in conditions of stagnating markets, the search for lower costs of production can lead to the swifter relocation of capacity than would otherwise be the case – and so increasing shares of the trade in the hands of newcomers.

The 1980s have seen many examples of this. The largest is China, with a rate of increase in textile and garment exports of 10 per cent per year since 1979, increasing the country's share of US imports of this kind from 1 to 8 per cent (1978–82). Pakistan has now begun to expand in this field. Malaysia is already well known as a second-rank Newly Industrializing Country, raising its rate of growth from 4.4 per cent annually (1965–80) to 10.2 per cent in the 1980s. Thailand increased similarly from 8.5 to 9.2 per cent; in 1986 and 1987, Thai manufactured exports increased by 40 per cent per year (with garments and textiles up 81, footwear 73 and leather goods 208 per cent). Even India is currently expanding manufacturing output by close to 10 per cent annually. The examples are not restricted to Asia. As mentioned earlier, the small economy of Mauritius entered a fast growth phase in the 1980s, led by manufacturing (mainly textiles and garments); annual export growth rose from 3.4 (1965–80) to 10.4 per cent (1980–86); between 1984 and 1987, real GDP rose by 25 per cent and per capita income doubled (in current prices), the real standard of living improving by a third.

The rates of growth of exports of particular categories of commodities have continued to be high in the 1980s. Thus, the annual growth in exports of office and telecommunication equipment between 1980 and 1987 reached 15 per cent; for garments, 10.5 per cent; motor vehicles, 9 per cent; household appliances, 8.5 per cent; machinery and transport equipment, 6 per cent; chemicals, 6 per cent. In 1987, the star performer was the export of garments, rising by 30 per cent in that year.[8]

There are, of course, no guarantees that spurts of growth will be sustained in particular countries. We have the striking example of Colombia which increased its manufactured exports between 1968 and 1974 at the same pace as Taiwan, but then suddenly fell back to slow growth.[9] The issue is not now whether this country or that expands, but laying out the evidence for a change in the structure of world demand, a change that has persisted into an era of slow world growth and one where certain sets of notorious problems in developing countries – famine and debt in Sub-Saharan Africa, debt in Latin America – might lead one to underestimate the heterogeneity of performance. Growth continues in a significant number of countries, and growth that is also structural development based upon rising productivity.

'TRICKLE DOWN'

In terms of the history of capitalism, perhaps nothing implied so far about the redistribution of world economic activity would be surprising. With all the notorious unevenness and cyclical character of the system, up to the First World War, there were simultaneously strong tendencies to develop new areas. The spread of economic development from Western Europe to North America and Central Europe, to southern Europe and selected areas elsewhere illustrates this effect. With the 'natural' comparative advantage of high transport costs – and, as Gunder Frank has pointed out, the suspension of

European manufactured exports in time of world war – manufacturing developed in a number of economically backward areas. Employment in Brazilian textiles – with the additional protection of tariffs and an exchange rate free of the gold standard – increased from 2,000 in 1895 to 26,400 in 1905 and 53,000 in 1907. By the 1920s, Brazil met 64 per cent of its domestic manufacturing supply (and over 90 per cent of its traditional manufacturing); much of the machinery employed in the coffee industry was locally made.[10] In India, the factory textile industry grew rapidly up to the 1920s when the country was estimated to possess the third largest textile industry in the world; by then, the textile labour force was big enough to be politically significant. The same is true in China which still commemorates the first great general strike following the May 30th movement. China had, from a low base point, very high rates of growth of manufacturing output in the interwar years, exaggerated by the development of Japanese heavy industry in Manchuria.[11] These beginnings in many countries (but not all) may initially have been restricted to light industry in the main and may have inflicted upon the workforce conditions of appalling severity, but they did represent a spread of manufacturing capacity even in the years of stagnation between the world wars.

What is surprising is that this possibility of geographical spread of manufacturing through the operation of capitalism was held to have ceased by the time of the Second World War. In the perception of the Left and the liberal centre, the market was dominated by geopolitics, and thus the hold of the dominant States on the main areas of manufacturing – in Europe and North America – was seen as permanently preventing relocation of all but the most trivial elements of manufacturing (which would primarily be light manufacturing). Why did this view develop?

The experience of the more advanced developing countries, particularly those in Latin America, was that, under the impact of the Great Depression of the interwar years, the prices of their raw material exports collapsed precipitately (whereas the prices of European manufactured exports did not) and they were blocked out of their main markets in Europe and North America by protectionism. The European States also assumed powers over the movement of capital. The cumulative debts and the level of servicing payments forced most of the Latin American countries to default. The only counteraction possible was to slash imports, erect barriers to import growth and control currencies. Thus, 'import-substitution industrialization' was not freely chosen as a strategy; it was forced upon governments by necessity. Furthermore, it was the politics of the dominant powers which had inflicted this damage on what were seen now as dependent economies.

A not dissimilar evolution of ideas took place in Europe and North America. Competitive markets were displaced by the building of national (or imperial) economic fortresses (and the language of war came to dominate economic relationships). The movement of capital and finance was tightly restricted, currencies controlled, external trade regulated. An era of State capitalism, based upon external controls, large public sectors and officially encouraged cartelization, was introduced and persisted in certain respects in Europe even as late as 1960. Governments overwhelmingly stressed the need for national economic independence. Not until after 1945, when the United States, with unprecedented political and military power and a strong economic interest, began to prise open the European empires, were the first moves made towards greater liberalization.

Thus, elements of autarchy were forced upon the Latin Americans by the Great Depression and confirmed by the following period of war economies. All were dedicated to safeguarding or achieving a basis of national economic independence that supposedly corresponded to political independence. In developed countries, it was assumed that the State and its political interest dominated and ought to dominate economies and markets. It was scarcely surprising that the newly independent former colonial possessions of Europe sought to follow exactly the same model. To do otherwise, it was thought, was to risk long-term stagnation, and the experience of the 1930s was there to support this proposition.

The process of internationalization of the world economy that had seemed so clear in 1914 (albeit divided among empires) was frustrated by war and slump. It was this unanticipated check that in part frustrated Marxist prognostications concerning world capitalism. Before 1914, economic internationalization was taken for granted and, indeed, the idea of national *economic* independence was seen as both utopian and reactionary. In the debate on the national question between, on the one hand, Rosa Luxemburg and the Left (including Bukharin, Radek, etc.) and, on the other, Lenin and the Bolshevik majority, neither side for a moment entertained the idea that there was any sense in national economic independence. The dispute was between Luxemburg who derived from the end of national economic independence the implication that there could be, in Europe, no political independence either so that European revolutionary national liberation now made no sense, and Lenin who argued that the one did not follow from the other:[12]

> The domination of finance capital and of capital in general is not to be abolished by *any* reforms in the sphere of political

> democracy; and self-determination belongs wholly to this sphere. This domination of finance capital, however, does not in the least nullify the significance of political democracy as a freer, wider and clearer *form* of class oppression and class struggle.

Furthermore, implicit in Lenin's account of imperialism[13] is an assumption of the geographical spread of manufacturing. Europe and North America were becoming rentier or bondholding States, while the proletariat would be concentrated in the 'backward and colonial countries'; the inhabitants of the developed countries would then be reduced simply to a servicing role, setting 'the seal of parasitism on the whole country which lives by the exploitation of the labour of several overseas countries and colonies'. It was a theme later developed by M. N. Roy and R. Palme Dutt for India as constituting that country's economic 'decolonization'; the British were, they said, encouraging the industrialization of their imperial possessions in order to build industrial reserves against the possibility of a working-class revolution in the metropolitan country.

With the benefit of hindsight, the perspective seems bizarre. World slump and very slow rates of growth of trade along with State capitalism in Europe and North America preserved and perhaps increased the dominance of the developed countries in world manufacturing as well as in finance, capital, and military capacity. In 1945, national State-managed capitalism, whether for war or peace, was taken as the norm by governments and economists. The discussiions around efforts to open the European economies and establish the Bretton Woods postwar system revealed the deep suspicions of Europeans that these were no more than attempts to establish American economic hegemony. Even Keynes, one of the architects of the new order, resisted the new trends. One of his 1943 government memos reads,[14]

> I am, I am afraid a hopeless sceptic about the return to nineteenth century *laissez faire* . . . I believe that the future lies with (1) State trading for commodities; (2) international cartels for necessary manufactures; and (3) quantitative import restrictions for non-essential manufactures.

If generals are always fighting the last war, ministries of finance and economists are always reacting to the last slump. In 1945, just as in 1918, the prognostications based upon the past were wrong. From 1947, as everyone knows, the world economy entered a phase of unprecedented and unanticipated growth that lasted for much of the following quarter of a century. As in the last half of the nineteenth century, the expansion of trade was significantly faster than the growth of production. But this time, the heart of the growth was not inter-industry exchanges (say, raw materials for manufactured goods) but intra-industry exchanges, dominated by manufacturing (and led by the engineering and chemicals industries). Indeed, the developed now displaced the developing countries as the major exporters of raw materials. In manufacturing, the opening of developed national economies began to create a single sector, with specialized parts in different countries.

The growth was so fast and lasted so long that it produced an unprecedented geographical shift in manufacturing capacity. We have seen something of this in relation to developing countries. But, relatively, this was quite small; between 1950 and 1980, the developing country share of world gross manufacturing production (excluding the Eastern bloc) increased from 12.7 to 17.9 per cent. More significant was the relative decline in the old established manufacturing powers, which seemed to continue the process of the nineteenth-century shift in shares. Between 1880 and 1913, the British share of world manufacturing exports declined from 41.1 to 29.9 per cent (while the United States increased from 7.8 to 12.6, and Germany from 19.3 to 26.5 per cent). In 1948, the United States produced, in exceptional conditions of postwar economic ruin in Europe, 47 per cent of gross world production (again excluding the Eastern bloc for lack of comparable data), and 33 per cent in 1987. In 1950, the US economy produced 76 per cent of world manufacturing output, and 28 per cent in 1979 (North America with Europe in the same period fell from 97 to 65 per cent). Even in the period 1970–85, this shift in manufacturing capacity has continued, as shown in Table 8.4. In sum, newcomers, whether classed as developed or developing countries, increased their share of world manufacturing capacity from 31 to 42 per cent in a mere fifteen years (ten of which were no longer in the high growth phase of the world economy).

However, there seems to be a qualitative change in what we call 'manufacturing'. The elaboration of linkages within manufacturing industry is such that most plants make the inputs for other plants. This separation and specialization has, as is now well known, permitted the dispersal of plants to utilize locational advantages for a particular stage. The World Bank's *World Development Report 1987* offers a picture of this internationalization of the individual commodity in a chart showing the 15 countries which directly contribute parts to the assembly of a European Ford Escort automobile. If we had details of an earlier round, countries supplying the 15 with components for their output, we would find more and more of the

Table 8.4 *Value added in manufacturing (% of total, current dollars)*

	1970	*1985*	*% Increase 1970–85*
Developing countries			
Total	14.7	20.1	
(1) Low-income	5.7	5.9	361
(2) Middle-income	9.0	14.2	557
Developed countries			
Total	85.3	79.9	336
(1) Old-established	68.6	58.2	306
(2) Newcomers[a]	16.7	21.7	426
(Excluding the Eastern bloc)			

[a] This is inevitably arbitrary, but includes Spain, Ireland, Finland, Italy and Japan.

world involved. Unfortunately, the level of disaggregation of world trade makes it difficult to go very far in identifying the specialization of different manufacturing locations, let alone allowing anticipation of dynamic changes that flow from innovations both in production and transport, as well as changes in government policies and exchange rates. The most that can be seen is the decline or increase in shares of aggregated sectors – as with Japan's current loss of labour-intensive manufacturing to Thailand, Malaysia, Indonesia, relocation of middle-skill manufacturing to Taiwan and Korea, and high-skill to North America and Europe. Nor is there some smooth progression from one stage to another in the chain of skill intensity, a kind of queue of countries waiting to move through predetermined phases of the product cycle. Governments are continually trying to jump the queue. China exports satellites as well as textiles and garments; India computer software; Malaysia automobiles.

The development of specialized roles in the creation of a commodity has important implications for government and business behaviour. For example, the change builds into the structure of manufacture the need to keep borders open, for the exports cannot be produced without imports. Thus, it is easily comprehensible why the major US automobile manufacturers led the campaign to prevent limitation in the import of automobile components. In the developed countries manufacturing seems to be moving towards what used to be seen as the characteristic of developing countries – manufacture through the assembly of imported parts. Conventional government policy is accordingly more limited than in the past, for reducing imports cuts inputs into both domestic consumption and exports. Hitherto, it has been customary for governments to regard external trade as a residual, what is left over after domestic consumption has been met. But in an integrated manufacturing economy, external transactions become fundamental to domestic activity.

INTERNATIONALIZATION

However, the growth of manufactured exports and the integration of manufacturing industries in different countries is not necessarily the most advanced form of internationalization in the world economy, although it is undoubtedly one of the most important for developing countries. Financial markets have long been more advanced in this respect, particularly with the prodigious growth of offshore markets, now of a size that places them beyond the effective management of the combined resources of the developed country governments.[15] Within that growth of a world pool of liquidity, world debt has provided powerful forces of centralization on particular markets for individuals, companies and sovereign borrowers.

Furthermore, the liberalization of capital movements has permitted an accelerated integration of capital resources, making it increasingly difficult to identify the nationality of larger corporations. (Both the criteria with which to identify nationality and the significance of nationality are in any case becoming obscure.) The generalization is too broad, for corporations stand in different relationships to the heart of nationalism, the State. The size of the US defence budget, for example, obliges a range of large corporations to relate directly, and patriotically, to the Federal Government in a way that is not true of others. The United States is in a special position in another way since it is overwhelmingly the largest market, so that all world corporations are likely to find it necessary to locate significant operations there; all multinational corporations, regardless of origin, are obliged to be 'American' in some sense.

For smaller powers, the operation of the markets seems to dilute the nationality of corporations. In Europe there is growing confusion on this question – illustrated in the different attitudes of the British and French Governments on whether Nissan (Britain) is a Common Market or Japanese company. The British Government agonized, and the Defence Minister resigned, over whether Westland helicopters should be 'American' (owned by a consortium of companies, the two largest being registered in the United States and Italy) or 'European' (another consortium, let by two companies, one registered in France and one in Germany). Should Landrover become 'American' or 'German'? Fortunately we were spared public agonizing over whether Rowntrees chocolate should become 'Swiss' (it has become so, without notable change). The confusion illustrates some of the difficulty in seeing the State as an executive committee of the national bourgeoisie, rather than a competitor for the favours of an international bourgeoisie.

Hitherto, these processes of increased international integration have tended to affect North America and Europe, while the latecomers, Japan and the more advanced developing countries, have retained a much clearer national separation. However, the remarkable appreciation of the Yen has forced companies in Japan to internationalize swiftly. In the case of manufacturing, it used to be the case that only some 3–4 per cent of the value of the manufacturing output of Japan was undertaken outside the country, compared to 18–20 per cent for the United States. Now the outflow from Japan of direct foreign investment in manufacturing has tripled between 1986 and 1989 (45 per cent to the United States, 20 per cent to Europe and 15 per cent to Asia). The outflow in other forms of finance has, of course, been much greater.

As noted earlier, the Four Tigers have also become exporters of capital (as well as continuing to be importers). They are among the creators of new national pools of capital (and their own multinational corporations) which are likely to be increasingly significant and, again, indicate the 'trickle-down' effect of capitalist growth. It is difficult to quantify this phenomenon, but the International Finance Corporation survey of the capitalization of developing country stock exchanges offers some surrogate measures. Thus, Taiwan has become one of the top twelve stock exchanges in the world, its capitalization now equal to over half that of London. For the 30 leading developing countries, capitalization has grown from $95 billion in 1984 to $377.4 billion in 1988; and in terms of the volume of transactions, the total for the 30 is now equal to a sixth of Tokyo's.[16]

There are other components of internationalization where integration is slower. In the field of labour, the Four Tigers have, under the impact of labour scarcities, begun to attract legal and illegal immigration (see Note 3), a key sign of 'maturity'. At the opposite extreme, the cities of the United States in general, and California in particular, lead the rest of the world in the remarkable cosmopolitanization of the workforce. One of the continuing strengths of US capitalism, in contrast to Japan and Europe, is its recruitment of labour from the rest of the world, from the highest to the lowest levels of skill.

In the case of import controls, governments are economically motivated to permit free entry while politically obliged to cheat on the rules to a greater or lesser extent. With immigration, it is the reverse; the rules imply tight control and this is popularly supposed to represent political wisdom, while the practice allows, to a greater or lesser extent, systematic cheating. The contradictions appear stark, however. Hong Kong, with an officially estimated labour shortage of 130,000 workers, is nonetheless simultaneously moving towards the compulsory repatriation of Vietnamese boatpeople. Singapore's growth depends upon an inflow of unskilled immigrants (in construction, domestic service, hotels and restaurants), yet it treats unskilled immigrants extremely harshly and is currently threatening illegal immigrants with whipping and expulsion. Japan, with a currently estimated 200,000 or so illegal immigrants, is officially opposed to immigration. However, the demographic reshaping of the population will make for a considerable labour scarcity, particularly in the young and unskilled categories, so that it will hardly be possible to operate the economy after the year 2000 without some form of immigration.

In fact, the ageing of the populations of the developed countries collides with existing immigration regulations. Most governments are expecting a decline in the active labour force, and a sharp decline in the young worker group, while aged dependants increase. This simultaneously affects the labour force in standard manufacturing and in low paid services (including those provided for the aged), as well as the activity rates required to meet the increased burden of pensions for an enlarged retired population. This would suggest a number of reforms; for example, lengthening the working life and the continued export of manufacturing capacity to developing countries (or increased imports). But there still remains a component of the labour force which cannot be substituted, ranging from the armed forces to construction and services. This would suggest developed country governments will be obliged to liberalize immigration controls.

Access to services with low labour costs can be obtained in other forms of internationalization. It may become possible for more parts of the Third World to become, like Florida, a location for the retired (this already occurs to some extent). The international tourist trade, now one of the largest earners of foreign exchange in the developing countries, can be seen as also a means to secure access to cheap services. Of course, all these sectors of activity collide directly with the old idea of national independence and conjure up images of subordination and indignity. However, in economic terms, they also represent, albeit on a very unequal basis, a redistribution of economic activity tending, even if under very limited circumstances, towards the greater equalization of income.

Thus, in sum, while one can easily identify powerful political pressures to restore the old form of economic nationalism in the developed countries, there would appear to be strong structural features that not only resist this but continue to impel the world system towards greater integration. Short of generalized collapse, the reactions to the Great Depression – separating out economically distinct national or imperial economies from the world system – are unlikely to be repeated (which is not to say that there cannot be a major slump). This means that the opportunity for a redistribution of manufacturing towards developing countries has a reasonable chance of continuing, and while this may not entail, in conditions of slow world growth, such dramatic cases as that of South Korea, it does provide a perspective for the growth of capitalism in those countries able to participate in the trend.

In sum, the economic promise of capitalism may still not have been exhausted.

EXPLANATIONS

What were and are some of the factors which encouraged the geographical spread of certain sub-sectors of manufacturing capacity to developing countries? One of the more obvious was the break-up of empire and its enforced economic disciplines. An unprecedented number of new States were created, with the political autonomy which is a precondition for most governments to manage their economies. Many made major attempts at improving the skills of the labour force (the literacy rate of developing countries improved from 33 per cent in 1950 to 50 per cent in 1979) and building an appropriate infrastructure (power, water, drainage, irrigation, highways, sea and air terminals, etc.). The achievements have been astonishing. Never before have such enormous improvements been made so rapidly as those undertaken by the newly independent governments (achievements which are starkly contrasted with those of the imperial period). Furthermore, the physical condition of their populations has also improved remarkably. While a significant proportion may have experienced no improvement, and some a deterioration, for the majority the changes were sufficiently radical to make for dramatic improvements in the figures for average life expectancy, one of the most sensitive indices of, among other things, protein intake.

Many of these changes were concentrated in particular localities, cities or regions, thus implying higher standards there than the average. Accordingly, some of the conditions were achieved for attaining the same (or even better) levels of labour productivity in the developing as in the developed countries. Simultaneously, many governments were making great efforts to industrialize, based in the 1970s on rising levels of domestic savings (as opposed to an inflow of foreign capital).

These changes were the results, in part, of government action. But there were other important factors that occurred independently of governments. Thus, the costs of transport and communications fell rapidly. The importance of this was enhanced by innovations in transport equipment, reducing fuel consumption and so the cost of moving freight. This effect was increased by the sustained efforts to reduce the average weight of goods moved (particularly by the continuous reduction in the use of steel per unit of output). As movement became cheaper, less hazardous, speedier, the possibility of spreading the geographical location of manufacturing plants grew, initially for goods of low weight and high value. Now transport economies have radically transformed stock policies, allowing for the 'just-in-time' system.

There have also been – as noted earlier – important changes in breaking down the protectionism of the developed countries. The decline in economic borders between the dominant powers allowed for a new pattern of specialization among them, creating a single interdependent manufacturing economy. The minority of developing countries with the industrial capacity, and the social orders, able to exploit this new structure of demand, were the incidental beneficiaries, a position enhanced by special rights, bilateral treaties, a generalized system of preferences, etc. Indeed, the United States, and to a lesser extent, Europe, encouraged part processing abroad of domestically manufactured products (in the case of the United States, under tariffs 806.3 and 807).

However, many of these factors would have facilitated the redistribution of manufacturing capacity, but would not have caused it. For that we must assume not only general growth in the world system, but a change in the structure of demand. This possibly arose out of the growing shortages of supply in labour-intensive sectors of manufacturing within the developed countries. Buyers from Europe were driven to search out new sources of, initially, garments. Hong Kong, completely open to external demand changes, responded and was driven into the process of self-transformation. The other three of the Four then copied Hong Kong through deliberate State intervention. This State-directed process of the three shaped the growth to expand heavy industry disproportionately, and to build an old-style 'national' economy, rather than to emulate Hong Kong's narrow range of specializations.

The 1950s were the crucial period for this transition. It was then that, in Europe, the impact of rapid growth transformed the demand for labour. The agricultural workforce was swiftly drawn into non-agricultural activity. The period saw the start of the transfer of married women from household activity to paid employment. And it was also the beginning of the drawing in of migrant workers from abroad. The geographical catchment area of the European labour market extended outwards from the core of the 'Golden Triangle' (Amsterdam-Cologne-Paris) to southern Europe (Italy, Spain, Portugal, Yugoslavia), to North Africa and the East Mediterranean (Algeria, Tunisia, Morocco, Greece and Turkey), and even further into West Africa and the Middle East. Sweden drew workers from Finland, and then southern Europe. Even slow-growing Britain recruited from its former colonies. Thus, the first impact of internationalization in the postwar period was felt in the supply of semi-skilled and unskilled labour (the classifications imposed at the destinations, not at the sources, of migration). The search for highly skilled labour (the 'brain drain') was, early on, from a global rather than geographically restricted area of recruitment.

The drawing in of new workers to labour-intensive sectors of production in the developed countries – agriculture, mining, construction, some services and, later, assembly industries – appears to have been precipitated by the same forces which impelled buyers and manufacturers to search out new sources of manufacturing abroad. The possibility of low-cost locations in turn stimulated the technical and managerial innovations to divide processes between labour- and skill-intensive locations. So profitable did this reorganization become that it was not deflected by the return of high unemployment to the developed countries in the late 1960s. The expected wage, appropriate to the education and skills of the labour force, made it uneconomic to restore the old forms of manufacturing.

By the 1970s, the developed countries had become locked in a process that appears to be irreversible. Despite slump and stagnation, the system has remained relatively open, in contrast to the years of the Great Depression. Furthermore, integration has increased in the period of slow growth. The new structure is not stable in detail. Competition can continue to change the advantages of particular locations,and this is especially important where the time period of the turnover of capital is short (so that companies can relocate frequently). The relative advantage of different countries can quickly change, returning some segments of manufacturing from developing to developed countries, but this does not now affect the structure as a whole. Furthermore, the process is far from complete. For example, much of the labour force of India, China, Bangladesh, Indonesia and Pakistan are not engaged. If they became so, this could profoundly change the relative pricing of the factors of production on a world scale (and so the nature of the appropriate technology).

The change in the structure of world demand does not, of course, explain why some countries rather than others have been able to exploit the process to achieve domestic self-transformation (although the role of Hong Kong as the only completely open economy in the 1950s, must be significant – it is the first straw in the wind). But the question as to which countries were able to respond has to take for granted the change in external demand, which is a factor of much greater significance for the world as a whole. It has transformed not only economies but economics, shifting theoretical concerns from the problems of managing national economies to operating in an open world market. It has even more dramatically transformed policy, to a greater or lesser degree, in all countries. Indeed, probably never before in the history of capitalism has the world market been of such obsessive concern for governments. The scaffolding of public power is being removed and economic independence, as an aim of governments, is fading.

THREE INCIDENTAL OBSERVATIONS

One of the implications of the preceding account is that the postwar changes make the past criteria for assessing the power of States slightly suspect. Thus there might be grounds for scepticism about, for example, the view that the United States is in relative decline as measured by the share of world manufacturing undertaken within American borders. By another measure, American power has grown. For example, while the process of growth in the more advanced developing countries has *not* been spearheaded by multinational corporations, nor primarily by the import of capital from the developed countries (the movement of capital and of multinational corporations to these countries is the response to growth rather than the cause of it), nonetheless the growth is a response to market demand in the developed countries. Furthermore, the wrecking of many developing country economies in the crises of the 1970s and 1980s has made this dependence even greater than before. Table 8.5 shows that only five of the 24 largest developing country exporters of manufactured goods have experienced a decline in the share of exports going to the developed countries.

Table 8.5 *Value of manufactured exports ($1 billion or more, in order of absolute size), and proportion of exports going to developed countries, 1980 and 1986*

	Value of manuf. exports, 1986	*% going to developed countries*	
		1965	*1986*
Taiwan	$35.9bn	47	78
Hong Kong	32.7	71	60
South Korea	31.9	68	75
PR China	20.0	—	32
Singapore	14.7	9	55
Brazil	9.1	40	56
Yugoslavia	8.3	24	30
Poland	8.2	—	19
India	7.2	55	59
S. Africa	7.1	94	—
Hungary	6.5	11	23
Israel	6.1	67	71
Portugal	5.7	59	91
Malaysia	5.0	17	69
Mexico	4.9	71	90
Turkey	4.4	83	57
Thailand	3.9	39	60
Greece	3.1	56	75
Indonesia	3.0	25	50
Philippines	2.8	93	74
Pakistan	2.3	40	65
Argentina	1.8	45	37
Morocco	1.1	63	53
Tunisia	1.1	19	70

Source: Ibid., Table 14.

The category of developed country is misleading since in this case it conceals the fact that the key markets are in the United States and, to a lesser extent, Japan and Australia. In the case of the United States, the leading exporters supply between 20 and 28 per cent of total manufactured imports, compared to 4.9 per cent in 1964 (an average annual rate of increase of 26 per cent). In the mid-1980s, the United States took a third of the manufacturing output of the developing countries and 60 per cent of their manufactured exports (at the same time, they took 40 per cent of US manufactured exports).[17] For Japan, imports from the leading developing countries accounted for 18 per cent of all manufactured imports, as against 1.6 per cent in 1964 (an annual increase of 28.7 per cent). In key sectors, the proportions are much larger.

Furthermore, the technical intensity of these imports is increasing. Taking this factor relative to the exports of the leading developing countries to the OECD group as a whole, the imports can be divided as follows according to skill intensity:

	high	medium	low
1964	2.2%	15.9%	81.6%
1985	25.0	21.6	53.2

Source: OECD; see note 17 to chapter 2 here.

(Of course, the total of these imports as a proportion of total domestic supply in the OECD group remains very small – 2 per cent, and 2.6 per cent for the United States.)

US manufactured imports are now equal to roughly a third of its manufactured output (manufactured exports are equal to a fifth). Many of these imports are not a direct supply to retail consumption, but are inputs to domestic manufacture. Figures are not available to disaggregate this component as a measure of American integration in international manufacturing processes. However, there are figures for imports under tariff schedules 806.30 and 807.00, commodities which start their manufacture in the United States, are processed abroad and then return for completion. These imports grew consistently faster than imports in general during the 1970s, and rose from 9–10 per cent of total imports in the early 1980s to 17 per cent in 1987. (While general imports grew by 24 per cent, items under these two schedules grew by 140 per cent.) Some 90 per cent of the imports concerned came from Canada, Japan and Mexico, but there were also important items imported from Europe and East and South-East Asia.[18]

Thus, it can be argued that the United States is emerging as the vital centrepiece of a global economy, more fully internationalized than any of its leading rivals and mediating the growth of both the Pacific and Atlantic economies. (And Europe still remains an important export market for the United States – $76 billion in 1988, or double the exports to Japan – and US registered companies in Europe sell goods worth some $450 billion annually.) While opinion tends to focus on what are seen as the negative aspects of current growth – a dependence upon an inflow of funds to compensate for a low rate of domestic savings, the trade and budget deficits – the reverse is also true. The world depends overwhelmingly upon the United States both in trade and finance.

Even in conventional terms, the picture is often distorted by national egotism. Despite all the complaints, US companies have continued to acquire assets in Europe and Japan at a significantly higher rate than the acquisition of assets in the United States by foreign companies.[19]

The second observation concerns the method of analysis of the emerging world order. Commentators frequently seem to take for granted the existence of clear-cut national entities, combining the State – with military, political and economic power – a discrete segment of world capital with an unambiguous loyalty to the State, and a share of the world's territory and population. This complex is fused into a reasonably self-evident national interest, which confronts unequivocally a clear-cut set of foreign interests. Writers speak of the national entity being 'inserted' into the world market (and, no less suspiciously, of the world market 'penetrating' the domestic economy), as if the two sides were distinct and unproblematic. So it must seem from the slit trenches of the competing national governments, but outside this narrow world, more scepticism is appropriate.

With the integration of capital, markets and production, alliances of the competitors increasingly cut across national demarcations. Robison,[20] in his study of Indonesia's ruling order, identified a series of competing clusters of interests combining a section of the military (with its own industrial interests), parts of the central bureaucracy, some public corporations, some private Chinese capital (with different networks abroad), supported by different foreign aid programmes and particular foreign multinationals. The contest over different strategies involved different clusters, cutting across the national/foreign divide. Thus, in the late 1960s, the public oil corporation, Pertamina (under Ibn Sutowo), together with Krakatau Steel, provided the focus for a cluster of interests strongly promoting an import-substitution industrialization strategy based on a heavy industry programme and associated with Japanese interests, some private and some official. Its opponents, dominated by importing and trading interests, fought for a 'free trade' alternative, with support from different parts of the military and civil bureaucracy, other public corporations, some US interests, again both public and private (although it is also possible that US heavy industry interests would support the first alternative), as well as the World Bank and the International Monetary Fund. The buoyancy of oil prices gave the government sufficient autonomy to back the Pertamina strategy, so patronizing the interests of one cluster, while, in the 1980s, the decline in oil revenues forced compromises favouring the alternative. Thus, the method has the merit of disaggregating the blunt concepts of 'the State', 'the private sector', 'the multinationals' and so on, to show dynamic coalitions related to different power and profit interests. Robison also shows how, at crucial moments, outside forces are recruited to strengthen a case – as when students were mobilized to demonstrate against the visit of Japanese Prime Minister Tanaka.

Indonesia is by no means a model for all developing countries, let alone all countries. But the method does cut across the nationalist assumptions, which are increasingly misleading in analysis.

The third observation is that an integrated world manufacturing economy not only leads to the rapid growth of the urban working classes in the developing countries but also to some measure of synchronization of the rhythms of class struggle. Between late 1973 and 1976, an unprecedented number of worker struggles occurred. National strike rates ran at record levels in many countries (in particular, in Italy, Australia, India, the United States, Ireland, Britain, Japan, West Germany and Norway). In terms of average days lost per 1,000 employed, for the fourteen largest developed countries, the figure rose from 450 (1964–6) to 611 (1967–71) to 687 (1972–6). In Burma, Malaysia, Jamaica and in southern Africa, there were bloody skirmishes, and in Nigeria, a public sector general strike. In Thailand, a general strike led to the overthrow of the military regime (annual man days lost in disputes, running at below 18–20,000 between 1956 and 1972, rose to half a million in 1972 and nearly three quarters of a million in 1974). In Chile, a revolution was destroyed; in Portugal, it was bought off. In the succeeding years, the synchronization has grown weaker, but there have still been major worker confrontations – notably in Brazil, in Iran in Khomeini's ascent to power, in India, in Korea (in 1980 and 1987–8); in Indonesia in 1979. The old mole continues to rise from the depths from time to time, and the more successful capitalism is, the more frequent those appearances.

At each stage, most of the movements in developing countries were interwoven with peasant and national struggles, usually with important student participation. It would be quite wrong to suggest that the scene was monopolized by workers. Indeed, quickening of the tempo of growth, as in India, can produce an increase in that appalling mixture of national-caste-religious-communal and worker struggles which characterizes some of the more endemic fissures in the social structure (as in Gujerat and Assam in recent years). The relevant point here is to indicate that the continued growth of the system is transforming the world social structure and the potential political alternatives. History is very far from over.

PROSPECTS

What are the prospects for the continued redistribution of manufacturing to the developing countries? It was argued earlier that the emerging structure of world trade would not seem to present economic obstacles to continuation. Of course, this does not mean that all countries have equal means to participate. As noted earlier, many were severely damaged in the period of slow growth in the 1970s and 1980s – most notoriously in Sub-Saharan Africa where the severity of conditions can only encourage pessimism. Many of them have scarcely enough capacity to keep going – and to keep famine at bay – let alone to inculcate the disciplines required to develop manufactured exports. Their vulnerability to external changes is extreme.

However, the possibility of continued growth of manufacturing for the more advanced developing countries is qualified. The integration of the system, the removal, as it were, of the economic shock absorbers of the State, means the increased synchronization of major fluctuations. Thus, a severe slump in the developed world could not easily be offset in the developing (as, in part, happened for the Latin American countries after the Great Depression). The great growth of manufactured exports in the 1980s depended, as noted in the last section, on the growth of the US market. There are doubts as to whether this can continue, and Europe seems unlikely to make up any American decline. Furthermore, the present debts of the US Government add an element of instability to the situation; a financial crash in the US would be very damaging for the developing countries.

Debt has also been seen as a more general problem affecting the possibility of continued manufacturing growth. Certainly cumulative debts and the heavy burden of debt servicing involved severely affects the prospects of growth by pre-empting a major part of export revenue and acting as a generally deflationary force. The debt problem is too enormous a subject to be treated within the confines of the present paper. However, in terms of the present theme, contraction or stagnation in domestic markets need not affect the possibility of continued redistribution of manufacturing. Mexico provides a good example of this, for, along with the slump in the domestic economy, there has been rapid growth of manufacturing capacity on the border with the United States (employment increased from some 120,000 in the early 1980s to around 400,000 by 1989). Indeed, it was precisely the effect of the 1982 conjuncture which forced a devaluation of the peso. This led to a radical reduction in the dollar value of wages on the border – in hourly terms, from

$1.42 in 1980 to 0.88 cents in 1986 – so leading to a rapid increase in employment.

Some observers have argued that competition from the new developing country manufacturers has forced their developed country rivals to innovate to match their cost advantages. Capital-intensive – even automated – production, it was said in the early 1980s, was capable of matching these costs, even in garments. However, the growth of developing country manufacturing (including garments) does not seem to have been affected so far (nor has the rate of growth of US imports slackened). Rather there has been a new marriage of automated fabric cutting in the US with making-up in South-East Asia (so that the US value added as a proportion of the total value for garment imports under tariffs 806 and 807 is the highest for all commodities: 54–69 per cent).

Others suggest that the development of 'economies of scope', the production of tailor-made advanced manufactured goods, with great speed of change in the production cycle, will restore the comparative advantage of the developed countries. However, the developing country share of manufacturing supply is still small and would not seem to be affected by this change which will be, at least initially, in the upper end of the market. Furthermore, tailor-made production will almost certainly depend on some standardized components, which will permit new combinations between developed and developing country manufacturing. Nor are the pricing results of innovations yet clear – how far increased capital costs of automated production will outweigh the advantages of low labour costs. Finally, as we have seen, developing country capital may also move to markets in developed countries, and developed country production may move to the newly emerging markets in the more advanced developing countries.

Apart from generalized slump ending the process, the real question marks concern the political and social orders rather than economic circumstances. The process of growth has produced, as discussed in the preceding section, new and politically significant working classes that have begun to exercise some influence on events. The willingness to accept the extraordinarily harsh working conditions that the growth of manufacturing has hitherto required cannot be taken for granted. Secondly, the emergence of a world labour market – with wages tending in certain sectors to become more uniform between countries – forces groups of workers in many different locations to compete for work. The downward pressures on wages could be severe, particularly for unskilled labour, giving employers a major increase in bargaining power. The world's trade unions are ill-equipped to organize in an international context in the face of opposition on the part of governments.

The issue affects all countries that participate in the manufacture of the same commodities. The emergence of sizable black economies in the developed countries – particularly in Italy, where it is known as the 'Third World' economy – is a possible sign of this downward pressure on wages, a measure of homogenization between labour conditions for certain forms of production in developed and developing countries. The gruelling character of the labour regime this entails then raises questions concerning the stability of the social orders presiding over the process. The speed and extent as well as the militancy of the struggles in South Korea in 1987 is a vivid demonstration of the pent-up frustrations that flow from enforced growth. Thus, class conflict could be engendered on a much larger scale as a result of the spread of manufacturing, particularly where the State uses its power deliberately to underprice labour.

How far will protectionism in the developed countries affect the continued spread of manufacturing? It is by far the easiest method to explain unemployment and the need to hold down wages to blame foreigners rather than the incompetence of native employers. Political support is relatively painlessly secured by restricting imports, even where this damages the welfare of the mass of the population and those sectors of manufacturing which use the banned imports, as well as protecting uncompetitive segments of manufacturing. Often protectionism is introduced slowly, as a kind of creeping paralysis, without clear-cut decisions being taken. Thus, between 1981 and 1985, some 35–40 per cent of Korea's exports came under restrictions of various sorts. Developing country exports are particularly vulnerable because they are concentrated in a fairly narrow and highly visible range of goods, and the countries concerned have relatively little bargaining power.

The Reagan Administration saw the biggest increase in protectionism in the United States since President Hoover. Import controls were used as a means to offset the effects of the other policies of the Federal Government which so radically cheapened imports. One estimate suggets that a quarter of US imports are now affected, as compared to half this at the beginning of the Administration. About 40 per cent of Japan's exports are now affected (cutting, it is said, US imports from Japan by $6 billion in 1986).

There are thus well-founded reasons to fear the Uruguay Round of trade negotiations may fail, particularly as regards agriculture and services. In agriculture the most severe damage is done to the poorer developing countries by the European Community's dumping of subsidized exports abroad, and the US application of import quotas to protect domestic producers. There are other fears that the Single

European Market, the US–Canada Free Trade Agreement, and ideas of an East Asian economic federation will increase the general protectionism.

However, while it would be wrong to underestimate these threats, there are grounds for limited optimism. So far protectionism does not appear to have reduced US imports significantly nor prevented very high growth of manufactured exports by a number of developing countries over the period 1986–9. Where such exports have been affected is, as noted earlier, by the restrictions of the Multi Fibre Arrangement. Even so, room has been made in the market for new lower-cost exporting countries, not currently restricted. And even where these mechanisms cannot be employed, reclassifying imports and even smuggling them have been means to escape controls. It is not clear how far governments can systematically control imports in an integrated system, except through a blanket control on all imports.

More generally, developed country markets and manufacturing output are dependent upon imports, so that cuts directly affect current output and reduce employment, particularly in the United States. Furthermore, some of the pressure has been relieved by the retooling of affected industries – for example, steel and automobiles – and their return to profitability. None of this affects agricultural protection, however. One result is to discourage agricultural exports from developing countries and increase the pressure for them to expand manufacturing.

As for the idea of protectionist regions, it is still the case that the major trading and financing powers are too heavily interlocked into each other's markets to risk *general* trade wars. Japan, the United States and Europe are overwhelmingly interdependent, and any attempt by one to isolate itself economically from the other two would produce catastrophic consequences for all three. Short of collapse – in which case protectionism is only one of many problems – the three major participants still have a powerful interest in keeping the system open, thus safeguarding the niches occupied by developing countries.

CONCLUSIONS

The theories which guide the economic policies of governments take their shape from the experience of the past. Thus, the policies of developing country governments in the early stages were powerfully affected by a version of nineteenth-century experience and the effects of the Great Depression. The imperial powers, it was said, had forced upon a major part of the globe the task of supplying European manufacturing industry with raw materials, based upon the dominant position of metropolitan capital and enforced by metropolitan armies, with markedly asymmetrical gains from the relationship. The Great Depression then exposed the vulnerability of raw material exporters to developed country government action in cutting imports and capital exports. From this was derived a condemnation of monoculture, which spread to include all specialization; opposition to 'capitalism' – that is, to international trade and foreign capital; and attempts to build a fully diversified industrial economy, based upon the growth of the domestic market, as the foundation of an economic independence to parallel political sovereignty. Around this set of imperatives, networks of interests grew up, a capitalism dependent not upon external 'centres' so much as the local State.

Meanwhile the system transformed itself again. The developed countries, where metropolitan capital was concentrated, became the major exporters of raw materials. This led Hong Kong to stumble upon a change in the structure of world demand which brought swift industrialization, and the three other Little Tigers then exploited this lesson to implement part of the old programme of economic independence (a diversified economy with a heavy industrial base). They did so, however, not through the domestic but through the international market – but with import substitution continuing to protect their domestic markets. This eclectic formula relied entirely on the change in world demand, and the gamble paid off. Probably one of the most striking indices of its success is in the increase in real wages and thereby, the average level of protein consumption; 14-year-old South Korean boys have added 11 centimetres to their average height since 1965.

The economic formula – leaving aside the much more difficult social and political preconditions – seemed in retrospect much simpler than had been expected: an undervalued exchange rate, cheap labour, some manufacturing base, inputs into exports that were either subsidized or obtained from the cheapest world source, an adequate infrastructure and a responsive bureaucracy. That is with the benefit of hindsight; President Park and his associates were quite pessimistic about exports in the early 1960s, and genuinely surprised at their success.

Now, with much more erratic rates of change in world trade, debts and protectionism, it is more difficult. For many countries, particularly some of those in Sub-Saharan Africa, the strategy seems ruled out by the lack of a manufacturing base and the means to make one. But it is still possible, as is demonstrated by some of the newcomers who began the process in the 1980s (for example,

Mauritius). The overall case now no longer depends upon the fortunes of the Gang of Four.

The success of the Four turned upon world demand at a particular historical moment. It is for this reason that both the neoclassical and Left–Liberal accounts fail satisfactorily to explain the process of growth and tend to swing between what are supposedly exclusive options – import substitution *or* export promotion. The key for Korea was the opportunistic mix, quite a lot of luck and favourable world demand.

Of course, none of the successes in the task of economic development imply that capitalism has suddenly become harmonious, without uneven development. Only that, for example, Baran's assessment[21] that capitalism was no longer capable of the development of an underdeveloped country is wrong in at least some important cases. Nor does success mean that the Newly Industrializing Countries offer a means to resume the growth in the world economy of the period 1947–74. The newcomers are still too small to affect world profit rates.

The world is still marked by great inequality between States. Some have a privileged access to a disproportionate share of the surplus generated in the world system, and with it are able to bribe, bully and threaten to achieve their purposes. But the more developed they are, the less *economic* independence from the world system they possess. Indeed, such a concept seems today quite unrealistic. With the benefit of hindsight, we can see that programmes of import-substitution industrialization which, it was thought, would create economic independence, were in fact a prelude to reincorporation at a more advanced stage, whether achieved by deliberate policy choice or by force through the debt mechanism. The mercantilist phase which seems always to be the policy framework for the first phases of national industrialization, was not a means to avoid capitalism, but to build it.

The 'geopoliticization' of the world market seemed self-evident in the rise of imperialism and through the first half of the twentieth century. The economic seemed always subordinate to the political, the market to the State, the world to Washington. The concept led the Left astray, marrying its purposes to the struggle to achieve and defend the national independence of the new ruling orders of the former imperial possessions. But the process of capital accumulation on a world scale was not the creature of particular States nor particular institutions (the multinational corporations, the IMF, etc.). The moment capitalist growth resumed, the market re-emerged as the dominant force, reshaping the world in quite unanticipated ways. Recognizing the change is the first step to rebuilding an effective critique.

9

Mexico and the Pacific Rim Region

THE PACIFIC RIM: THE UNITED STATES AND JAPAN

The concept of a Pacific Rim region derives in part from a recognition of an emerging network of economic relationships, in part from rival foreign policy strategies by the dominant powers, the United States and Japan. Within the network of economic relationships, this chapter examines trade in the main, but some reference will also be made to the related flows of capital and migrant labour. Part I discusses the overall picture of economic flows in the region, and Part II, Mexico's external economic relationships.

In fact, insofar as the Pacific Rim exists, it is an interaction between more narrowly defined territorial locations – for example, California and Tokyo–Osaka, with offshoots in particular regions of other countries (for example, Guangdong Province in south China). There are also strong bilateral interactions between particular countries, such as Canada and the United States and Mexico and the United States. The essence of the Pacific Rim region in fact more usually excludes Mexico and the rest of the Latin American countries, and is seen as a relationship between Seoul, Singapore and San Francisco, with an extension to Sydney.

As a region, the Pacific Rim is overwhelmingly dominated by the two major economies, just as the economic interactions are dominated by their bilateral exchanges in trade and finance. This is illustrated in Table 9.1 where the respective shares of the fifteen leading countries of the region are displayed in terms of the regional product and export values for 1987, and value added in manufacturing for 1986. Just over 83 per cent of the regional product and value

Originally published as 'México y las Relaciones Económicas Exteriores de la Cuenca del Pacífico', Cuadernos de Política Internacional No. 50, Instituto Matías Romero de Los Estudios Diplomáticos (Secretería de Relaciones Exteriores, Gobierno de los Estados Unidos de México), Mexico City, February 1990, pp. 5–35.

added in manufacturing was held by the two leading powers, and nearly 54 per cent of the export value. Only in export values was the disproportion somewhat reduced, with the four Newly Industrializing Countries holding nearly a fifth of the region's total (of course, shares of regional population would show a quite different picture). In fact the disproportions are greater than appear, because the two largest economies are also major operators outside the area.

Table 9.1 *Countries of Pacific Rim, percentage of regional GDP, MVA and value of exports*

	Per cent Share of Regional					
	Domestic Product 1987		*Manufacturing Value Add, 1986*		*Export Value, 1987*	
'The Americans'						
Mexico	1.7		1.8		2.3	
Canada	4.5	60.7	3.5	54.6	10.4	40.8
United States	54.5		49.3		28.1	
Asia						
Japan	28.8		33.8		25.6	
China	3.6		5.4		4.4	
NICs						
South Korea	1.5		1.7		5.3	
Singapore	0.2	2.1	0.3	2.5	3.2	19.6
Hong Kong	0.4		0.5		5.4	
Taiwan	NA		NA		5.7	
ASEAN[a]						
Indonesia	0.8		0.6		1.9	
Philippines	0.4	2.2	0.4		0.6	5.9
Malaysia	0.4		NA		2.0	
Thailand	0.6		0.6		1.3	
ANZ						
Australia	2.2	2.6	1.7	2.0	2.8	
New Zealand	0.4		0.3		0.8	

[a] Singapore is included under NICs (Newly Industrializing Countries)
Figures do not sum to 100 due to rounding.

Source: Calculated from *World Development Report 1989*, World Bank, Washington DC, 1989, Tables 3, 6 and 14.

(a) Trade

In the 1980s, the volume of world trade increased annually by 4 per cent (while production increased by 2.5 per cent), but world manufactured exports increased by an annual 10 per cent in volume, and over 16 per cent in value (and manufactured output by 6.5 per cent). Within this flow, capital goods increased faster still (at 20 per cent per annum in value) to attain a share of 30 per cent in world merchandise trade.[1]

(i) *United States*. An important component in this trade in manufactures was a response to the growth of demand in the United States; by the second half of the 1980s, US imports of manufactured goods equalled nearly a third of domestic manufactured output. The leading Newly Industrializing Countries (NICs) increased their share of these imports to some 20–28 per cent (compared to 4.9 per cent in 1964), at an annual rate of growth in the 1980s of 26 per cent. By the mid-1980s, the US took a third of the manufactured output of the less developed countries and 60 per cent of their exports. The largest part of this trade is with Mexico and East and South-East Asia.

The shares of this trade with the different groups of countries in the Asian Pacific Rim and the differences in rates of growth are shown in Table 9.2.

Table 9.2 *Shares of US–Asian Pacific Rim trade with different groups of Asian countries and rates of growth, 1978–88 (%)*

	1978	*1988*	*Growth 1978–88*
Japan	51.1	47.4	206.6
NICs	27.7	35.5	284.2
ASEAN	11.7	7.1	137.5
China	2.2	5.5	566.7
ANZ	7.3	4.9	150.0

Source: Calculated from data in International Monetary Fund, *Direction of Trade Statistics, Yearbook, 1889,* IMF, Washington DC, 1989 (nominal dollar values;.

The table shows the relative decline of the less developed ASEAN group (still relatively dependent upon raw material exports, particularly oil for Indonesia), and the equally developed ANZ, but the much more rapid growth of the NICs, and, from a low base point, China.

The aggregate figures, however, conceal radical changes in the nature of these trading relationships. Traditionally, manufactured exporters traded finished goods. But the fastest rates of growth of US imports and exports is in part-processed goods, indicating a technical integration of US manufacturing activity with manufacturing abroad. The most important element here are US imports under tariff categories 806 and 807 (where import duties are levied only on the value added abroad on goods which originate and complete their manufacture in the US). In the early 1980s, imports under this heading constituted 9–10 per cent of total US imports (with very high rates of growth in the 1970s). With extraordinarily high rates of growth in US imports (24 per cent annually) in the 1980s, goods entering the country under these two tariffs increased by 140 per cent a year (to reach 17 per cent of the total). The growth was statistically exaggerated by a change in the regulations in 1986.

Roughly two-thirds of the imports under these two tariff schedules come from Mexico, Canada and Japan, indicating the core zones of the US's integration with foreign manufacturing. The commodities of particular importance in this respect, however, are not spread across the spectrum of manufacturing output, but are highly specialized. Vehicles and machinery are dominant (rather than labour-intensive manufactured goods), as shown in Table 9.3.

Table 9.3 *Share of particular commodities in US imports under tariffs 806 and 807, 1987 (%)*

Motor vehicles	56.9
Semi conductors	13.6
Motor parts	10.8
Other machinery and equipment	8.0
Internal combustion engines and parts	7.6
Other electrical equipment	1.6
Furniture, mattresses, pillows	0.8
Scientific instruments	0.4
Other	0.5

Source: Calculated from data in *Imports under Items 806.30 and 807.00 of the Tariff Schedule of the United States, 1984–87*, US Department of Commerce, Washington DC, December 1988.

The share of different countries in the largest component of the trade (under 807), and the rates of growth between 1984 and 1987 are as shown in Table 9.4.

Table 9.4 *Shares of the leading Pacific Rim countries in 807 imports, 1984–7 (%)*

	1984	*1985*	*1986*	*1987*	*Rate of growth*
Mexico	36.2	51.8	55.0	35.2	176
Canada	10.1	10.7	15.0	30.4	542.9
Japan	2.9	5.4	13.3	3.2	200.0
South Korea	8.7	3.6	1.0	3.2	66.7
Singapore	4.4	3.6	1.2	3.2	133.3
Malaysia	11.6	3.6	1.5	4.8	75.0
Philippines	7.2	1.8	1.0	2.4	60.0
Dominican Rep.	1.5	3.6	3.3	2.4	300.0

Source: Calculated from *ibid.*

The domination of motor vehicles partly explains the powerful, if fluctuating, role of Mexico and Canada as well as the striking growth of Canada's share, suggesting the relocation of the vehicle manufacturing capacity of US firms to the north.

More disaggregated data would serve to indicate how far the categories show competition between countries, how far an elaborate and changing pattern of complementary specializations. Changes in technology and relative pricing continually shift the interdependencies. At one stage, virtually finished garments might have predominated in US imports in this category, but US firms have acquired a comparative advantage in automated fabric cutting while parts of South-East Asia dominate the making up. The marriage of these two geographically distant specialities in a single manufacturing process has resulted in US-located plants recapturing a major part of the value added (the US share here, 54–60 per cent, is the highest of all commodities under these two tariff schedules).

The national figures are misleading in another way, for they show only the immediate source of supply. There is no reason to think that this exhausts the backward international linkages. Just as the US may finish goods imported from other countries, those countries may obtain components from yet a third range of suppliers, and so on in an increasingly complex chain of production. Furthermore, in the field of garments, goods are shifted to other countries before being exported to their final destination to escape Multi Fibre Arrangement quotas. The spreading of Japanese, Korean and Taiwanese capital in South-East Asia and elsewhere may well encapsulate this process within particular companies.

Mexico's output has related well to the growth of demand in the

US, and rates of growth have been high and changing relative to shifts in both demand and supply. Table 9.5 shows imports from Mexico in 1987 under 807 bunched in the middle ranges of capital and skill intensity, not in labour-intensive output: motor vehicles, electrical conductors, equipment for breaking and making electrical circuits, motors and generators and internal combustion engines.

Table 9.5 *US 807 imports from Mexico, shares of value by commodity, 1987 (%)*

Agricultural and forest products		1.7
Textiles, garments and footwear		6.0
Chemicals, coal and gas, rubber and plastic goods		0.8
Minerals and metals		2.1
Miscellaneous		6.4
Machinery and equipment		83.1
– of which:		
Motor vehicles	17.3	
Electrical conductors	9.5	
Internal combustion engines	7.8	
Television receivers	5.8	
Other television apparatus	4.6	
Motors and generators	5.2	
Articles for making/breaking circuits	5.0	
Tape recorders, etc.	4.6	
Office machines	33.3	
Semi conductors	3.0	
Motor vehicle parts	2.7	
Other machinery and equipment	14.3	

Source: Calculated from *ibid*, pp. B–59–61.

(ii) *Japan's trade* with the other countries of the Pacific Rim over the period 1978–88 is shown in Table 9.6.

The close and growing interlinking of the four NICs (South Korea, Taiwan, Singapore and Hong Kong) and Japan emerges clearly, as also the extraordinary performance of China. It is surprising that Australia and New Zealand have had higher rates of growth in trade with Japan than the ASEAN group. With the spread of Japanese manufacturing capital to the ASEAN (discussed later), it is likely that this is changing. Already, Japan takes some 18 per cent of the manufactured exports of the leading developing country exporters (compared with 1.6 per cent in 1964), and this is growing by 29 per

Table 9.6 *Shares of Japan's trade with the grouped countries of the Pacific Rim, 1978 and 1988, and rates of growth (%)*

	1978	*1988*	*Rates of increase*
North America	46.7	50.0	208.6
China	5.3	6.5	237.5
Four NICs	22.7	25.5	219.7
Four ASEAN	16.0	11.1	134.6
Two ANZ	9.3	6.8	194.7

Source: IMF, *Direction of Trade Statistics.*

(iii) *Other trade in manufactures.*

Table 9.7 *Changes in trade 1978–88 (%)*

	1978	*1988*	*incr.*		*1978*	*1988*	*incr.*
NIC trade with:				*ASEAN trade with:*			
N. America	40.0	45.4	284		41.4	41.7	138
Japan	35.8	29.4	206		27.6	26.2	146
China	5.3	13.9	660		5.2	4.8	133
NICs	—	—	—		22.4	25.0	162
ASEAN	13.7	8.8	162		—	—	—
ANZ	5.3	2.5	120		3.4	2.4	100
	Averages:		256				145
China's trade with:				*ANZ trade with:*			
N. America	15.0	23.0	567		41.7	31.9	150
Japan	40.0	25.7	238		16.7	42.6	500
China	—	—	—		8.3	4.2	100
NICs	25.0	44.6	660		20.8	12.8	120
ASEAN	10.0	4.1	150		12.5	8.5	133
ANZ	10.0	2.7	100		—	—	—

Source: Calculated from IMF, *Direction of Trade Statistics.*

cent per year. However, Latin America – with only 2.7 per cent of Japan's external trade – plays a very small role in this expansion of Japanese manufactured imports.

Table 9.7 displays some of the disproportionalities in the trading patterns, reflecting both shifts in competitive positions and peculiar specializations. The NICS' trade with the more advanced countries grew very strongly, whereas the trade of the ASEAN group grew most swiftly with the NICs. However, lest this seem the result of a simple difference in degree of development, China's performance cuts across, with remarkable increases in trade with North America and, even more, with the NICs (where its relationship with Hong Kong must dominate this result). ANZ trade was relatively sluggish except for the remarkable increase in trade with Japan.

Trade in services has also grown very rapidly, partly to provide the means for the movement of both goods and people. The growth of air traffic and container movement has been particularly rapid, supported by remarkable declines in the costs of mobility. Richard Cooper[2] offers estimates of the decline in air fares and air freight; for the first, a decline in the San Franciso–Hong Kong air fare from $12,700 in 1937 (1985 prices) to $1,094 in 1987, with a prospect of a further 90 per cent fall by the year 2000; for the second, a decline from $5.33 per tonne/mile in 1943 to $0.39 in 1985, with a possible further decline of two thirds by the turn of the century.

One important and growing element here is international tourism, expanding worldwide from 25 million (arrivals) in 1970 to 360 million in 1987 (with total receipts of the order of $160 billion). The overseas visits of the Japanese, who come relatively late to this movement, are now expanding rapidly; one estimate suggests that the number of Japanese overseas tourists will shortly reach 10 million, and another, that their cumulative expenditure abroad in the five years to 1992 could reach $55 billion, much of it spent in the countries of the Pacific Rim.

(b) Direct Foreign Investment

Capital owned by companies registered in the United States (henceforth 'US capital') has long played a powerful role in Central America and Mexico, and in Singapore, the Philippines and Indonesia. This has been both in manufacturing and services. However, the Pacific region has traditionally been much less important than Europe and Latin America; under a quarter of the overseas earnings of US companies come from the Pacific area.

Capital held by companies registered in Japan has played a role in the growth of the NICs and in raw material extraction in Indonesia.

However, in the 1980s, with an appreciating Yen (and rising wages in Japan), Japanese capital has made a major expansion abroad, particularly to the US (with 40 per cent concentrated in California).

The respective cumulative investment totals by 1988 are given in Table 9.8.

Table 9.8 *Pacific Rim: US and Japanese cumulative investment, 1988 ($bn)*

North American investment in:		Japanese investment in:
North America	—	53
Japan	14	—
Australia	12	6
NICs	10	8
ASEAN	8	5
China	?	2

This shows the two powers as roughly equal in the Asia Pacific Rim, with the United States tending to have slightly larger and more diversified holdings. However, the picture in particular countries could diverge far from the aggregate; Japanese investment (and aid) to Thailand is said now to be ten times that of the United States. Japanese and Hong Kong Chinese capital is currently expanding swiftly in western Canada. The major asymmetry arises in the investment of the two major powers in each other. However, Japanese capital exports expanded far more rapidly in the 1980s, increasing, for example, by 62 per cent in 1988 (and possibly reaching $50 billion worldwide in 1989 – compared to $4.6 billion in 1980).

Furthermore, Japanese companies are now establishing manufacturing plants abroad on a large scale, the more advanced in North America (and to a much lesser extent, in Europe), the less advanced first in the NICs, now in the ASEAN group and to a lesser extent in China. Part of the output of these plants is being exported to Japan. The most recent official survey of Japanese business abroad[3] estimates that 16 per cent of the output of companies abroad is exported to Japan (compared to 11 per cent in 1983), 55 per cent to the local market and 30 per cent elsewhere.

Japanese firms have also moved some operations from the NICs to ASEAN in search of lower-cost locations. Thus, Uniden (makers of mobile telephones) have shifted manufacture from Taiwan and Hong Kong to the Philippines and China. Other companies have replaced them to supply the local NIC markets with higher value manufacturing, retailing and distribution. Some companies have established complementary production sites in more than one ASEAN country. Hitachi manufactures semi-conductors in Malaysia for video recorders made in Singapore. Mitsubishi assembles vehicles from parts made in several countries in South-East Asia. Following the ASEAN decision to halve tariff rates on components manufactured in other member countries, this trend has been enhanced. Toyota, for example, is expanding its diesel production in Thailand to supply assembly in Malaysia. Its Indonesian petrol engine production supplies assembly in Malaysia and the Philippines. The company estimates that the value of its international component trade inside the company in ASEAN will reach $100 million in three years (compared to $5 million in 1989), and radically reduce its imports from Japan. Furthermore, the larger Japanese companies were according a much greater degree of local autonomy to regional headquarters abroad, as well as establishing research and development facilities there.

Japanese investment in the United States is partly designed to escape protectionism. Thus, for example, since 1980 Japanese companies have built ten car plants there and 130 vehicle component factories. By 1989, output in the States from these companies had reached over one million units (15 per cent of total US output), and was expected to reach 2.5 million by 1995. There was even greater production in the field of consumer electronics.

Furthermore, the NICs are becoming significant exporters of capital to North America but also to lower-cost production sites in South-East Asia, the Caribbean and Central America. An additional motive here in the garment-exporting business is to locate where quotas under the Multi Fibre Arrangement are not fully used. The appreciation of the new Taiwan dollar and the Korean Won have added to the effects of rising real wages (particularly in the sudden increase in Korean wages in 1987).

Taiwan's export of capital in 1988 was officially put at $219 million (an increase of 81 per cent on 1987), but estimates of the inflow at destination put the figure at between $2.2 and 3.5 billion. In manufacturing, the favoured sectors were electronics, petrochemicals, textiles and garments, footwear and toys,and the destinations, the Philippines, Thailand, Malaysia and Indonesia. There was a further large increase in 1989 and the total outflow could be as high as $7 billion.

Hong Kong's textile firms have been particularly mobile. It is estimated that they employ between 1.5 and 2 million workers in the south China province of Guangdong where, in 1988, the predominantly female labour force cost their employers roughly one-eighth of the Hong Kong level. The rapid growth of China's garment exports since 1978 is partly attributed to this role of Hong Kong firms, as also the rapid growth elsewhere (for example, in Mauritius and Lesotho in southern Africa).

Capital flows establish networks of interdependent specializations that bind countries together in single production systems and underpin the growth of trade.

(c) Migration

The flow of direct foreign investment in search of low-cost production sites is often matched by a reverse flow of relatively low-cost labour. Possibly the most extreme form of this exchange is on the Mexican–US border, but a similar phenomenon also affects the Asian Pacific Rim.

In Japan, increasing real labour costs threaten the elimination of a mass of activities – from companies too small to move abroad and insufficiently capitalized to automate production, to activities which are immobile (personal and public services, entertainment, construction, mining and agriculture). As in North America and Europe at an earlier stage, the rate of growth of the economy inevitably draws in workers, legally or illegally.

It is estimated that illegal immigration in Japan is now running at one to two hundred thousand people per year. Much of the labour force in bars and restaurants is said to be Filipina, and Pakistanis and Sri Lankans work on construction sites. Farmers contract to take Filipinas as wives (Japanese women are presumably now reluctant to accept farmer husbands). At the other end of the occupational scale, a significant number of Taiwanese and Korean doctors are said to practise illegally.

There is a pressure group – including small businessmen – to relax immigration controls, so far without success. However, demography is working in the same direction; the ageing of the Japanese population is sharply reducing the supply of young labour, while the educational system is even more swiftly reducing the unskilled.

The Korean Government is beginning to worry about the same demographic phenomenon, and the Singapore Government has spent a decade seeking to reconcile a high rate of economic growth, a low rate of population growth and tight immigration controls. In Taiwan, there is thought to be an annual inflow of illegal unskilled workers from South-East Asia of between 12 and 30 thousand. In Hong Kong, despite the expansion of production facilities in China and other parts of the world, in mid-1989 the leading business federation estimated a labour shortage of 200–250,000, particularly unskilled workers on construction sites, in hotels, personal services, manufacturing and retailing. The government estimate of labour shortages was 130,000.

On the other side of the Pacific, the United States' prodigious appetite for immigrant workers continues unabated. This includes not only the temporary illegal migrants from Mexico and Central America, but also the continued inflow of Asians, increasing from just over one million in the mid-1960s to 6.5 million in 1989 (with a heavy concentration in California). Immigrants do something to reduce the effects of the ageing of the American population.

(d) Foreign policy dimensions

So far this account has been concerned with what appears as the spontaneous results of a market-driven system – in particular, the outcome of differential labour costs and changing exchange rates. However, the phenomenon is influenced also by the attempts of governments to shape the processes to their own advantage. In particular, the two dominant powers are competing to shape the Pacific Rim in their own interests, and other governments are reacting to this with separate purposes.

The US Government, for long the most dominant power on the East Asian seaboard, has highly specific interests in simultaneously ensuring the security of the Asian seaboard while reducing the burden of its direct defence, in reducing the scale of US imports from the region and seeking to penetrate the markets of its regional partners. However, the administration is also aware of latent antagonisms which could obstruct co-operation, and has been keen to prevent the creation of a pole of opposition to its own interests (particularly if led by Japan). It has most recently been employing the Australian Government as a surrogate representative of its policy aims.

The Japanese approach has been to seek to create an economic alliance not, in certain respects, unlike the Co-prosperity Sphere advanced as the economic rationale of Japanese imperialism before the Second World War. An underlying fear in some Japanese government circles is that the two other large economic zones in the world economy will move to degrees of economic integration that exclude the Japanese. The development of integration in Europe up to 1992 – now infused with the heady vision of a Europe encompassing the Eastern bloc – and the Free Trade Agreement between the US and Canada (with the possible ultimate inclusion of

Mexico) are seen as possible steps in this direction. Secondly, it is assumed that the Japanese predominance in manufacturing will not persist indefinitely, given the growth of cheaper NIC output, the shortage of labour (particularly the young workers required to staff manufacturing industry), rising real wages in Japan, and the expected propensity of Japanese consumption to rise and savings to fall. The current account surplus, it is thought, may be eliminated in the 1990s through increasing imports (from offshore locations of Japanese companies), increased Japanese spending abroad, and increased capital exports.

Within the Japanese Government, there have long been identifiable frictions in approach between the Ministry of International Trade (MITI) and the Foreign Office (Gaimusho). MITI's emphasis has been upon creating swiftly an economic federation in East and South-East Asia as the basis for the diaspora of Japanese manufacturing capacity and a possible defensive region. Gaimusho has been more preoccupied with sustaining co-operative diplomatic relationships and not exacerbating relationships with the United States or ASEAN, nor causing such fears in Europe and America that moves to protectionist federations there are encouraged. It was from Gaimusho that the first modest initiatives in the field began with the first conference of the Pacific Free Trade Area (PAFTAD) in 1968 to encourage regional co-operation.

From the MITI approach has emerged a much more vigorous – indeed, *dirigiste* – initiative to employ the Japanese aid programme (rapidly becoming the largest bilateral programme in the world) and trade and investment policies to create an interdependent economic region, the centre of which would be Japan. The programme was launched by the Minister of International Trade in Bangkok in January 1987 as the New Asian Industrial Development Plan, under the direction of MITI. An ASEAN–Japanese Development Fund outlined the funding basis for the Plan for the ASEAN countries.

The Plan was to be directed from Tokyo through bilateral relations with each of the selected Asian powers, so that the Japanese Government alone would view the whole project. So far, participants have included Thailand, Malaysia, Indonesia, the Philippines, China and India.

The Plan led to the elaboration of a series of stages. First, Japanese officials would visit the country concerned, make a study of its industries, identify those with the potential to be internationally competitive and design a master plan for investment and the transfer of technology by Japanese companies, backed by the aid programme and by Japanese technical expertise. The study would include recommendations on the policy changes required to support the programme, and the joint membership of a steering committee to oversee implementation. In some cases, Japanese officials would be seconded to government industrial ministries (for example, two Japanese officials in the International Co-operative Agency are at present working in the Thai Department of Industrial Promotion, and one in Malaysia's Industrial Development Agency).

The second phase of the planning process was the preparation of guidelines for the development of each of the industries selected, with programmes of supporting infrastructure, legal provisions, tax and incentive measures to attract Japanese investors. Loans for the physical infrastructure were the responsibility of the Japanese Overseas Economic Co-operation Foundation; technical support came from the Japanese International Co-operation Agency; management, production technology, marketing, promotion and distribution expertise were to come from JETRO (which also arranged direct investment through its Asian Industrialization Project). Finally, training budget allocations were set aside to train local staff in Japan through the Association for Overseas Technical Scholarship Programme.

However, MITI's intentions – to create geese flying in V formation, with Japan at the point of the V – are not the same as their realization. The cruel domination of Korea and Taiwan up to 1945, the Japanese invasion and occupation of China in the 1930s, and the wartime occupation of South-East Asia, do not make it easy to reconcile the clashes of national interest. The complex relationship between Japan and China (which both the US and Thailand at one stage saw as a counterweight to Japan) illustrates how difficult it will be to fashion a Japanese economic federation. Furthermore, the US Government is concerned to prevent any Japanese domination, to the point of sending three Cabinet Ministers to the first meeting of the Asia Pacific Rim Conference in November 1989 (an Australian initiative, undertaken even though the Japanese Government had earlier formulated an alternative proposal).

Furthermore, all the powers of the region are highly dependent, in economic, military and political terms, upon North America and Europe, none more so than Japan itself. It is difficult to conceive of circumstances where geographical proximity would come to outweigh these powerful external links. Particularly in view of the enormous economic weight of Japan within the Asian region; the largest gross domestic product outside Japan, that of China, is still only just ahead of the value of sales of Japan's largest company, Dai–Ichi Kangyo (and the third, that of Australia, is nearly 30 per cent less).

There are, of course, some tendencies to regionalism, and influential voices have argued that, for example, reciprocal managed trade is the dominant form now,[4] and regional trading blocks should dominate world trade and supersede GATT.[5] However, it is difficult to see how the present open trading system could be transformed into regions short of a general economic collapse.It is not just Japanese firms that source output from East and South-East Asia; American and European firms also do so. On the other hand, the threat of regionalism is a useful bargaining weapon in negotiations.

MEXICO'S EXTERNAL ECONOMIC RELATIONSHIPS

Introduction: the NICs

As noted above, there are three important flows to be considered in the market-driven economic integration of territories – exchanges of commodities and services (exports and imports), the movement of capital and the migration of labour. Here attention will be mainly devoted to some of the features that mark the first flow, trade.

The world economy is dominated by three major regions – what we have called, 'the Americans', Europe and now the East Asian seaboard. The closer countries are to these regions, other things being equal, the more likely it is that they will be drawn into regional interactions. Thus, Mexico's involvement in the US economy should hardly occasion surprise.

To compare the relative sizes of the three regions in trade terms, let us adopt the group of three Americans – Mexico, the United States and Canada – as the standard of measurement. The respective percentage share of the three in the combined elements below are as follows:

- (i) Combined gross domestic product (1987): Mexico 2.8; Canada 7.5; United States 89.7.
- (ii) Combined value added in manufacturing (1986): Mexico 3.5; Canada 7.1; United States 90.1.
- (iii) Combined export value (1987): Mexico 5.7; Canada 25.4; United States 68.9.

Thus, Mexico and Canada, compared with the United States, are slightly 'overindustrialized' for their size of product and considerably more export-oriented.

By way of comparison, the figures for 11 industrialized countries of western and southern Europe are as followas:

- (i) Gross domestic product (1987): 93 per cent of the Americans.
- (ii) Value added in manufacturing (1986): 101 per cent of the Americans.
- (iii) Export value (1987): 299 per cent of the Americans.

Thus, the Europeans are very slightly more industrialized relative to the Americans, and very much more export-oriented. Indeed, Europe has the dominant position in world trade, with fully 45.8 per cent of total world exports compared to 15 per cent for the Americans (although the Americans take 21 per cent of world imports, 17 per cent of them for the United States alone). Of course, the differences in exports are partly a function of disparities in size; what is internationally traded between the much smaller European economies is domestically exchanged in the United States. If we now compare the new and rapidly rising region of the Asian Pacific Rim (11 countries), the shares are:

(i) Gross product (1987): 65 per cent of the Americans.
(ii) Value added in manufacturing (1986): 84 per cent.
(iii) Export value (1987): 145 per cent.[6]

Thus, the Asian group (dominated by Japan in economic terms, but China in population), with a product two-thirds the size of the Americans, has already surpassed four-fifths of the manufacturing capacity and half as much again in export production. If we added the respective rates of growth[7] over the past three decades, we would then see a remarkable narrowing of the gap between the three groups, but especially between the Americans and the Asians.

The Asian performance is closely related to the fact – discovered more by accident than design in the 1950s – that the comparative advantage of the older industrial countries in certain sectors of manufacturing was in decline. The reasons for this need not concern us here.[8] The United States (and Britain) led the way in this respect, and initially West Germany and Japan were the first beneficiaries (leading to the relative 'overindustrialization' in both – they have long been net importers of services; this is now changing). But even the spectacular performance of Japan was, as is well-known, superseded by the growth of four other Asian exporters of manufactured goods (South Korea, Taiwan, Hong Kong and Singapore). The four 'Little Tigers' had much smaller domestic markets than Japan and relied on home demand very much less; world trade from the beginning was the source of growth. Finally, other parts of East and South-East Asia followed suit in the 1970s and 1980s. China's phenomenal growth (10.4 per cent per year for gross domestic product between 1980 and 1987, and 11.7 per cent for exports) has now been followed late in the 1980s by long-stagnating India (currently expanding by between 6 and 9 per cent). Thus, despite the notorious problems of the 1980s, high growth in certain developing countries is by no means exhausted.

The composition of the manufactured exports of the developing countries also changed nearly as radically as the volume. They have become increasingly capital- and skill-intensive. In the late 1950s and the 1960s, the trade was dominated by labour-intensive products. But in the 1970s, as the decline in comparative advantage in the developed countries spread from goods where prices depended upon the cost of labour to those where this was much less true (that is, affecting the basic industrial structure), so the NICs transformed the skills of their labour force and their industrial structures in order to exploit this change.

The change in the skill content of NIC exports is shown in Table 9.9.

Table 9.9 *Changing composition of NIC exports to the OECD group – manufactures by technology level (% change)*

Technology level	*1964*	*1980*	*1985*
High	2.2	21.5	25.0
Medium	15.9	18.5	21.6
Low	81.6	59.8	53.2
Total	100	100	100

Source: Table 2.4, *The Newly Industrializing Countries: Challenge and Opportunity for OECD Industries*, OECD, Paris, 1988, p. 24.

In the 1980s, with a continued relatively high rate of growth in manufactured exports, some of the key commodities in this trade, in order of rates of growth, were office and telecommunications equipment, motor vehicles, machinery and transport equipment. Despite the heavy protection against garment imports in the OECD countries, this trade, of vital importance for developing countries, also expanded quite rapidly (and by an heroic 30 per cent in 1988). Other key items included household appliances and chemicals.

The Asian NICs expanded rapidly in the field of capital goods. Sixty per cent of their exports in this sector are in the fastest growing sub-sector, office and telecommunications equipment (compared to 30 per cent for the OECD group). This is one of the factors behind their high growth rates in the 1980s.

Table 9.10 *(a) Sectoral shares in Mexico's exports to the United States, selected years (%)*

Sector	*1970*	*1975*	*1980*	*1985*	*1987*
Foodstuffs	47.8	21.2	11.3	9.1	11.7
Raw Materials	10.7	10.0	5.0	4.2	3.9
Fuels	5.0	12.1	52.9	41.5	19.4
Manufactures	30.7	50.7	28.4	42.3	61.2
Other	5.8	6.0	2.4	2.9	3.8
Totals	100.0	100.0	100.0	100.0	100.0

(b) Changing share of selected items

Item	*1970*	*1975*	*1980*	*1985*	*1987*
1. Chemicals	47.8	21.2	11.3	9.1	11.7
2. Semi-finished goods	25.9	14.3	12.1	11.5	13.0
(a) Metal manufactures					
Steel	6.7	1.6	0.9	1.3	1.6
3. Machinery	33.9	48.4	5.3	51.8	46.9
(a) Engines	2.9	2.6	1.8	11.1	8.1
(b) Electrical mach.	23.5	35.0	4.2	31.8	28.5
Electr. mach. & switchgear	4.2	6.5	9.3	9.0	8.4
Telecommns eq.	6.9	15.0	19.3	9.1	6.4
Transistors	9.3	8.3	3.9	2.8	2.5
(c) Heavy ind. mach.	0.3	1.9	2.2	0.8	1.0
(d) Business mach.	5.3	5.2	2.5	3.7	3.8
(e) Scientific instru.	0.9	1.6	2.7	2.3	2.6
4. Transport	3.5	7.1	5.5	10.4	16.4
(a) Road vehicles	2.5	5.3	5.4	10.2	16.2
(b) vehicle parts	2.5	4.7	5.1	5.8	5.2
5. Consumer goods					
(a) Consumer electronics	4.6	1.3	1.4	6.9	7.4
(b) Apparel	9.8	11.7	8.3	4.5	4.3

These are only a minority of selected subsectors and some of their constituent commodities and therefore do not sum to 100.

Source: Calculated from the absolute figures in Directorate of Intelligence (Central Intelligence Agency), *OECD Trade with Mexico and Central America*, US Government, Washington DC, January 1989, Table 14.

Mexico

(i) Manufactured exports

Mexico, with its close proximity to a country which is both the world's largest market and which has experienced one of the largest declines in comparative advantage in some sectors of manufacturing, would have had to struggle very hard to escape the trend to a growth in manufactured exports, particularly since it is one of the middle-income countries best positioned in terms of its existing industrial structure to exploit the trend.

In 1965, 16.5 per cent of its total exports were manufactured goods – 5 per cent, sugar; 2.6 per cent, textiles, garments and footwear; 3.9 per cent, chemicals; 2.2 per cent, iron and steel (and 51 per cent, agricultural primary commodities, and 20 per cent, minerals). By 1970, the share of manufactured exports had risen to 31 per cent of the total, and to 51 per cent by1975 (see Table 9.10). Thus, the tendency towards the international integration of manufacturing was already developing swiftly between Mexico and the United States in the early 1970s.

The predilections of Mexican governments were not, however, in this direction. They constantly emphasized issues of economic independence rather than interdependence, industrialization on the basis of the domestic market rather than external demand (although import-substitution strategies could always be subverted by unfavourable market conditions operating across the long open border with the north). Manufactured exports grew apparently by default.

What checked, and indeed reversed, the process of Mexico's technical integration with the manufacturing economy of the north was the discovery of significant oil reserves. Oil exports (and borrowing on the basis of potential exports at a continuing high price) provided the rationale for a renewed dash for national industrialization. In this sense, President Lopez Portillo was the last of the Cardenistas. However, in contemporary terms, the meaning of this version of economic nationalism had become transformed – it was possible only with increased reliance on raw material exports, preeminently oil. Thus, in exporting terms, Mexico regressed while enormously increasing the vulnerability of the economy to the concatenation of circumstances that brought the boom to an end in 1982.

After that date, the need to service the debt and the long boom in the United States pulled the Mexican economy violently in the opposite direction, resuming the pattern that existed before 1975. In the 1980s, Mexico's exports of manufactured goods expanded in

Table 9.11 *(a) Mexican imports from the United States, percentage share by sector for selected years*

Sector	*1970*	*1975*	*1980*	*1985*	*1987*
Foodstuffs	8.6	11.0	16.2	9.9	7.2
Raw materials	8.0	6.6	5.2	5.5	5.4
Fuels	4.1	4.2	2.3	4.3	3.5
Manufacturing	74.8	74.4	74.1	77.1	80.0
Other	4.5	3.7	2.2	3.2	3.9
Total	100.0	100.0	100.0	100.0	100.0

(b) Share of selected items

Item	*1970*	*1975*	*1980*	*1985*	*1987*
1. Chemicals	13.4	13.4	13.7	13.5	11.8
2. Semi-finished	13.3	13.2	18.0	12.8	14.5
(a) metal manufs.	5.8	6.6	10.4	4.0	4.3
3. Machinery	42.9	40.6	40.5	46.4	49.1
(a) Electr. mach.	11.3	12.1	9.7	19.5	23.3
(b) Heavy mach.	1.2	9.3	10.6	7.0	6.2
(c) Business mach	2.7	2.4	2.4	4.7	4.6
4. Transport	19.4	21.2	18.5	17.3	15.2
5. Consumer goods	11.0	11.5	9.5	10.0	10.2

(many items are omitted, so the totals do not sum to 100)

Source: Ibid., calculated from Table 13, pp. 49–52.

volume terms by an heroic 79 per cent (despite a significant deterioration in the terms of trade in the middle of the decade. Table 9.10 presents the story in terms of sectoral shares in Mexico's exports to the United States – with manufactures declining fromn 51 per cent in 1975 to 28 per cent in 1980, and then returning to 61 per cent in 1987. (Of course, part, but only part, of this shift is spurious in volume terms, because the 1970s experienced buoyant raw material prices and the 1980s stagnant or declining ones.) In the second part of the table, a selection of sub-sectors of manufactured exports is presented both to show the effects of the crisis and the increasing skill content of exports. Machinery exports, for example, fell from 48 per cent of the total of manufactured exports in 1975 to 5.3 per cent in 1980, then returned to 50 per cent in 1985; electrical machinery moved from 35 to 4.2 to 32 per cent. There are perverse trends also: commodities that did not follow the same tendency. Furthermore, if we take garments as a surrogate for labour-intensive production, they showed a steady decline in share (from 12 per cent in 1975 to 4.3 per cent in 1987), perhaps reflecting the process affecting the Asian NICs of a continuing loss of comparative advantage in this sector, to the gain of poorer countries.

The growing technical sophistication and capital intensity of Mexico's manufacturing exports is shown in the fastest growing sub-sectors. Thus, scientific instruments moved its share from 0.9 to 2.6 per cent between 1970 and 1987; computers from 0.6 to 1.2; aircraft engines from 0 to 7.7 per cent, etc.

Table 9.11 shows the other side of the coin, Mexico's imports from the United States. In the period of boom, 1975–80, manufactured imports increased by 289 per cent, but this was partly to service a rapid growth in consumption rather than to upgrade production. After 1982, the increased sophistication of exports required an increasing sophistication in imports, but this cannot be demonstrated in the figures here because of the problems of aggregation. However, the import figures also show that part of the cost of the stress on industrialization has been a neglect of agriculture, particularly in the supply of basic foodstuffs. In this field, the comparative advantage of the United States is strong – reflected in Mexico's import of some 12 million tonnes of grain in 1989.

Thus, in the 1980s Mexico experienced a prodigious growth in exports of manufactured goods while simultaneously increasing their technical sophistication. It did so by exploiting the growth in the North American market in the same way as the Asian NICs. Whereas slump suddenly exposed the manufacturing weakness of Britain (fully 17 per cent of its industrial capacity was closed in 1979–80), it was boom that revealed this in the United States. Industrial capacity was incapable of meeting the growth in final demand, and indeed of producing domestic output without a rising volume of imported components. Manufactured imports now roughly equal a third of manufactured output. However, in those important areas where US manufacturing retains its advantage there is continued growth. (Manufactured exports are still equal to a fifth of output; the US remains, of course, the second largest exporting country in the world after West Germany.)

Mexico's role in the US economy is exaggerated because its

northern border runs alongside two regions with among the highest medium-term rates of economic growth in the country, California and Texas. California, with 13 per cent of US national income (if it were an independent country, it would have the seventh largest GDP in the world), experienced continued rapid expansion in the 1980s. On an index of 1982=100, its gross product reached 140 by 1988, and was expected to cross the 150 mark in 1989. It is the largest recipient of Japanese capital – $8 billion in non-bank assets, employing an estimated 70,000. With the vital assistance of legal and illegal immigrants from Mexico and computer engineers from Taiwan, Greater Los Angeles has now become the largest manufacturing area in the country (the immigrants have played a crucial role in raising American employment and incomes).[9]

As noted earlier, the aggregation of traded items does not allow us to identify very clearly the different patterns of specialization between Mexico and the United States (the statistical illusion is that they are exchanging the same things, for example 'machinery'). This obscures the technical integration that is taking place, so that we cannot easily see the Mexican input to US output (and vice versa). However, integration can partly be seen in the growth of *maquiladoras* (in-bond assembly plants), which are in part devoted to participation in joint production processes. Employment here has grown from 123,000 in 1982 to 412,000 in 1989 (it is now equal to 15 per cent of Mexico's manufacturing employment and, with a rapid rate of growth, is tilting the regional balance of the country towards the north). Its contribution to Mexico's external earnings has risen from 2.5 to 5.3 per cent (1970–86). Furthermore, contrary to fears expressed earlier, the nature of the operations involved has become increasingly technically sophisticated. It is less dominated by US-registered small labour-intensive operations, and more – as befits the Mexican comparative advantage generally – by larger operations, with a middle range of skills and a wider diversity of ownership. Mexico now cannot compete with the poorer countries on low wages. The other side of the picture is imports to the United States under tariffs 806.00 and 807.30, which we have already examined (see Tables 9.3–9.5).

The US share in Mexico's external trade has tended to decline in the long term from its peak of 88 per cent during the Second World War to a low of 56 per cent in 1982 (but up again to 65 per cent in 1988). This possibly reflects the role of oil in Mexico's exports; the larger it is, the greater the diversity of outlets. Mexico's share of US trade is much smaller – 2.3 per cent in 1940, 6.4 per cent in 1982 and 4.9 per cent in 1986 – but still large enough to make it the third largest US trade partner after Canada (23.6 per cent) and Japan. Nonetheless, the asymmetry of the relationship in trade terms enhances Mexico's vulnerability to US protectionism.

Diversification away from the US has come in increased trade with other members of the OECD group, particularly Europe and Japan, not with the fast growing countries of East and South-East Asia. In 1988, 6 per cent of exports went to Japan and over 10 per cent to Europe. Exports to eight of the high growth countries of the Asian Pacific Rim (excluding Japan) totalled only 1.6 per cent of total exports in 1986 and 1987.[10] Japan in the main imported raw materials (three-quarters of the imports were crude oil with a 1986 value per tonne of $96), while exporting high value capital machinery (with a value of $4,525 per tonne). China, on the other hand, proved a growing market for Mexico's manufactured goods.

(ii) Other elements

Trade in commodities is only part of the important advantage that Mexico now derives from its proximity to the United States. There is also illegal trade which is, for obvious reasons, difficult to quantify. The range of estimates for Mexico's unrecorded economic activities varies from 26 per cent of GDP by CEESP (Centro de Estudios del Sector Privado) (excluding unrecorded remittances from the US, tax evasion and revenue from narcotics) to 50 per cent by the Confederation of Industrial Chambers.

Trade in services is also of increasing importance. Tourism, targeted to increase by nearly 10 per cent per year up to 1994, is a key revenue earner. It tends still to be dominated by North Americans although there are faster growing areas of demand.

The *maquiladoras* may also begin to attract an increasing volume of service activities (there was always some of this – one of the earliest Ciudad Juarez factories was for sorting coupons). For example, it has been rumoured that some bank and airline data-processing functions may be relocated south of the border in In-Bond areas, and this may be the beginning of the movement to Mexico of more software programming for companies in the north (India and possibly other developing countries are competitive in this field). From casual observation on the frontier, Mexican medical services seem to be of growing importance to meet the considerable increase in demand from aged Americans wintering on the northern side of the border. As an export, this has great potential since US medical services are notoriously highly priced and are easily undercut in Mexico (to reverse the process whereby the Mexican rich go to the US for medical treatment). In the future, the border may see lines of hospitals along the Mexico side (with retirement homes attached), perhaps with emergency ambulance services to collect patients from deep within the US. The paradox of Mexico providing the means to save gringo lives would startle the country's ancestors, but it would symbolize Mexico's arrival as a Great Power.

As is well known, two-thirds of the foreign investment in Mexico is of US origin. Japanese investment has increased swiftly, particularly in heavy industry and infrastructural development, and vehicle and household appliance manufacture, but it is still only 8–9 per cent of Japanese investment in Latin America as a whole (the largest share is in Panama, the second in Brazil), and it seems unlikely that it will displace West Germany in second place in Mexico in the immediate future.

However, Mexico may expect, depending upon the policy framework, to see a rising inflow of capital from Asia more generally to establish plants to supply not just the United States but also Japan and other parts of the world with the middle range of technically sophisticated manufactures. If East Asia can supply the North American market, Mexico, given particular patterns of specialization, could supply East Asia.

(iii) Mexico–US relations

The US is already dependent upon Mexico in a number of ways, and that dependence is likely to increase for several reasons. One of the more obvious lies in demography. The North American population is ageing and its young age group contracting, at a time when almost 80 per cent of Mexico's nearly 85 million are below the age of 40. Whether the migration is of Americans and their capital south or Mexicans and their exports north in response to this imbalance, is partly a choice open to the Mexican Government, a mark of the very considerable increase in Mexico's relative power in the relationship. Or again, if agricultural liberalization results from the current Farm Bill and the Uruguay or later rounds of trade negotiations, it is likely that American agricultural products will come under stronger competition from imports. Hitherto, there has been a tendency for the dependence of US farms on Mexican illegal migrants to decline, but a change in the competitive context could reverse this, leading to Mexico's labour supply, particularly of unskilled workers, becoming crucial whether they farm in Mexico or in the US.

In the past, the opportunities were much more limited and scarce, but now the advantages appear to be favouring Mexico. Exploiting the economic relationship with the US and diversifying relationships away from the US at the same time is only feasible with growth. That is also required to ease some of the more horrifying conditions of the relationship – such as the cruel hypocrisy of the movement of labour across the border. It is possible that it can only be achieved by conceding the free movement of capital, but Mexican business is now strong enough to dispense with the cocoon of protection and to welcome technological improvements from abroad.

The argument is predicated on the assumption of a continuing integration of world capitalism, and the emergence of a single global economy. The process would seem now to be too far advanced for the governments of the developed countries to halt or reverse it. Their domestic output is increasingly dependent upon imports. Of course, they will continue to use their greater power in the system to seek to gain advantages through bullying and cheating on the supposed rules of free trade (as with the Multi Fibre Arrangement), but even so, they are obliged to accept the main process which is taking place.

Thus, the emerging world order offers striking opportunities for renewed and rapid economic growth in Mexico. This paper has stressed the potential, since so much has been written about the obstacles to growth and the severe problems of the country – from debt, high interest rates, low oil prices, to inequality of incomes, corruption, pollution and the stubborn persistence of poverty. Only some of these problems are ameliorated by growth, and some will undoubtedly be made worse. But in the long struggle to employ all who want to work at levels of productivity capable of sustaining tolerable incomes, Mexico's evolution as a major manufacturing power is an important step forward.

CONCLUSIONS

Hitherto, the Pacific Rim has been seen as almost entirely an Asian phenomenon – whether as regional framework for US interests in East and South-East Asia or the wider regional interests of Japan. Mexico has scarcely participated. It is not a member of the new Australian or Japanese initiatives. Its share of trans-Pacific trade and capital movements is small, and there is no trans-Pacific migration. There is a danger that Mexico may be seen as no more than a North American dependency in the relationships which are emerging, and may miss opportunities for wider economic diversification.

Like the NICs of East and South-East Asia, as also the ASEAN group (with Singapore a member of both), Mexico has an interest both in checking the influence of one great power by a relationship with the other, and in offsetting the domination of both major powers by diversifying its economic and political relationships. However, it is also in competition with the NICs, particularly in the US market, and no doubt, in the future, in the Japanese market. At a disaggregated level there are growing areas of specialization (as there are among the developed countries) in the middle level of skill and capital-intensive production that would provide the basis for trade and capital movements between Mexico and the two larger NICs, Korea and Taiwan. Mexico's access to the US market and to US technology also makes it an attractive location for Korean and Taiwanese manufacturing, just as Korean and Taiwanese proximity to Japan might make them attractive locations for Mexican offshore production for the Japanese market. Joint Mexican–Korean enterprises might be a useful institutional form here. Mexico also has areas of special expertise that could be important to Asia – in the oil industry in Indonesia, for example. (In the past Mexican hybrid seed has transformed grain production in much of Asia.)

In sum, while Mexico needs to continue to exploit to the full its relationship with the US market, it also has an interest in political and economic diversification – both to Japan and to the NICs and ASEAN countries.

Notes

1. Economic Development and Urbanization

1. Dr Rakesh Mohan, Indian Planning Commission, point made orally on his 'Industry and Urban Employment (a preliminary exploration of available data for India, 1961–1983)', Paper for a Conference, Poverty in India, University of Oxford (Institute for International Development), Oxford, October 1987 (mimeo).
2. United Nations: *Urban and Rural Population Projections, 1950–2025: the 1984 Assessment,* United Nations, New York, 1986.
3. See my 'Some Trends in the Evolution of Big Cities: Studies of the USA and India', *Habitat International*, Vol. 8, No. 1, pp. 7–28, Pergamon Press, Oxford; republished here pp. 69–96; also for Brazil, Andrew M. Hamer, *Brazilian Industrialization and Economic Concentration in São Paulo: A Survey*, Discussion Paper (Report No. UDD 14), Urban Development Department, Operational Policy Staff, World Bank, Washington DC, October 1982 (mimeo).
4. For an early outline of the case, see B. F. Hoselitz, 'The Role of Urbanization in Economic Development: Some International Comparisons' in Roy Turner (ed.) *India's Urban Future*, California University Press, Berkeley, 1962, pp. 157–81.
5. For an excellent critique of the data and interpretations of Mexican materials on unemployment and urban–rural migration, see Peter Gregory, *The Myth of Market Failure: Employment and the Labour Market in Mexico,* World Bank Research Publication, Johns Hopkins University Press for the World Bank, Baltimore and London, 1986.
6. Adam Smith, *An Inquiry into the Nature and Causes of the Wealth of Nations,* R. H. Campbell and A. S. Skinner (eds), Clarendon Press, Oxford, 1976, Vol. 1, p. 31.
7. On the urban lead in productivity for modern cities, see 'Urbanization and Economic Development', in George S. Tolley and Vinod Thomas (eds), *The Economics of Urbanization and Urban Policies in Developing Countries*, World Bank Symposium, World Bank, Washington DC, 1987, pp. 15–30. On the Indian case, see: Satyendra Verma, 'Urbanization and Productivity in Indian States', in Edwin S. Mills and Charles M. Becker

(eds) *Studies in Indian Urban Development*, World Bank Research Publications, Oxford University Press (for World Bank), Washington DC, 1986, pp. 103–36.

8. David Ricardo, *On the Principles of Political Economy and Taxation*, edited with an introduction by R. M. Hartwell, Penguin, London, 1971, pp. 324ff.
9. Karl Marx, *Capital*, introduced by G. D. H. Cole, Vol. 1, Everyman, London, 1930, p. 371.
10. *Ibid.*, p. 373.
11. *Ibid.*, Vol., II, Foreign Languages Publishing House, Moscow, 1957, p. 781.
12. See: A. Erlich, *The Soviet Industrialization Debate*, Harvard University Press, Cambridge, Mass., 1960; also M. Lewin, *Russian Peasants and Soviet Power, a Study in Collectivization,* George Allen & Unwin, London, 1968, and E. H. Carr and R. W. Davies, *Foundations of a Planned Economy*, 1928–1929, Macmillan, London, 1969.
13. Nicolai Bukharin, 'Notes of an Economist (at the beginning of the new economic year)', translated with an introduction by Keith Smith, *Economy and Society* 8:4, Routledge, London, 1979, pp. 446–500.
14. E. Preobrazhensky, *The New Economics*, translated by Brian Pearce, with an introduction by Alec Nove, Clarendon Press, Oxford, 1965.
15. See Mihael Manoïlesco, *Le siécle du corporatisme*, Felix Alcan, Paris, 1934; and *The Theory of Tariff Protection*, London, 1937.
16. Raúl Prebisch's arguments were presented in a report of the United Nations Economic Commission for Latin America, *The Economic Development of Latin America and its Principal Problems,* 1950; *Economic Survey of Latin America 1949,* Part 1, 1951; *Problemas teóricos del crecimiento económico*, 1952.
17. Among the best known were: A. Emmanuel, *Unequal Exchange: A Study of the Imperialism of Free Trade*, Monthly Review Press, New York, 1972; Samir Amin, *Accumulation on the World Scale: a Critique of the Theory of Underdevelopment*, Monthly Review Press, New York, 1974, 2 vols.; A. Gunder Frank, *Dependent Accumulation and Underdevelopment*, Monthly Review Press, New York, 1979.
18. I. M. D. Little, T. Scitovsky and M. Scott, *Industry and Trade in Some Developing Countries*, Development Centre, OECD/Oxford University Press, London, 1970.
19. *Why the Poor Stay Poor: Urban Bias in World Development*, Temple Smith, London, 1977.
20. *Terms of Trade and Class Relations*, Frank Cass, 1977.
21. *The Organisation of Space in Developing Countries*, Harvard University Press, Cambridge, Mass., 1970.
22. Robert Z. Lawrence, *Can American Compete?* The Brookings Institute, Washington DC, 1984.
23. J. Vernon Henderson, *International Experience in Urbanization and its Relevance for China*, World Bank Staff Working Paper 758, World Bank, Washington DC, 1986; and 'The Analysis of Urban Concentration and Decentralization: the Case of Brazil' in Tolley and Thomas, *The Economies of Urbanization*, pp. 87–93.

24. But see the now sadly out-of-date: on New York, S. M. Robbins and N. E. Terleckyji, *Money Metropolis*, Harvard University Press, Cambridge, Mass., 1960; and on London, John H. Dunning and E. Victor Morgan, *An Economic Study of the City of London*, Economists' Advisory Group, Allen & Unwin, London, 1971.
25. Cited in Donald L. Foley, *Controlling London's Growth: Planning the Great Wen, 1940–1960*, University of California Press, Berkeley and Los Angeles, 1963, p. vi.
26. See, in particular, Part I, The Demographic Transition in: *The World Economy: History and Prospects*, Macmillan, London, 1978, pp. 1–44.
27. This is an underlying thread in his *Civilization and Capitalism, Fifteenth to Eighteenth Centuries*, William Collins, London, 1981 (3 volumes).
28. See World Bank, *China: Socialist Economic Development* (nine volumes, mimeo) *Annex B, Population, Health and Nutrition*, Report No. 3391–CHA, World Bank, Washington DC, 1 June, 1981.

2. Urbanization and Economic Development

1. *Report of the National Commission on Urbanisation*, Government of India, New Delhi, Aug. 1988, Vol. 1, p. 2.
2. See United Nations, *Global Review of Human Settlements, Statistical Annex*, prepared by the Statistical Office, Dept. of Economic and Social Affairs, United Nations, New York, 1976; Kingsley Davis, *World Urbanization, 1950–1970*, Population Monograph Series 4 and 9, University of California Press, Berkeley, 1972, 2 vols; and United Nations, *Methods for the Projection of Urban and Rural Population*, Manual VII, Population Studies 55, United Nations, New York, 1977.
3. Koichi Mera, 'An economic policy hypothesis of metropolitan growth cycles: a reflection on the recent rejuvenation of Tokyo', *Review of Urban and Regional Development Studies*, 1/1, Tokyo, January 1989, pp. 37–46.
4. For example, see Chart I for 1965–1970 data (Degree of urbanization compared with GNP per capita), Annex 1, in World Bank, *Urbanization: Sector Working Paper*, World Bank, Washington DC, June 1972, p. 73; Figure 2.1 (Level of urbanization and GNP/CAP for 11 countries in 1975) in Bertrand Renaud, *National Urbanization Policies in Developing Countries,* World Bank Staff Working Paper 347, July 1979, p. 16; and George S. Tolley, 'Urbanization and Economic Development', and Allen C. Kelley and Jeffrey G. Williamson, 'What Drives City Growth in the Developing World?' in George S. Tolley and Vinod Thomas (eds), *The Economics of Urbanization and Urban Policies in Developing Countries*, World Bank, Washington DC, 1987, pp. 15–31 and 32–35.
5. Edwin S. Mills, 'An Aggregate Model of Resource Allocation in a Metropolitan Region', *American Economic Review*, 57, 1967, pp. 197–210.
6. David Keeble, 'The Changing Spatial Structure of Economic Activity and Metropolitan Decline in the United Kingdom', in H. J. Ewers, J. B.

Goddard, and H. Matzerath (eds), *The Future of the Metropolis – Berlin, London, Paris, New York: Economic Aspects*, Walter de Gruyter, Berlin and New York, 1986, p. 183.

7. Mills and Song identify Korean urbanization as larger than would be predicted (in the Chenery–Syrquin model) by reason of the unusually large international sector, particularly manufactured exports, in the generation of South Korea's gross national product. See Edwin S. Mills and Song Byung-Nak, *Korea's Urbanization and Urban Problems, 1945–1975*, Harvard University Press, Cambridge, Mass., 1979.
8. Edwin S. Mills and Charles M. Becker, *Studies in Indian Urban Development*, World Bank Research Publication, Oxford University Press for the World Bank, Oxford, 1986, Tables 4–5, p. 67.
9. See his 'The sizes and types of cities', *American Economic Review*, 64, 1974, pp. 640–56; 'Industrial bases and city size', *ibid.*, 73, 1983, pp. 164–8; 'Urbanization in developing countries: city size and population composition', *Journal of Development Economics*, 22, 1986, pp. 264–93; 'Aspects of urban concentration in Brazil', in Tolley and Thomas, *The Economics of Urbanization*; and *Urban Development: Theory, Fact and Illusion*, Oxford University Press, Oxford, 1988.
10. Robert Z Lawrence, *Can America Compete?*, Brookings Institute, Washington DC, 1984.
11. *Studies in Indian Urban Development*, p. 133.
12. See the model of Kelley and Williamson, in Tolley and Thomas, *The Economics of Urbanization*, p. 43.
13. Figures cited in Per Ljung and Catherine Farvaque, *Addressing the Urban Challenge: A Review of the World Bank FY87 Water Supply and Urban Development Operations*, General Operations Research, INU 13, World Bank, Washington DC, March 1988.
14. *Report of the National Commission*, Vol. 1, p. 2.
15. See also Rakesh Mohan, 'Urbanization and India's Future', *Population and Development Review* 11(4), October 1985, pp. 619–45.
16. For an examination of an earlier period for the 22 leading developing country exporters, see 'A global manufacturing system', in my *The End of the Third World: Newly Industrializing Countries and the Decline of an Ideology*, Tauris 1986/ Penguin 1987, pp. 93–117.
17. OECD, *The Newly Industrializing Countries: Challenge and Opportunity for OECD Industries*, OECD, Paris, 1988.
18. *Industria Maquiladora de Exportación*, Instituto Nacional de Estadistica Geografica e Informatica, Aguascalientes, February 1990.
19. See Table 7, GATT, *International Trade 1987–88*, GATT, Geneva 1988, Vol. 1, p. 12.
20. World Bank–UNDP, *Africa: Adjustment and Growth in the 1980s*, World Bank, Washington DC, March 1989.
21. M. Q. Dalvi, *Zambia's Transport Policy: Main Issues, Approach and Options*, Working paper No. 1, UNDP/DTCD Transport Planning Project, Ministry of Power, Transport and Communications, Government of the Republic of Zambia, May 1988 (mimeo).
22. World Bank, *World Development Report 1989*, Oxford University Press for the World Bank, Oxford, 1989, p. 14.

23. United Nations, *Patterns of Urban and Rural Population Growth*, Dept. of International Economic and Social Affairs, United Nations, New York, 1980.
24. S. Cochrane and D. R. Vining Jr., 'Recent trends in migration between core and peripheral regions in Developed and advanced Developing Countries', *International Regional Science Review*, 1988, and Mera, 'An economic policy hypothesis'.
25. For a comparison of trends in urbanization in the United States and India, see the following chapter in this volume.
26. Moonis, Reza *et al.*, 'India: Urbanization and National Development', in M. Honjo (ed.), *Urbanization and Regional Development*, Maruzen, Singapore, 1982.
27. I. M. D. Little, T. Scitovsky and M. Scott, *Industry and Trade in Some Developing Countries*, Development Centre, OECD/Oxford University Press, London, 1970.
28. Michael Lipton, *Why the Poor Stay Poor: Urban Bias in World Development*, Temple Smith, London, 1977. For an opposite case, see Ashok Mitra, *Terms of Trade and Class Relations*, Frank Cass, London, 1977.
29. The generalization goes beyond the known evidence and may not apply equally to all countries or to the same country at all times. The data for the United States are reasonable clear for the periods studied. Comparisons of this kind are difficult because of higher urban price levels and variation in the degree of monetization of rural consumption. See Thomas, Vinod, *The measurement of spatial differences in poverty: the case of Peru*, World Bank Staff Working Paper 273, World Bank, Washington DC, 1978.
30. John Harriss, 'Urban poverty and urban poverty alleviation', *Cities, International Quarterly of Urban Policy*, 6/13, August 1989, pp. 186–94.
31. *Report of the National Commission on Urbanization*, Vol. II, p. 89.
32. National Institute of Urban Affairs, *Urban Poverty Survey*, NIUA, New Delhi, 1987.
33. For a striking example from Calcutta's public transport, see *The World Development Report 1988*, Oxford University Press for the World Bank, Oxford, 1988, p. 144.
34. Planning Commission, *Report of the Task Force on the Financing of Urban Development*, Government of India, New Delhi, 1985 (mimeo).
35. W. Arthur Lewis, *Evaluation of the International Economic Order*, Discussion Paper 74, Woodrow Wilson School Research Programme in Development Studies, University of Princeton, 1977, pp. 39–40.
36. Johannes F. Linn, 'The costs of urbanization in developing countries', *Economic Development and Cultural Change*, 30/3, Chicago, April 1982, pp. 625–48.
37. Remy Prud'homme, 'Does Paris subsidize the rest of France?' in Ewers, Goddard and Matzerath, *The Future of the Metropolis*, pp. 285–96.
38. For an early version of this case, see B. F. Hoselitz, 'The role of urbanization in economic development: some international comparisons' in Roy Turner (ed.), *India's Urban Future*, California University Press,

Berkeley, 1962, pp. 157–81.

39. Philip Amos, *African Development and Urban Change*, Development and Project Planning Centre, University of Bradford, October 1988, p. 14 (mimeo).
40. For a summary of the research evidence, see Subbiah Kannapan, in *Finance and Development*, International Monetary Fund and World Bank, Washington DC, January 1989, p. 47.
41. *The Myth of Market Failure: Employment and the Labor Market in Mexico*, World Bank Research Report, Johns Hopkins University, Baltimore, 1986.
42. United Nations, *Fifth Population Enquiry among Governments: Monitoring Government Perceptions and Policies on Demographic Trends and Levels in relation to Development as of 1982*, Population Division, United Nations, New York, 1984, p. 19.
43. On the argument that transport improvements encourage migration by removing obstacles, see Bertrand Renaud, *Economic fluctuations and speed of urbanization: a case study of Korea, 1955–1975*, World Bank Staff Working Paper 270, World Bank, Washington DC, November 1977.
44. See Kyu Sik Lee, *The location of jobs in a developing metropolis: patterns of growth in Bogota and Cali, Colombia*, Oxford University Press for the World Bank, Oxford, 1989, and Michael Murray, *Subsidizing Industrial Location: A Conceptual Framework with Application to Korea*, World Bank Occasional Paper 3, Johns Hopkins University Press for the World Bank, Baltimore, 1988, and the discussion in *Urban Edge: Issues and Innovations*, 13/6, July 1989, pp. 1–5.
45. See the influential – surprisingly so, given its doubtful methodology – *Community Cost of Industrial Location in Bombay and Nasik*, by G. Kulkarni and A. Kulkarni, SICOM, Bombay, 1968.
46. 'To argue that growth transmission is mostly or fully restricted to the hinterland of a growth center is to maintain that regional or subregional city systems have a high degree of closure, i.e. a low degree of interaction with urban units situated elsewhere in the national system' – Alan Pred, *City Systems in Advanced Economies*, Wiley, new York, 1977, p. 95.
47. 'It is precisely because we will not invest in a city such as Gwalior that Delhi still continues to grow; it is because Warangel is left undeveloped that Hyderabad is bursting at the seams . . .'; or again, 'The Commission is confident that, if sufficient investment is made . . . then, by the end of the Ninth Plan, the urban settlement pattern of India would have substantially changed and the imbalances of the present metro-dominated system would have been greatly reduced' – *Report of the National Commission on Urbanization*, Vol. 1, p. 6.
48. For example, the contributors to United Nations, *Population Distribution Policies in Development Planning*, Department of International Economic and Social Affairs, Population Studies No. 75, United Nations, New York, 1981.
49. See the discussion in *World Development Report 1988*, Oxford University Press for the World Bank, Oxford, 1988, pp. 158–67, and on the

decentralization of educational and health services, pp. 131–41.

50. Per Ljung and Jun Zhang, 'The World Bank support for institutional and policy reform in metropolitan areas: the case of Calcutta', Paper for the XVII Triennale di Milano (Policy Strategies and Projects for Metropolitan Areas), Milan, 1988 (published in *Habitat International*, Vol. 13, No. 3, 1989, pp. 5–14).

3. Some Trends in the Evolution of Big Cities

1. A case presented, for example, in B. F. Hoselitz, 'The role of urbanisation in economic development: some international comparisons', in Roy Turner (ed.), *India's Urban Future*, California University Press, Berkeley, 1962: for a critique, see N. V. Sovani, 'The analysis of "over-urbanization"', in N. V. Sovani, *Urbanization and Urban India*, London, 1966.
2. For the Chinese sources, see my *The Mandate of Heaven, Marx and Mao in Modern China*, Quartet, London, 1978, pp. 46–7, 108–5. For Fidel Castro's views, contrasting with Marx's 'idiocy of rural life', see 'The city is a cemetery of revolutionaries and resources', cited by Régis Debray, *Revolution in the Revolution?*, Pelican edition, London, 1968, p. 67; and also 'The peasant possesses a virgin mentality, free from an assortment of influences which poison the intellect of citizens in the city. The revolution works on these fertile intellects as the rain works on the soil', *Obra Revolucionaria*, Havana, 7 March 1961, p. 24.
3. The problem of the changes in the meaning of the concept, 'family', are discussed instructively by Norah Carlin in 'An unnatural practice', *Socialist Review* 50, London, January 1983, pp. 18–23.
4. The data used here are drawn in the main from: 1980 Census of Population, Supplementary Reports, PC80–S1–5, *Standard Metropolitan Statistical Areas and Standard Consolidated Statistical Areas, 1980*, Bureau of the Census, United States Government Printing Office, Washington DC, 1980.
5. Hawley calculates that the areas of more rapid population growth in Metropolitan Regions changed from Central City Areas (1900–10) to a 5-mile ring around central city areas (1910–20), to a ring between 5 and 10 miles from central cities (1920–50), and thereafter, to 10 miles and beyond. See Amos H. Hawley, *The Changing Shape of Metropolitan America*, Glencoe Ill., 1956, pp. 14–16. Compare a comment on the emerging European pattern in the 1950s: 'a general description of what is happening in the modern industrial world is that the macro-location of industry and population is tending towards an ever increasing concentration in a limited number of areas; their micro-location, on the other hand, is towards an ever increasing "diffusion" or "sprawl"' – Colin Clark, Fiona Wilson and J. Bradley, 'Industrial Location and Economic Potential in Western Europe', *Regional Studies* 3, 1960, p. 197.
6. The 'Three Great Differences' were those between rural and urban

people, worker and peasant, mental and manual labour – *cf. The Mandate of Heaven*, pp. 50–51.

7. The peak years for manufacturing employment in various industrialized countries, with the proportion of the labour force involved, was: USA 1973 (32.5%); Holland 1965 (28.2%); France 1974 (28.1%); Belgium 1965 (33.9%); Italy 1975 (32.6%); West Germany 1961 (34.7%); Japan 1975 (25.8%); Britain 1966 (34.9%). See my 'Deindustralization', *International Socialism* 8, London, Winter 1980, pp. 72–81.
8. *Employment and Earnings*, Bureau of Labor Statistics, US Department of Labor, Washington DC, March 1982.
9. See Table 21, World Bank, *World Development Report 1983*, Oxford University Press for the World Bank, Oxford, 1983.
10. The phrase is that of Robbins and Terleckyi, in S. M. Robbins and N. E. Terleckyi, *Money Metropolis*, Harvard University Press, Cambridge, Mass., 1960; see also J. H. Dunning and E. Victor Morgan, *An Economic Profile of the City of London*, Allen and Unwin, London, 1971.
11. This point is illustrated in more detail in my *Of Bread and Guns: the World Economy in Crisis*, Pelican, London, 1983.
12. Data in this section are drawn from: Census of India, *Provisional Population Trends, Rural–Urban Distribution*, Series–I, India, Paper 2 of 1981, R. Padmanabhan, IAS, Delhi, 1982.
13. A point well demonstrated by Rakesh Mohan and Chandrashekar Pant in: 'Morphology of Urbanization in India: some results fromn the 1981 Census', *Economic and Political Weekly*, Bombay, XVII/38–39, 18 and 25 September, 1982; see also Rakesh Mohan, 'Coming to Terms with Urbanization', *Cities*, London, 1/1, August 1983, pp. 46–58.
14. A point noted by Mills and Becker who infer that: '. . . a large initial population discourages further city growth, starting at initial populations somewhat below one million.This evidence is in opposition to the view that large cities grow rapidly because they are large.' Edwin S. Mills and Charles Becker, *Indian City Sizes and City Growth*, Discussion Paper (Report No. UDD4), Urban Development Department, Operational Policy Staff, World Bank, Washington DC, February 1983.
15. See my *Economic Development, Cities and Planning: the Case of Bombay*, Oxford University Press, Bombay, 1978, pp. 21–2.
16. Infrastructural decisions are much stressed by Andrew Hamer in his account of the disproportionate growth of São Paulo – see Table IV.3 and discussion in Andrew M. Hamer, *Brazilian Industrialization and Economic Concentration in São Paulo: a Survey*, Discussion Paper (Report No. UDD14, mimeo), Urban Development Department, Operational Policy Staff, World Bank, Washington DC, October 1982, p. 46.
17. The 'black economy' is not, of course, the same as what is implied in the phrase 'informal sector'. The first was developed to identify the scale of tax evasion rather than unrecorded petty miscellaneous manufacturing and trade (which may or may not be black or grey). Recent estimates of the size of the American workforce engaged in the 'black economy' make it of some significance – *cf. Of Bread and Guns*, pp. 137–9: a

recent estimate puts it at 23% – *cf.* R. de Grazia, *Le Travail Clandestin*, International Labour Organization, Geneva, 1983.

18. Geoffrey Charlish, 'Why Silicon Valley Continues to Breed Success', *Financial Times*, London, 10 August, 1983, p. 14.
19. The phrase was advanced by Rakesh Mohan as the desirable aim of policy, in: *The Strategy for Housing and Urban Development: Some New Perspectives* (unpublished, mimeo), Planning Commission, New Delhi, June 1982, p. 43.
20. '. . . within Brazil, a pattern of deconcentration is becoming evident: first areas close to the most favoured metropolises have emerged; second, more distant metropolises have begun to grow steadily . . . [but] As long as balance of payments considerations, or other such macroeconomic concerns play a dominant role in spatial matters, Brazil will continue to be an economic archipelago, more closely linked than before, but, nevertheless, an archipelago' – Hamer, *Brazilian Industrialization*, p. 10.
21. Alonso, writing at the beginning of the 1970s, observed then: 'Direct policies to modify this geographical distribution [of population] have been generally ineffective and sometimes counter-productive because they have underestimated or misjudged the connections among elements of the system along dimensions other than the geographic. Conversely, many policies and public actions whose main thrust is not territorial turn out to have strong consequences which are normally not intended'. W. Alonso, 'Problems, Purposes and Implicit Policies for a National Strategy of Urbanization', in Sara Mills Mazie (ed.), *Population Distribution and Policy*, V. Research Reports, US Commission on Population Growth and the American Future, Government Printing Office, Washington DC, 1972, p. 645.
22. *Ibid.*, p. 636.
23. Harry W. Richardson, *Population Distribution Policies*, Paper for the International Seminar on Small Cities and National Development, New Delhi, 24–29 January 1983, United Nations Centre for Regional Development, Nagoya, 1982, p. 7. For a useful and broadly sceptical discussion of population distribution policies, see United Nations, *Population Distribution Policies in Development Planning*, UN/UNFP Workshop, Bangkok, 4–13 September 1979, United Nations, New York, 1981.
24. Bertrand Renaud, *National Urbanization Policies in Developing Countries*, Staff Working paper No. 347, World Bank, Washington DC, July 1979, pp. iii–v.
25. Richardson, *Population Distribution*, p. 20.
26. On US data for the 1960s, see *National Growth and Development*, Second Biennial Report to Congress, Committee on Community Development, The Domestic Council, US Government Printing Office, Washington DC, December 1974.
27. For example, see Advisory Committee on Intergovernmental Relations, *Urban and Rural America: Policies for Future Growth*, US Government Printing Office, Washington DC, 1968.
28. See for a description of the regional measures, Bernard Chinitz,

'Regional Economic Development: the Title V Program', *Canadian Journal of Regional Science* 1/2, Toronto, 1978, pp. 107–23.

29. In India this is apparent from the Census results for 1971 for Bombay, Madras and Calcutta. For a different example, see Kalmann Schaefer, assisted by Cheywa R. Spindell, *Urban Development and Employment in São Paulo,* Urbanization and Employment Research Programme, World Employment Programme, Working Paper, International Labour Organization, Geneva, June 1975; the work of Hamer already cited; and the masterly overview in Zilton Luis Macedo, *Industrialization and Urbanization in the State of São Paulo, 1950–1970*, unpublished Ph.D. thesis, University of London, London, 1983.
30. Mills and Becker, *Indian City Sizes*.
31. For a summary and discussion of some of the recent innovations, see K. Young and Charlie Mason (eds), *Urban Economic Development, New Roles and Relationships*, Public Policy and Politics Series, Macmillan, London, 1983.
32. For a critical discussion, see Neil Smith, 'Gentrification and Uneven Development', *Economic Geography* 58/2, April 1982, pp. 139–55.

4. On the 'Petty Bourgeoisie'

1. Frederick Engels, *Revolution and Counter-Revolution in Germany*, 1851–2, in Karl Marx/Frederick Engels, *Collected Works* (hereafter *CW*), Vol. 11, p. 9.
2. *Ibid.*
3. Engels, *Two Years of Revolution, 1848 and 1849*, 1850, *CW*, Vol. 10, p. 361.
4. *Ibid.*
5. Engels, *The Constitutional Question in Germany*, 1847, *CW*, Vol. 10, p. 85.
6. Engels, *Revolution and Counter-Revolution*, pp. 88–9.
7. *Ibid.*, p. 10.
8. Engels, *The Constitutional Question*, p. 88.
9. Karl Marx, *The Eighteenth Brumaire of Louis Bonaparte*, 1852, *CW*, Vol. 11, pp. 130–1.
10. Karl Marx, letter to P. V. Annenkov, 28 December 1846, *CW*, Vol. 38, p. 105; stress in original.
11. Karl Marx, letter to Sorge, 19 October 1877, in *Correspondence of Marx and Engels, Selected 1846–1895,* London, 1934, p. 350.
12. Engels, *Revolution and Counter-Revolution*, p. 89.
13. Marx, *The Eighteenth Brumaire*, p. 130; stress in original.
14. *Ibid*, p. 133; stress in original.
15. Karl Marx and Frederick Engels, *Address of the Central Authority to the League*, March 1850, *CW*, Vol. 10, pp. 280–1.
16. *Ibid*, p. 282.
17. Trotsky's account of this is among the most perceptive – cf. L. D. Trotsky, 'Fascism, Stalinism and the United Front, 1930–1934',

republished in *International Socialism*, Aug.–Sept. 1969, and Carr's commentary, Note B, 'Trotsky and the rise of Hitler', in E. H. Carr, *The Twilight of the Comintern, 1930–35,* Macmillan, London, 1982, pp. 433–6. On the interesting case of Mussolini, erstwhile Marxist, whose political fortunes were transformed from a rootless search for a class basis for his restless ambitions to Fascist dictator when he connected with the frustration of the north Italian petty bourgeoisie, see Ernste Nolte, *Three Faces of Fascism* (transl. from German by Leila Vennewitz), Weidenfeld, London, 1965, pp. 202 ff.

18. Marx–Engels, *Werke* 4, 484, cited in Special Note F, 'The alleged theory of the disappearance of the Middle Classes', in Hal Draper, *Karl Marx's Theory of Revolution*, Vol. II, *The Politics of Social Classes*, Monthly Review, New York, 1978, p. 519.
19. Karl Marx, *Theories of Surplus Value*, Part II, Lawrence and Wishart, London, 1969, p. 573.
20. Draper, *Karl Marx's Theory*, p. 623.
21. On the documentation of this, see Tony Cliff, *Lenin*, Vol. 1, *Building the Party*, Pluto Press, London, 1975, Chapter 8, pp. 168–182.
22. V. I. Lenin, *The defeat of Russia and the revolutionary crisis*, 1914–15, *Lenin, Collected Works*, Vol. 21, p. 380; stress in original.
23. See, for example, 'the new middle class' ('an unfortunate term') as described by Rudolf Hilferding in 1910 in *Finance Capital, a study of the latest phase of capitalist development*, translated and republished, Routledge, London, 1981, pp. 347 ff. Max Weber most vividly identified some of the ideological imperatives of the public segment of this stratum in 'Politics as a Vocation', and 'On Bureaucracy'; cf. *From Max Weber, Essays in Sociology*, translated, edited and introduced by H. H. Gerth and C. Wright Mills, Routledge, London, 1948, pp. 77–178 and 196–244. Others wrote extensively on the subject in the 1950s and 1960s – for example, see Serge Mallet, *La nouvelle classe ouvrière*, Collections Esprit, Editions du Seuil, Paris, 1963. The same issues have resurfaced in Britain in current discussion of 'the end of the working class' in the Labour and Communist parties.
24. For discussion of the trends in Britain, see my 'Deindustrialization', *International Socialism 7*, Winter 1980, pp. 72–81.
25. Cited by Chris Harman, 'Farewell to the working class?' *Socialist Worker*, London, 16 April 1983.
26. A slightly random selection of 'proletariats' would include: Frantz Fanon: 'In colonial countries, the peasants alone are revolutionary, for they have nothing to lose and everything to gain. The starving peasant, outside the class system, is the first among the exploited to discover that only violence pays. For him, there is no compromise, no possiblëcoming to terms', *The Wretched of the Earth*, Penguin, London, 1965, p. 48; and Paul Sweezy: 'The masses in the exploited dependencies constitute a force in the global capitalist system which is revolutionary in the same sense that Marx considered the proletariat of the early period of modern industrialization to be revolutionary', 'The proletariat in today's world', *Tricontinental*, 91/1968, p. 33; and Régis

Debray: 'The guerrilla force is completely independent of the civilian population in action as well as in military organisation; consequently, it need not assume the direct defence of the peasant population', *Revolution in the Revolution?*, Penguin, London, 1968, p. 41.

27. 'China's Economic Strategy', *Monthly Review*, New York, July–August 1975, 27/3, p. 9.
28. This is not the place to discuss the issues, but the record is summarized in Dipak Kumar Das, *The national and colonial question: from Marx to the Second Congress of the Communist International*, unpublished Ph.D. thesis, University of Calcutta, 1980; cf. also Ian Cummins, *Marx, Engels and National Movements*, Croom Helm, London, 1980.
29. As an example of the absurd muddling of language, consider Kenneth Kaunda's justification of new policy: 'now Government is yours, industries are yours, the whole economy is yours . . . to run and manage effectively and successfully . . . it is as this background . . . that I find it imperative in the interests of the nation as a whole to announce a wage freeze until further notice and . . . an embargo on strikes', *Towards complete independence*, text of a speech to the National Council, UNIP, August 1969.
30. Carr, *The Twilight* . . ., pp. 151–2.
31. For an attempt to identify it, cf. my 'Marxism-Leninism-Mao Tse-Tung Thought', republished as 'Conservatism and the East', Chapter 5 in *Beliefs in Society, The Problem of Ideology*, Penguin, London, 1971.
32. 22 December 1941, Address to the Shensi-Kansu-Ninghsia Border Region Assembly, translated by Boyd Compton in *Mao's China, Party Reform Documents, 1942–44*, Washington State University Press, Seattle, pp. 247–8.
33. Cited by N. B. Krishnan, *Far Eastern Economic Review*, Hong Kong, 26 May 1983, p. 46.
34. F. G. Bailey, *Politics and Social Change, Orissa in 1959*, University of California Press, Berkeley, 1963, pp. 166 ff.
35. These issues are documented in detail in my *The Mandate of Heaven: Marx and Mao in Modern China*, Quartet, London, 1978.
36. 'The task of our New Democratic system is . . . to promote the free development of a private capitalist economy that benefits instead of controlling the people's livelihood, and to protect all honestly acquired private property', *On Coalition Government*, 24 April 1945 (in the original version, not the subsequently edited one). cf. extracts included in Conrad Brandt, Benjamin Schwartz, John K. Fairbank, *A Documentary History of Chinese Communism*, Athenaum, New York, 1967, pp. 303–4. What would Marx have made of 'honestly acquired private property'? He would not have seen the morality of its acquisition as in any way relevant to its abolition.
37. *Correct the 'Left' errors in land reform propaganda*, 11 February 1948, in Mao Tse-tung, Selected Works, Peking, Vol. IV, p. 197.
38. *Ibid.*
39. *General Report*, Peking Municipal People's Government on Agrarian Reform in the Peking Suburban Areas, 21 November 1950, translated in

Current Bulletin, Hong Kong, No. 72.
40. *Socialism and the Peasantry*, 1905 in *Collected Works*, Vol. 9 (1962 edition), p. 315.
41. *Letters from Afar*, 11 March 1917, *ibid.*, Vol. 23, p. 326.
42. *Telegram to the headquarters of the Loyang Front after the recapture of the city,* 8 April 1948, in *Selected Works*, IV, p. 248.
43. Karl Marx, Preface to *A Contribution to the Critique of Political Economy*, from the extract in *Karl Marx, Selected Writings*, edited by T. B. Bottomore and Maximilien Rubel, Penguin, London, 1963, p. 68.
44. A phenomenon not quite as new as is often supposed. Marx noted: 'In England at the end of the seventeenth century, they [different elements in the process of primitive accumulation] arrive at a systematical combination, embracing the colonies, the national debt, the modern mode of taxation, and the protectionist system. These methods depend in part on brute force, for example, the colonial system. But they all employ the power of the State, the concentrated and organised force of society, to hasten hothouse fashion, the process of transformation of the feudal mode of production into the capitalist mode, and to shorten the transition'. *Capital*, Vol. 1, (S. Moore transl.), Foreign Publishing House, Moscow, n.d., p. 751.
45. The economic underpinning of this argument, with empirical demonstration, is laid out in my *Of Bread and Guns: the World Economy in Crisis*, Penguin, London, 1983.

5. The International Migration of Labour

1. Compare the contemporary tolerance of the passport as a means of labour control to Marx's comment on internal labour passports:

> The excess of despotism reached in France will be apparent by the following regulations as to working men.
>
> Every working man is supplied with a book by the police – the first page of which contains his name, age, birthplace, trade or calling, and a description of his person. He is therein obliged to enter the name of the master for whom he works, and the reasons why he leaves him. But this is not all: the book is placed in the master's hands and deposited by him in the bureau of the police with the character of the man by the master. When a workman leaves his employment, he must go and fetch this book from the police office; and is not allowed to obtain another situation without producing it. Thus the workman's bread is utterly dependent on the police. But this again is not all: this book serves the purpose of a passport. If he is obnoxious, the police write 'bon pour retourner chez lui' ['Valid for return home'] in it, and the workman is obliged to return to his parish!
>
> . . . No serfdom of the feudal ages, no pariahdom of India has its parallel
>
> Karl Marx/Frederick Engels, *Collected Works*, Vol. 10, p. 578.

2. This phenomenon is usually related to apparently accidental changes in the birth rate, reflected later in changes in the size of labour force. In fact, there is often no correlation with birth rates – for example, Greece, Spain, Portugal and Yugoslavia have the same sort of birth rates as those countries to which their nationals have migrated.

   'Surplus workers' is the obverse of 'lack of the means to employ' (or 'capital deficit'), just as 'scarcity of labour' means 'excess of the means to employ' (implying an excess demand for goods or services, 'capital surplus'). But differences of this kind have existed for a very long time, so they can hardly account for particular movements of workers at particular times. There are many areas, in any case, with a 'capital deficit' but hardly any emigration.

   Furthermore, the argument implies that it is the 'surplus' workers, the unemployed, who move, when frequently it is not. 'Scarcity' implies a general spread of unfilled vacancies in labour-importing countries, when such a situation never exists, only particular scarcities in particular trades. The argument also assumes that the existing labour force in destination countries is 'fully utilized' when it never is nor could be outside the realm of theory. There are always sections of the population which could be employed if the wage and conditions offered were good enough – women working at home, people under the age of 15, the sick, invalided and retired. If the price of labour, the wage, were to rise high enough, it would induce a movement of workers out of low into higher paid jobs (as happened in Germany, France and the United States with agricultural workers in the 1950s and 1960s). Alternatively, jobs can be exported or subcontracted abroad, as today when the Lancashire millowners are trying to subcontract garment making to the Mediterranean countries (the 'outward processing' system).

   Thus, the occurrence of 'scarcity' or 'surplus' does not *explain* the movement of workers; on the contrary, it is the movement which alone gives rise to the invention of these terms.
3. In Britain, the numbers in higher education have roughly doubled every twenty-five years in this century. Between 1955 and 1970, numbers were doubling every eight years. On comparative expenditure and enrolments, see:

Increases in higher education
(average annual growth rates) (%)

	Dates	1. Expenditure	2. Enrolments
France	1958–68	13.3	9.8
W. Germany	1957–66	16.3	5.0
Italy	1950–65	15.0	3.9
Japan	1950–65	11.1	6.9
UK (England & Wales	1950–66	9.8	5.1
US	1955–67	11.4	7.5

(*OECD Observer,* No. 50, Feb. 1971, p. 15.)

Decasualization reduces the labour hours available if we assume that casual workers formerly took several jobs without working the same number of hours as they previously worked in more than one job.

4. The 1971 survey of 47,000 industrial units, employing between one and four workers, and covering 116,000 workers in all, showed:

1.	Value added	Rs. 104 million
2.	Hired labour costs	Rs. 66 million (at Rs. 1,375 per year)
3.	Imputed wage for employers and family labour	Rs. 93 million
4.	Profits	Rs. 55 million
5.	Actual return to employers family labour	Rs. 38 million (or Rs. 559 per person)

(A. N. Bose, *Calcutta and Rural Bengal,* Minerva, Calcutta, 1978.)

5. The Report of the Inspector General of Recruiting, following the Boer War, noted 'the gradual deterioration of the physique of the working classes from whom the bulk of recruits must always be drawn', cited R. M. Titmuss, *Essays on the Welfare State*, London, 1958.

6. Distribution of the Gross Domestic Product, 1976

	GNP per capita, 1976 US$	Public Consumption %	Private Consumption %	Gross Domestic Investment %
Japan	4910	9	57	33
US	7890	17	64	16
France	6550	13	62	23
W. Germany	7380	18	55	24
USSR	2760	—	—	—
UK	4020	19	60	17

7. One estimate of the net subsidy from immigrant homelands to West Germany puts the figure for workers who have moved between 1957 and 1966, and 1968 and 1973 (there was a net outflow of foreign workers in 1967) at US$33 bn (1962 prices). Remittances returned to the homelands in the same period were US$8.8 bn. There are no estimates of the immigrant net contribution to West Germany's gross domestic product. Another estimate, solely for highly skilled and professional immigrants to Britain, Canada and the United States, 1961–72, puts the subsidy at US$46 bn.

8. This migration increases shortages of casual labour during the harvesting in parts of Spain which encourages the larger farmers to buy labour-saving equipment, which in turn increases emigration: 'to their paternalist relationship with the big landlords, has been added a further dependence on the European trade cycle'. Bernard Kayser, *Manpower Movements and Labour Markets* (Report), OECD, 1971, p. 196.

9. In a study of Cologne in Germany, a writer notes: 'the throng of foreign workers does not form a single quantitative supplement, elastic by

definition: on the contrary, it is for the most part an essential force in the economy because of the sectors of which it is in possession. For the main feature of immigrant manpower on the labour market is its practically irreversible specialization: it seems out of the question that, even in a period of crisis, nationals should demand again for themselves jobs which have become considered inferior and abandoned to the foreigners' (*ibid.*, p. 175).

10. It is for this reason that Böhning describes immigrant labour as a 'conjunctural shock absorber', (W. R. Böhning and D. Maillat, *The Effects of Employment of Foreign Workers,* OECD, Paris, 1974, p. 28.
11. Compare Victor Serge's observation on the exiled:
'I have witnessed the birth of the enormous category of "stateless persons", that is, of those men to whom tyrants refuse even a nationality. As far as the right to live is concerned, the plight of these men without a country . . . can be compared only to that of the "unacknowledged man" of the Middle Ages who, since he had no lord or sovereign, had no rights and no protection either, and whose very name became a kind of insult', *Memoirs of a Revolutionary, 1901–1941*, translated by Peter Sedgwick, (to whom much thanks for pointing out the passage), Oxford, 1963, p. 373.
12. And once their labour power was exhausted, they must carry their bodies off, out of the territory of the State. General Circular No. 235 of 1967 stipulated that: 'as soon as they become, for some reason or another, no longer fit to work or superfluous in the labour market, they are expected to return to their country of origin or the territory of their national unit where they fit in ethnically (even) if they were not born and bred in the "Homeland"' (cited in M. J. Andrews, 'Crossroads: A consequence of ideology or urbanization' unpublished dissertation, May 1979).

6. Newly Emergent Bourgeoisies?

1. Prebisch's principal works on these questions were undertaken under the auspices of the United Nations Economic Commission for Latin America (ECLA). They included: *The Economic Development of Latin America and its Principal Problems*, United Nations, New York, 1950; *Economic Survey of Latin America 1949*, Part 1, United Nations, New York, 1951; *Problémas teóricos y praticos del crecimiento económico*, United Nations, New York, 1952.
2. One version of this is presented in detail in A. Emmanuel's *Unequal Exchange: a Study of the Imperialism of Free Trade*, Monthly Review Press, New York, 1972. See also Samir Amin's *Accumulation on a World Scale: A Critique of the Theory of Underdevelopment*, Monthly Review Press, 2 vols, New York, 1974.
3. For a more detailed refutation of this theory, see my 'Theories of Unequal Exchange', *International Socialism*, 33 (London), Autumn 1986, pp. 111–22, and chapter 7 of this volume.
4. Baran, *Political Economy of Growth*, pp. 194–5.

5. *Ibid.*, p. 225.
6. Cited by E. H. Carr in *The Bolshevik Revolution, 1917–23*, Macmillan, London, 1950, Vol. 1, p. 4.
7. Still one of the best accounts of this is R. A. Brady, *Business as a System of Power*, Columbia University Press, New York, 1943.
8. This is explored in more detail in my *Competition and the Corporate Society: British Conservatives, the State and Industry, 1945–64*, Methuen, London, 1972, pp. 23–74.
9. J. M. Keynes, *Essays in Persuasion*, London, 1931, pp. 41–2, reprinting his 1924 Sidney Ball lecture in the University of Oxford.
10. J. M. Keynes, *The General Theory of Employment, Interest and Money*, Macmillan, London, 1936, p. 376.
11. In *The Middle Way: A Study of the Problem of Economic and Social Progress in a Free and Democratic Society*, Macmillan, London, 1938.
12. N. Bukharin, *Imperialism and World Economy*, Moscow, 1917, English transl., Merlin Press, London, 1972.
13. See the two leading examples – Andrew Shonfield's *Modern Capitalism: the Changing Balance of Public and Private Power*, Oxford University Press for the Royal Institute of International Affairs, London, 1965 and J. K. Galbraith, *The New Industrial State*, Hamish Hamilton, London, 1967.
14. See, for example, Leroy Jones and Il Sakong, *Government, Business and Entrepreneurship in Economic Development: the Korean Case*, Studies in the Modernisation of the Republic of Korea, 1945–75, Council on East Asian Studies, Harvard University Press, Cambridge, Mass., 1980, p. 296.
15. M. K. Datta-Chaudhuri, 'Industrialization and foreign trade: the development experience of South Korea and the Philippines', in Eddy Lee (ed.), *Export-led industrialization and development*, International Labour Organisation, Bangkok, 1981, p. 56.
16. See Chapter 2 of my *The End of the Third World: Newly Industrializing Countries and the Decline of an Ideology*, I. B. Tauris and Penguin, London, 1986/1987, pp. 30 ff.
17. Shin Byung Hyun, deputy Prime Minister and Minister of Planning, in his address to the 13th meeting of the International Economic Consultation Organization for Korea, 16 July 1984, reported in *Economic Bulletin*, Economic Planning Board, Government of the Republic of Korea, Seoul, July 1984, p. 12.
18. Excellently analysed in Merle Lipton, *Capitalism and Apartheid: South Africa 1910–84*, Gower/Maurice Temple, Aldershot, 1985.
19. See my *The End of the Third World*, pp. 87–9.
20. In *Capitalism and Apartheid*.
21. This is argued in greater detail in my *Of Bread and Guns: the World Economy in Crisis*, Penguin, Harmondsworth, 1983.

7. Theories of Unequal Exchange

1. William Stafford (John Hales), *A Compendious or Briefe Examination of Certayne Ordinary Complaintes of Divers of Our Country Men in These our Days*, 1581, pp. 4 and 6, cited by I. I. Ruben, *A History of Economic Thought*, Ink Links, London, 1979, pp. 44–5.
2. See Alexander Hamilton, *Report on Manufactures*,. 1791, and Friedrich List, *National System of Political Economy*, 1841.
3. Mihail Manoïlesco, *Le Siècle du Corporatisme*, Felix Alcan, Paris, 1934, p. 30.
4. *Capital*, Vol. I, London, 1930, pp. 371–2.
5. *The German Ideology*, 1846, as cited in Eric Hobsbawm (ed.), *Pre-capitalist economic formations*, Lawrence & Wishart, London, 1964, p. 127.
6. E. Preobazhensky, *The New Economics* (trans. Brian Pearce), Clarendon Press, Oxford, 1965.
7. Prebisch's position in the late 1940s and early 1950s is presented in: Economic Commission for Latin America, (i) *The Economic Development of Latin America and its Principal Problems*, United Nations, New York, 1950; (ii) *Economic Survey of Latin America 1949*, Part I, United Nations, New York, 1951; (iii) *Problemas teóricos y prácticos del crecimiento económico*, United Nations, New York, 1952; and (iv) *International Cooperation in Latin American Development and Policy*, United Nations, New York, 1954.

   For an account of the evolution of his thought, see Joseph L. Love, 'Rául Prebisch and the origins of the doctrine of unequal exchange', *Latin American Research Review*, XV, 3, 1980, pp. 47–72.
8. Thomas Balogh, *Dollar Crisis, Causes and Cure*, Blackwell, Oxford, 1949, and G. D. A. MacDougall, *The World Dollar Problem*, Macmillan, London, 1957.
9. G. Myrdal, *Economic Theory of Underdeveloped Regions*, Macmillan, London, 1957.
10. H. Singer, 'The distribution of gains between investing and borrowing countries', *American Economic Review* 40, May 1950, pp. 473–85.
11. Lewis's most famous contribution was 'Economic development with unlimited supplies of labour', *The Manchester School*, May 1954.
12. Paul Baran, *The political economy of growth*, Monthly Review Press, New York, 1957.
13. Samir Amin, *Accumulation on a World Scale: a critique of the theory of underdevelopment*, Monthly Review Press, New York, 1974, 2 volumes.
14. A. Emmanuel, *Unequal Exchange: A Study of the Imperialism of Free Trade*, Monthly Review Press, New York, 1972.
15. A. Gunder Frank, *Dependent Accumulation and Underdevelopment*, Monthly Review Press, New York, 1979.
16. 'Black Reformism: the theory of unequal exchange', in *Capitalism and Theory*, Pluto, London, 1974, pp. 95–116.
17. Fifth Session (28 July 1919), in *Second Congress of the Communist International: Minutes of the Proceedings*, I, New York, London, 1977, p. 135.

18. An idea shared by right-wing Italian nationalists in the early 1920s and both a founder of the Communist Party of China (Li Ta-chao) and a right-wing Kuomintang leader (Tai Chi-t'ao) – cf. M. Meisner, *Li Ta-chao and the Origins of Chinese Marxism*, Harvard University Press, Cambridge, Mass., 1967, p. 145, and C. Brandt, *Stalin's Failure in China, 1924–1927*, Harvard University Press, Cambridge, Mass., 1958, p. 57.
19. *Capital*, Moscow, n.d., I, p. 216 (my emphasis).
20. See 'Black Reformism'.

8. The End of Economic Nationalism

1. In 1950, South Korea's per capita income was $146 (in 1974 prices), compared to Nigeria's $150, Kenya's $129, Egypt's $203, Brazil's $373, Mexico's $562, Argentina's $907. If we compare an index for these figures (Argentina = 100) and compare it to per capita gross national product (current prices) in 1986, this is the result:

	1950	1986		1950	1986
Argentina	100	100	Egypt	22	32
Mexico	62	79	Nigeria	17	27
Brazil	41	77	Kenya	14	13
			S. Korea	16	101

2. Jagdish Bhagwati, with Anne Krueger, 'Exchange control, liberalization and economic development', in Jagdish Bhagwati edited by Gene Grossman, *Dependence and Interdependence, Essays in Development Economics*, Basil Blackwell, Oxford, 1985, Vol. 2, p. 70.
3. In Hong Kong, the leading business federation estimates a labour shortage of between 200,000 and 250,000 workers, particularly the unskilled for work in construction, hotels, services, manufacturing and retailing. The government estimates a shortage of 130,000 workers, 10,000 of them in the technician and skilled grades. Singapore has drawn in an unknown number of illegal immigrants which it is now busy trying to expel. The South Korean Government is worried at the medium-term decline in young workers. The Taiwanese authorities estimate illegal immigration, particularly the unskilled and from South-East Asia, at between 12,000 and 30,000.
4. Hong Kong firms are said now to employ 1.5 million workers in China's Guangdong province (where a third of Hong Kong's currency circulates). South Korea's 1988 overseas investment was officially put at $480 million (48 per cent going to the United States). The outflow is partly the result of a 25 per cent appreciation of the Won, and the investment has gone in part to develop capacity in the manufacture of textiles and garments, footwear, toys, etc. in Thailand, Malaysia, Mexico and the Caribbean. Taiwan's direct investment abroad increased by 81 per cent in 1988. Officially, the flow was put at $218.7 million, but estimates at

the destinations put the real figure at between $2.2 and 3.5 billion. Again, it is partly the result of a 40–45 per cent appreciation in the New Taiwan dollar. Thailand is a favoured destination, along with the Philippines and other locations in South-East Asia.

5. 'The experience and causes of rapid labour-intensive development in Korea, Taiwan, Hong Kong and Singapore, and the possibilities of emulation', in Eddy Lee (ed.), *Export-led Industrialization and Development*, ILO(ARTEP), Bangkok, 1981, p. 25.
6. Dependency theorists examine the East Asian experience in Frederic C. Deyo, *The Political Economy of the New Asian Industrialism*, Cornell University Press, Ithaca and London, 1987.
7. See 'A Global Manufacturing System', in my *The End of the Third World: Newly Industrializing Countries and the Decline of an Ideology*, Tauris, London, 1986, pp. 93–117.
8. Table 7, GATT, *International Trade 1987–88*, General Agreement on Trade and Tariffs, Geneva, 1988, Vol. 1, p. 12.
9. David Morawetz, *Why the Emperor's New Clothes were not made in Colombia*, World Bank Staff Working Paper, World Bank, Washington DC, 1982.
10. Celso Furtado, *The Economic Growth of Brazil: a Survey from Colonial Times*, University of California, Los Angeles and Berkeley, 1971.
11. John K. Chang, *Industrial Development in Pre-Communist China: a Quantitative Analysis*, Aldine Publishing Co., Chicago, 1969.
12. *Collected Works of V. I. Lenin*, p. 145.12.
13. *Imperialism: the Highest Stage of Capitalism*, in *Selected Works of V. I. Lenin*, V, London, 1936, p. 92.
14. R. F. Harrod, *The Life of John Maynard Keynes*, Harcourt Brace, New York, 1951, pp. 567–8.
15. Discussed in greater detail in my *Of Bread and Guns: the World Economy in Crisis*, Penguin, London, 1983.
16. *Emerging Stock Markets: Fact Book 1989*, International Finance Corporation, Washington DC, 1989.
17. Ernest H. Preeg (ed.) *Hard Bargaining Ahead: Trade Policy and Developing Countries*, Transaction Books for the Overseas Development Council, New Brunswick, 1985, p. xi.
18. The growth figures are exaggerated by the introduction of the Customs User Fee in December 1986, leading to the transfer of formerly duty-free goods to these schedules. See US International Trade Commission, *Imports under Items 806.30 and 807.00 of the Tariff Schedules of the United States, 1984–87*, Annual, ITC, Washington DC, December 1988.
19. The stock of direct investment by US-registered companies in Europe increased from about $70 billion in 1984 to $122 billion in 1987.
20. Richard Robison, *Indonesia: the Rise of Capital*, Allen and Unwin, London and Sydney, 1986. See also his 'Authoritarian States, Capital-Owning Classes and the Politics of Newly Industrializing Countries: The Case of Indonesia', *World Politics*, XLI/1, October 1988, pp. 52–74.
21. *The Political Economy of Growth*, Monthly Review Press, New York, 1957.

9. Mexico and the Pacific Rim Region

1. GATT, *International Trade: Annual Report 1989*, GATT Secretariat, Geneva, 1989.
2. In Leslie Castle and Christopher Findlay (eds), *Pacific Trade in Services*, Allen & Unwin (in association with the Pacific Trade and Development Conference Secretariat and the Australian National University), Sydney, 1988.
3. MITI, *Third Basic Survey of Business Activity Abroad*, Ministry of International Trade and Industry, Tokyo, 1988, mimeo; see also *Economic Statistics*, Bank of Japan Research and Statistics Department, monthly, and 'Japan's Changing Direct Foreign Investment', *Focus Japan*, 14/12, 1987, pp. 1–2.
4. Peter Drucker, 'The Futures that have already happened', *The Economist*, 21 October 1989, pp. 27–30.
5. See Lester Thurow, 'Must we manage trade?' *World Link*, World Economic Forum, Massachusetts Institute of Technology, June 1989; Rudiger W. Dornbusch, James Poterba and Lawrence Summers, *The Case for Manufacturing in America's Future*, Eastman Kodak, Rochester NY, 1988, and Rudiger W. Dornbusch, Paul Krugman, Yung Chul Park, *Meeting World Challenges: US Manufacturing in the 1990s*, Eastman Kodak, Rochester NY, 1989.
6. Calculated from *World Development Report 1989*, World Bank, Washington DC, 1989, Tables 3, 6 and 14.
7. As a mark of this remarkable growth, see the index of per capita gross national product for a selection of less developed countries between 1950 and 1986 (with Argentina, the richest in 1950, as 100):

	1950	1986		1950	1986
Argentina	100	100	Egypt	22	32
Mexico	62	79	Nigeria	17	27
Brazil	41	77	Kenya	14	13
South Korea	16	101			

8. See my *The End of the Third World: the Newly Industrializing Countries and the Decline in an Ideology*, Tauris, London, 1986, Penguin, London, 1987, and Viking, New York, 1988.
9. Kevin F. McCarthy and R. Burciaga Valdez, *Current and Future Effects of Mexican Immigration in California*, California Roundtable, Rand (R–3365–CR), Santa Monica, May 1986.
10. *Estadisticas del Comercio Exterior de Mexico, Informacion Preliminar*, January–December, 1987, Vol. 12, 1988, p. 28.